MOONS AND AUROCHS

Also by Alan Ogden

Romania Revisited,
On the trail of English Travellers 1604-1938.

Fortresses of Faith,
A pictorial history of the fortified Saxon churches.

Revelations of Byzantium,
The monasteries and painted churches of northern Moldavia.

Winds of Sorrow,
Travels in and around Transylvania.

The Discontented,
Betrayal, Love and War in Habsburg Hungary.

MOONS AND AUROCHS
Romanian Journeys

Alan Ogden

Orchid Press

Alan Ogden
MOONS AND AUROCHS: Romanian Journeys

First edition 2007

ORCHID PRESS
P.O. Box 31669,
Causeway Bay PO,
Hong Kong

www.orchidbooks.com

Printed in Thailand

ISBN-10: 988-97764-8-0
ISBN-13: 978-988-97764-8-0

HUNTING

I've never run after words.
All I have sought
Was their long
Silvery shadows,
Dragged by the sun through the grass,
Or drawn by the moon over the sea;
I've never hunted anything
But the words' shadows –
It is very skilful hunting
Learned from old folks
Who know
That there's nothing more precious
About a word
Than its shadow
And devoid of their shadows
Are the words that have sold their souls.

Ana Blandiana
Founder member of the Romanian Civic Alliance

Translated by Dan Duțescu

CONTENTS

FOREWORD

Moons and Aurochs is a somewhat disconnected account of a journey I undertook through Romania in October and November 2006. Halfway through my planned itinerary, I had to return to England and it was three months before I was able to go back, Despite these intervals, I hope the momentum for the reader has been sustained. It certainly was for me.

Why the moon? For the Slavic peoples who surround Romania, the sun is female and the moon male. But for Romanians, *luna* is feminine and *soare* is masculine, so in their folklore the moon is considered a beautiful girl, sister of the sun, shining at night, resting by day. According to legend, the sun wanted to marry his sister; as this was a sin, God stopped the wedding and took away some of the brightness of the moon, hiding her in the sea. The lovers never met again. During the course of my journey, I have tried to return some of the lustre that was cruelly erased from the image of Romania in the last half of the twentieth century by telling the story of my encounters with people who live and work there today, illuminating it with the history of some of her old provinces and regions.

Why aurochs, those great oxen from antiquity, a mix between a bison and a prize Spanish bull, whose images decorate the cave dwellings of prehistoric man? For the simple reason, this splendid species was once the symbol of the Principality of Moldavia and today has pride of place on one of the quarters of the Romanian Coat of Arms. Now it is extinct, the last specimens being recorded at the beginning of the seventeenth century in the great Polish royal forests of Jaktorowski. How did it die out? Domestic animals encroached on to its pasture, depriving it of food and bringing disease at the same time. I see a similar threat to Romania today. The EU is about to regulate the way of life for hundreds of thousands of Romanian country folk and their centuries-old tradition of self-sufficiency may likewise be on the verge of extinction.

☞ ☜

I would like to thank all those who helped me plan my journey by generously giving me their precious time and even more precious knowledge—Nicolae Ratiu, Michael Styrcea, Sherban Cantacuzino, Dennis Deletant, Moritz Fried, Michael Radomir, Canon Ian Sherwood, Simona Tatulescu-Cighir, Cristian Ferecatu, Jonathan Forbes, Adam Sorkin, Shona Kallestrup and Mike Morton; everyone who contributed to the narrative, particularly Virgil Munteanu, Sacha Ivanov, the Mikes family (Katerina, Grigor and Zsolna, Alexander), Czabo Apor, Abbot Mihail, The Marin family, Geza Tudos and Ioan and Delia Micurescu; John Akeroyd, Ana Blandiana and Luminita Cioaba for permission to quote their work; and, as in any travel book, the cast of characters who through just being around at the time endow colour and charm to ones pages for free—a big 'thank you' to all of them. Finally, I would like to thank my wife, Jose, whose support, enthusiasm and companionship have been inestimable, her god-daughter, Octavia Mackenzie, whose editing and proofing skills have been invaluable, and Andy Baker of Response Advertising for his entrancing front cover design.

Alan Ogden,
July 2007, London.

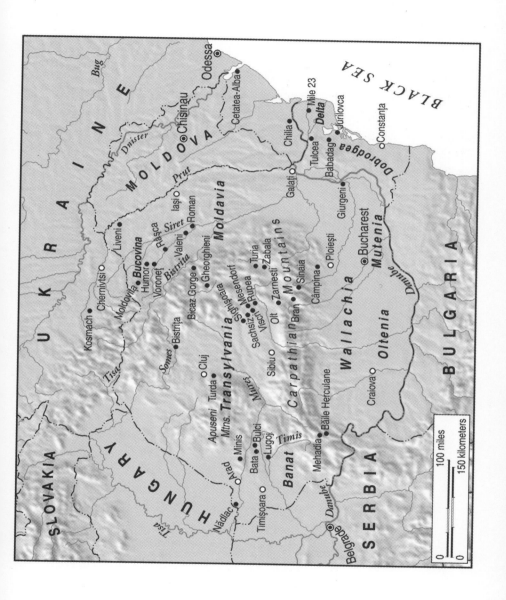

CHAPTER ONE

TRANSYLVANIAN THREADS AND RUSSIAN ÉMIGRÉS

Imagine a great hall—the cavernous sixteenth century Renaissance halls of Wawel Castle in Krakow come to mind—hung with resplendent wool and silken Brussels tapestries of different sizes and varied colour schemes, reds, blues and greens all vying with each other, but rather than illustrating the traditional seasonal themes and scenes from the Bible and antiquity, potted with birds, dogs, horses, shepherds, trees, lakes and castles, these tapestries depict life in an East European country. Romania is one such tapestry, a triptych with panels from Transylvania, Moldavia and Wallachia, each an intricately woven picture of people and places, of towns and countryside, of mountains and seas, of hills and plains, of the past and present. Its composition, needlework, texture and tones are far more complex than those of its neighbours, Bulgaria, Moldova, Ukraine, Hungary and Serbia. The secret to understanding Romania is to study the ravels of this tapestry, to visually unpick the weave and lay out the weft, and thereby reveal the elusive hand of history that designed today's Romania.

Crossing the border between Hungary and Romania at the village of Nadlac[1], forty miles to the East of the Hungarian city of Szeged, I tugged gently at my first loose thread to unravel the story of the Ratiu family, one of the proudest names in Romanian history. Indeed, if you follow the convulsive tale of the Ratius, you will concurrently track the precarious evolvement of the modern Romanian state. In 1331, one Indrei became *'nobilis'* of Nadlac by the decree of Voievod[2] Tamas of Szécsény and thus acquired some land. His descendant, Tamas of Nadlac, with a band of hardy Romanians fought the Turkish incursions into Croatia, hence the nickname Ratz (*Hrvac* or *Croat*). In 1394, Sigismund of Luxembourg, King of Hungary for fifty years and King of the Romans for fifteen, ennobled him[3] and the family adopted a suitably martial coat of arms—a leopard rampant with a sword in its right paw. Two years later, Sigismund, at the head of an immense army of 100,000 men, suffered a disastrous defeat at the hands of the Ottomans at Nicopolis, bringing his crusade to an abrupt and bloody end; indeed, it was to be the very last crusade. There is no record as to whether Tamas accompanied him but if he did, he was lucky not to be one of the ten thousand men beheaded in the Sultan's presence or one of the many thousands taken prisoner and sold into lifelong slavery.

I had first picked up the Ratiu thread in London, in Nicolae Ratiu's office on the eighth floor of an imposing office building overlooking Regent Street. The current head of the family, Nicolae had been a friend for several years and I had persuaded him to show me some of the family archives. Tracing his finger over family trees and occasionally referring to copies of princely letters, Nicolae outlined for me their extraordinary and, in the context of modern Romania, unique story.

After the disaster at Nicopolis, the Hungarian kings experienced a further setback when young King Louis was killed at the battle of Mohács in 1526, an event that led to the relinquishment of much of Hungary to the avaricious Ottoman Empire. The throne passed

---

[1]   Called *Nagylak* (Hungarian) until 1920.
[2]   Slavic for a local ruler or high official.
[3]   *Nobilis voivoda* or nobilis *kenezius*.

to his bother-in-law, Ferdinand Habsburg, Archduke of Austria and Holy Roman Emperor, whom the family continued to serve. In the 1570s, Petrus Ratz, at one stage the Emperor Rudolph's ambassador to Moscow, moved to Prague to be near the Emperor, who had made the city his imperial capital. By now Rudolf passed his days with his astrologers and astronomers, his 'edicts and dispatches accumulated the dust of weeks, unsigned upon his desk[4]', so Ratz did well in 1578 to progress in the nobility stakes. A second leopard's head and Mercury's messenger stick in the other paw were added to the family's existing coat of arms and a new coat of arms was given to Petrus and his descendants, showing a decapitated janissary's head—Tamas Ratz's crusader exploits had finally been recognised. The Ratz family became Ratz von Nadlac.

During the events that led to the brief unification of Transylvania, Wallachia and Moldavia in 1600, the Ratzs acted as intermediaries between the various warring parties. Nicolae showed me two letters, the first headed 'Instructions of the Ambassador of the illustrious and magnificent Lord Voivode Michael (of Wallachia) to His Most Sacred Imperial Majesty, Rudolph II, in the year of our Lord 1598 on Twenty First day of November'. In it, Michael implores the Emperor to mend his fences with Sigismund Báthory, the Prince of Transylvania, who had recently returned from self-imposed exile in Poland. The second, dated 16 December the following year and entrusted to the Lords George Ratz and John Zelestreii, is addressed to Rudolph's brother, Matthias. In it, Michael urges him to join forces with him to attack the very same Sigismund Báthory, who was now perceived as a threat by Michael. There can be few better examples of the dictum 'today's friend is tomorrow's enemy'.

In 1625, Gábor Bethlen, the first Prince of a truly independent Transylvania and a man always conscious of the need for friends rather than enemies, confirmed the family's nobility but a bitter row with George Rákóczi I, Prince of Transylvania, in 1653[5] resulted in

---

[4] C.V. Wedgwood: The Thirty Years War.
[5] The Ratiu family remain unsure about the exact date but are fairly certain the row broke out during an Election of a new prince by the Transylvanian Estates. They backed the wrong one.

disaster: he annulled their title and gave their lands at Nadlac to the Dobay family. Noble rank in Transylvania was not only desirable but essential in those days for without it, Romanians, who were not recognised as a *natio*[6] (a 'people' with political rights like Hungarians, Saxons and *Székelys*[7]), had to live outside the city walls. Although Prince Michael Apafi I of Transylvania restored the title to Vasile Ratz and his sons in 1680, their land remained confiscated and it was not until the early nineteenth century that a settlement was finally reached with the Bethlen family who had become owners of the Nadlac estates! By the end of the seventeenth century, the Ratzs had settled in Turda, a Transylvanian city well known for its twin virtues of salt production and religious tolerance. Indeed it had witnessed Europe's first declaration of such tolerance by Sigismund Zápolyai in 1568.

By now the Habsburg Emperors had finally expelled the Turks from Hungary and with their departure, the status of Transylvania as an independent principality also came to an end; the Diploma Leopoldinum promulgated in December 1691 effectively transformed it into an Austrian province. However, the two principalities of Moldavia and Wallachia on Transylvania's eastern and southern borders remained under Turkish suzerainty and their Greek Phanariot princes, appointed by the Sultans as 'commission men', taxed the hapless populace to such a degree of impoverishment that many emigrated West and North into Transylvania.

By 1761 according to an Imperial census, Transylvanian Romanians totalled 787,000, thereby forming a majority of the Transylvanian population. Yet still they did not participate in official political or religious life; under the Hungarian feudal system, they formed no *recepta natio* and thus had no political organization and likewise their religion, the Orthodox, did not rank as a *recepta religio*.

The agent for change came in the unlikely form of the Emperor Joseph. On the death of his mother and co-Regent, the Empress

---

[6] The Medieval notion of nationality was based on a wide range of distinctive customs, not just language.

[7] A people of Hungarian origin who arrived in Transylvanian around the twelfth century.

Maria Theresa, he turned his reforming zeal to Transylvania; he had been appalled at its backwardness on his visit there in 1773 when he received nearly 19,000 petitions. In 1781, he introduced *Concivilität*—citizenship for all—and the abolition of torture to extract confessions.

On his second Transylvanian visit in 1783, Joseph issued a decree of emancipation for the serfs, which the Hungarian nobility refused to implement thereby triggering a bloody peasants' revolt in return. Three Romanian leaders—Horia, Closça and Crişau—stepped forward to voice the collective concerns of the peasants. Events spun out of control as thousands of primitively armed peasants went on the rampage in the Abrud and along the Mures valley. By the time this outburst of anger had been brought under control, 230 castles and manor houses lay ruined or looted and over 100 members of the nobility murdered. Joseph now had to close Pandora's box. Horia and Closça were broken on the wheel, then disembowelled alive before an invited audience of 2,500 peasants; their limbs were stuck on pikes and distributed to the crowd as keepsakes. And the name of the priest who heard their confession? Ratz.

The forces of reaction, never far below the surface in the Habsburg Empire, found a more malleable leader in Joseph's successor, Leopold II. Whilst remaining sympathetic to the plight of the Transylvanian Romanians, the issue of Transylvania itself was put on ice for the alarming and thoroughly unsavoury revolution in France now dictated the Emperor's priorities: no more political experiments, only the restoration of law and order. When the leaders of the Romanians appealed to the Emperor in 1791 in a memorandum, the '*Supplex Libellus Vaalchorum*', asking for the recognition of the Romanians as a *natio* and for equal rights and privileges with the other *natios*, not surprisingly it was ignored.

For the next thirty years, the issue of Transylvania gathered dust on the Chancellery shelves in Vienna until 1835, when the Transylvanian diet was revived as a form of self-governance. The three *natios*—Hungarians, Székelys and Saxons—settled down to a collaborative government, which continued to exclude the

Romanian majority. When in 1840, Hungarian superseded Latin as the official language of the Hungarian Government and Parliament, the Transylvania Saxon Pastor, Stephan Roth, pointed out that when making a journey or visiting a market, 'before one tries to see whether one speaks German or the other Magyar, the conversation begins in the Wallach language' and published a book in 1842, *Der Sprachkampf Siebenburgen*, which argued in favour of Romanian as Transylvania's true primary language. For his plain speaking, the Hungarians subsequently executed him by firing squad on the battlements of Cluj in 1849.

With the introduction of Hungarian as a common language came a parallel demand by Kossuth, the arch proponent of Magyarisation, for the re-union of Transylvania with Hungary. As soon as the news of the February 1848 Revolution in Paris reached Bratislava, the Hungarian parliament decamped and returned to its ancient seat in Budapest and on 1 April the Union with Transylvania was proclaimed to the delight of the Hungarian minority and to the horror of the Saxons and Romanians. It was to prove a decisive moment for the Ratiu family and for the future of Romania.

Born just after the Peasants' Revolt in 1783, Basiliu Ratiu had established a reputation for himself as a leading Romanian intellectual — he had changed the family name from the Germanic Ratz to Ratiul — and a dynamic church leader. As bishop of Blaj and director of the seminary there, he played a prominent role in the extraordinary spontaneous demonstration by the Transylvanian Romanians in objection to the unilateral 'union'. When 6,000 Romanians gathered at Blaj in May 1848 to hear their leaders, it was Bishop Ratiu who cried "Now let us be free men!" Three weeks later, the crowd had swelled to 40,000 and was demanding proportional representation for the Transylvanian Romanian *natio*.

Unfortunately, by the spring of 1848, the tide of revolution had been stemmed; the Habsburgs had crushed the uprising in Milan (Savoy) and turned their attention to the far greater problem of how to suppress Hungarian independence. After quickly putting their own house in order by suppressing revolts in Prague and Vienna and by changing Emperors, the *Hofburg* gave the task of bringing Hungary back into the fold to two loyal Imperial Generals, Alfred Windischgrätz and his brother-in-law, Felix von Schwarzenberg. Both men had no time for the 'nationalities'.

Transylvania became a battleground. Kossuth appointed the diminutive but dynamic Polish General, Józef Bem, together with Commissioner Csány, to defend Transylvania against the Imperial troops. He then declared himself Governor of Hungary in April 1849, thus provoking the Habsburgs to invite the Russians to assist them. Two hundred thousand of the Tsar's men poured into Hungary from the North. Kossuth's 'hussars', brilliantly led by Bem, staged a courageous and desperate defence but, outnumbered two to one, were defeated by the Russians at Sighisoara in July. By October, Hungary itself had been reduced to the status of an Austrian province, with Transylvania ironically placed 'under the protection' of Vienna. The irrepressible Bem fled to Istanbul where he converted to Islam and under the name of Amurat Murad Pasha ended his days as governor of Aleppo.

But to the delight of Vienna, order had been restored in Transylvania—the Diet was stood down, a governor appointed and a visit arranged for yet another Habsburg Emperor. For now, the Saxons were the only happy *natio* in Transylvania for German had been reintroduced as the official language. Thus, it was no coincidence that when the Transylvanian diet was finally reconvened, it was in Sibiu, the twelfth century capital of the German settlers.

Suddenly there was a glimmer of hope for a lasting accord; the three languages—Hungarian, German and Romanian—were given equality, the Orthodox Church was put on an equal footing with its peers and the question of Romanian political representation addressed. But, with the Prussian victory over the Austrians at Sadová in 1866, the light soon faded. Ignominiously forced to hand Venice over to a 'defeated' Italy, Franz-Joseph had little option other than to settle with the Hungarians; if he didn't, the chances were that he would lose Hungary and the Empire would become an Austrian only affair. The result was a compromise—the *Augsleich* of 1866—when the Hungarians were given internal self-government and Austria-Hungary became a dual monarchy under the Habsburgs.

Dr Ioan Ratiu, Bishop Basiliu's nephew, had found himself in Budapest during the Year of Revolution. Ten years later he returned to Cluj where he was asked by the Romanian community of Transylvania to represent them in the Hungarian Parliament. Recognising the futility of participating in a foreign government, he founded the National Romanian Party (RNP) to fight for equality between Romanians and Hungarians. It was a far from easy objective; funds were scarce and the Augsleich had left the Romanian majority isolated—the Hungarians took comfort in being an equal partner in a powerful, unified empire and started to throw their weight about.

The feisty Bishop Basiliu's energy was far from spent. At the grand age of eighty-five, he signed the *Pronunciamentum* of Blaj in 1868, a declaration issued to celebrate the twentieth anniversary of the Romanian national assembly at Blaj, that memorable event in which he had played such a prominent part. The authors called for Transylvanian autonomy, a separate parliament and the application of the rights ratified at Sibiu in 1863-64. Once again, nothing resulted from this petition and the Bishop died in his eighty-seventh year, his dreams of Transylvanian autonomy and equality for the Romanian majority unfulfilled.

In April 1884, encouraged by the RNP, a new Romanian language newspaper *Tribuna* appeared on the streets of Sibiu. It pulled no punches—'we are not going to investigate whether the Romanians dissatisfaction is well-founded; there is no denying it exists as an elementary calamity'. Within four years, a libel suit had been brought by the authorities against the paper and its editor, Slavici, was duly imprisoned in the Danubian town of Vac. But Romanian nationalism was far from silenced; the war of words continued with a lively student pamphlet campaign and Ioan Ratiu was for the first time positive about progress—'Our grievances have been publicized all over Europe; it is not our fault that European public opinion has finally realised that something is rotten in this country.'

The frustrations of the Transylvanian Romanians were once again expressed in a Memorandum to the Emperor—'after 25 years of constitutional rule, the antagonisms are deeper than ever... (Romanians) can no longer trust the Budapest parliament or the Hungarian government'. A delegation of 237 Romanians, led by Ratiu, set off to Vienna in May 1892. Their purpose was to bring charges against Hungary's king to the attention of the Austrian Emperor; they were, of course, one and the same person. The sealed envelope containing the memorandum was deposited at the cabinet office from where it was forwarded to Budapest and then returned by the Prime Minister's office to Ratiu's home address—unopened.

Romanian failure was unexpectedly rescued by Hungarian stupidity—Turda's Hungarian community attacked Ratiu's house. This provoked an outcry and soon over 13,000 copies of the unread memorandum had been published in Sibiu with nearly 2,000 sent abroad. State prosecutors soon brought charges against the signatories as well as those who admitted responsibility for preparing it and a trial opened in Cluj in May 1894. In the great hall of the *Redout*, a splendid eighteenth century building usually the setting of glamorous winter balls, the defendants planned to turn what was billed as a routine libel trial into a major political confrontation. Ratiu made an impassioned speech, reminding his prosecutors 'a people is not an issue for discussion, it is for assertion'. The Hungarians and Romanian nations had been 'locked in litigious conflict for a hundred years' and there was 'another, higher court, a more enlightened and less prejudiced one, that will bring judgment: the jury of the cultured world, which one day will judge and condemn you with greater severity than this one can. If we are condemned in a spirit of impatience and by a racial fanaticism that has no equal in Europe, it will prove to the world that the Hungarians are a discordant element in the realm of civilization.'

After seventeen days, the trial ended. Four defendants were found not guilty and acquitted, but the others were found guilty. Ratiu was sentenced to two years imprisonment and Vasile Lucaciu to the maximum sentence of five. After the appeal court had rejected their collective plea for a judicial review, they started their sentences in late

July. Twenty years later, the outcome of the First World War was to find in the *memorandists'* favour.

In October 1918, the RNP met at Oradea and invoked the right of self-determination for the Romanians of Hungary, conveniently at the same time as President Wilson fully recognised the Yugoslavs and Czechoslovaks. The Habsburg monarchy had now finally dissolved into its component parts—Galicia and Ruthenia seceded—causing Hungary to disintegrate. The leaders of the Transylvanian Romanians convoked a National Assembly on 1 December in Blaj, without inviting the Hungarian and Saxon *natios* to attend. This assembly, cheered by thousands of peasants, declared for the union of Transylvania with Romania and adopted certain principles for the administration of the country, which were embodied in the so-called Resolutions of Alba Julia. The Hungarians, by now in total disarray, were powerless to resist.

Nicolae's grandfather, Augustin, deservedly became the first Romanian prefect of Turda and, in the family tradition of championing education, he founded a pioneering technical college there. But the euphoria of unification with Romania ebbed away in the 1940s when Transylvania was partitioned between the two Axis puppets, Admiral Horthy and Marshal Antonescu, and come the Soviet-backed Communist takeover of Romania in 1948, Augustin was arrested and sent to work on the infamous Black Sea canal, where he became ill and suffered catastrophic loss of memory. Found wandering around the streets of Bucharest, destitute, unwell and alone, by someone who fortuitously recognised him, the authorities sent him home to Turda, where for the next twelve years he was incarcerated together with his wife and daughter in a small dank cellar under the family house (now the Ratiu Foundation house). It was not until 1960 that conditions improved; he died in 1970.

Ion Ratiu, Nicolae's father, was marginally luckier; he avoided imprisonment but instead endured political exile for fifty years. After graduating with a law degree from Cluj University, he worked in London for his uncle, the politician, journalist, industrialist and diplomat Viorel Tilea, who was the Romanian Minister

Plenipotentiary in the United Kingdom. After the abdication of King Carol II in 1940, Ion, encouraged by Tilea to defy orders to return to Bucharest, asked for asylum in Britain and gained a scholarship to read economics at Cambridge. Tilea also stayed on and died in England in 1972; together with Ion, he had the proud distinction of losing his nationality twice, first for opposing the Fascists in 1940 and then the Communists in 1948.

Although Ion had been desperate to go back to Romania in 1947 to stand as a candidate in the parliamentary elections, the former Prime minister and leader of the Transylvanian branch of the National Peasants Party, Juliu Maniu, had warned him off. "We are doomed in Romania—you can do more for your country by staying outside." Ion heeded this advice, broadcasting for the BBC and writing an influential polemic *Moscow challenges the world* between 1946 and 1950.

After recovering from tuberculosis, Ion found work with a shipping company and in his spare time continued to draw attention to the plight of Romania. A passionate democrat whose key tenet was "I shall fight to the last drop of my blood to defend your right to disagree with me", he founded the British-Romanian Association in 1958 and in the same year started the Free Romanian Press, which in 1982 became the monthly *Romanul Liber*, dedicated to exposing the brutal reality of the Ceausescu regime. Courageously, Ion had identified Romania in his book *Contemporary Romania* in 1975 as 'a vassal state of the Soviet Union', giving the lie to the perceived wisdom that somehow Romania had managed to stay independent from Moscow. His campaign was so effective that after he launched the World Union of Free Romanians in Geneva in 1984, Ceausescu despatched an assassination squad of two DIE ladies to kill him. Although greatly amused at the time, it was nevertheless a relief for Ion when their mission was overtaken by events.

In 1990, after the fall of the Ceausescus, Ion put himself forward as the first opposition presidential candidate, contesting office with the former Communist minister of ideology, Ion Iliescu. When student agitators, orchestrated by the government, took to the streets, he told the BBC: "We are at long last emerging from a dictatorship that's lasted virtually forty-five years and we had hoped we could advance toward democracy and this is precisely why the young people shed their blood....Yet these demonstrations today make it look to me as if there is going to be a new attempt at taking over power from the people." Furious that "they (had) killed the dog but kept the chain", Ion persevered and was elected an MP for his home county of Cluj and served as Vice President of the Chamber of Deputies.

He also took *Romanul Liber* to Bucharest and started up a new daily paper *Cotidianul* in 1991. By 1996, when the democratically elected government of President Constantinescu took office, Ion, although no admirer of the new line-up, considered his 'job done' and immersed himself in domestic Romanian politics, becoming the Deputy for Cluj and Arad and roving ambassador to NATO as well as deputy speaker of the House of Deputies. When he died in January 2000, the world acknowledged the extraordinary role he had played in helping to bring freedom and democracy to Romania.

"Job done?" I quizzed Nicolae. "It doesn't quite fit with the story of the Ratius over the last 700 years."

"True. Two years ago, we as the Trustees of the Ratiu Family Foundation voted to establish an annual Ion Ratiu Democracy Lecture at Georgetown University in Washington in order to promote democracy not just in Romania but as a way of life worldwide. Our family's work and sense of civic duty will never be finished........"

The recipient of the Ion Ratiu Democracy Award in 2006 was the prominent Arab sociologist, Professor Saad El-Din Ibrahim. He had become the centre of international attention when he was arrested in 2000 on charges of accepting foreign funds without permission from the Egyptian government and for publishing information that 'tarnished Egypt's image'. A military court convicted him and he was sentenced to seven years of hard labour. In 2003, after eighteen months in prison, Egypt's highest criminal court acquitted him of all charges.

Appropriately the handkerchief of Ion Ratiu's mentor, Iuliu Maniu, hangs in a frame on the wall of Nicolae's London board room.

It was recovered after his death in 1953 from his prison cell in Sighet, along with a few other personal effects.

The Lebada Hotel in Bucharest, in which the Ratiu family is the principal investor, was about to close for two years, during which time it will be transformed into a Five Star conference hotel. Situated on a wooded isthmus protruding into Lake Panteleimon, its grandiose monumental architecture masks a whole history of differing uses. Based on an outer and inner quadrangular layout with a square campanile on its West side, there was a hint of its original seventeenth century monastic function as I walked among the limes and chestnuts and birches, their leaves now delicate yellow fingers. No longer the chanting of monks but the distant murmur of traffic reverberated around the cloister; the ubiquitous yelping and barking of dogs overlaid with the shrill chatter of sparrows provided the continuity of the intervening centuries.

Stripes of pale blues and light pinks slowly unfurled on the polished surface of the lake, like ribbons on a dark silver tray. Such stillness and tranquillity belied the terrible fate of poor St Panteleimon. Born in Nicomedia of a mixed marriage—his mother was a Christian and his father a pagan—the young Panteleimon studied medicine. Soon after his baptism, he healed a blind man and in doing so unwittingly incurred the wrath of the patient's ineffectual doctors who denounced him as a Christian. Finding himself in front of the rabidly anti-Christian Emperor Maximilian, Panteleimon fearlessly affirmed his Christian faith and for good measure healed a paralytic of long standing in front of the Emperor's very eyes. For his curative and miraculous efforts, he was promptly subjected to an appalling series of tortures, enough to fill a narthex wall with gruesome frescoes from top to bottom; stretched across a rack and burnt with candles; thrown into a pit of fire and then offered to wild animals; chucked into a river with a large stone attached to him (the stone floated). Finally he was condemned to death for refusing to renounce his faith. This sentence proved far from simple for each time the executioner's sword came into contact with the Saint, it broke as if made of wax. Only when Panteleimon had finished saying his prayers, did the executioner succeed in severing his head—the date was 27 July 304 and the young doctor was just twenty-nine years old.

His collect is apt:

> *"You emulated God's mercy, and He granted you the power of healing,*
> *O Panteleimon, victorious martyr of Christ.*
> *Heal our spiritual diseases through your intercession,*
> *And as we constantly cry out to the Lord 'Save us!',*
> *Take away the temptations which the enemy always places before our steps."*

If St Panteleimon was the inspiration of the monastery, its benefactor was a more mundane but equally remarkable individual, the eighteenth century politician, Grigore II Ghica, who occupied the thrones of both Wallachia and Moldavia no less than six times between 1726 and 1752. His grandfather, Gheorghe Ghica, was an Albanian and a former childhood playmate of Mohammed Köprülü, who had become the Sultan's Grand Vizier in 1656. Mohammed had bumped into his old friend in a Constantinople street and knowing him to be a worthy and reliable fellow soon had him installed as Prince of Moldavia in 1658, then of Wallachia in 1659. It was Gheorghe who moved the capital of Wallachia from Târgoviste to Bucharest.

Grigore added a manor house to his monastic foundation, distinguished not so much by its elevation but by the number of escape tunnels dug under the lake. In this respect, Ceausescu with his labyrinth of underground passages beneath the streets of Bucharest was merely continuing an old Romanian tradition. Lebada became a hospital in the nineteenth century, a use which continued until the end of the Second World War, when it was abandoned and then converted into a food store. It was only in 1987, when Romania was at the apogee of its Orwellian society, that it was perversely converted into a luxury hotel, designed to attract wealthy tourists.

This new function had two results according to its charming and softly spoken general manager, George Opris. First, the structure of the building was saved although the modernisation was achieved at the cost of somewhat garish taste. Second, the roundel drive at the front of the hotel needed an ornament, which facilitated the erection of a charming late nineteenth century fountain salvaged from the wanton destruction of central Bucharest in the 1980s by the Ceausescu regime hell-bent on building the grotesque complex of the Casa Alba presidential palace and its attendant ministries. On this Utopian pretext, monasteries and churches were demolished, including the eighteenth century Vacaresti Monastery, alongside family houses, blocks of flats and public buildings. Topped with a pair of storks cast in bronze, this little ornamental fountain has become a symbol of artistic and cultural survival.

Staying in a large hotel on the verge of closing down for refurbishment was a solitary experience; word had long gone round that the doors were about to shut and guests naturally had begun to shy away. The wide lofty corridors were empty and soundless, the dining room deserted, the bar abandoned by its clientele, the swimming pool-sauna-billiards complex locked; I wondered in its short life as a Communist party trophy hotel whether it had ever been full, whether there had ever been parties and laughter and bad behaviour.

Panteleimon is thankfully situated on the East side of Bucharest, which enables one to avoid the dense morning traffic as it angrily crawls into the city centre if, and only if one is heading for the Black Sea. I took the road to Badarog, passing scenes and sights that slowly accumulated into an endless panoramic slideshow of Romanian country life. Roadside shrines, with saints and bishops gaily painted on their walls, were easily mistaken for bus shelters with queues of patient ecclesiastic passengers; carts rumbled along, overloaded with rustling thickets of desiccated maize stalks. Sudden flurries of golden leaves fell from the lofty canopy of the poplar avenues that sentinel the roads in this fen-like landscape. In the villages, old women herded flocks of raucous turkeys, shepherds drove their sheep, elderly folk tended their solitary cow, horses and wagons busied by, housewives hauled handcarts stacked with heavy sacks, latticed maize stores bulged with earthy orange cobs. At one point of the journey, I noticed strange graveyards in two adjoining villages with large chunky stone crosses so tightly packed together that they appeared to lean on each other. Where were the ironwork crosses and neat graves beloved by both Orthodox and Catholic?

Then, as if it has been furtively hiding in the flat lands that separate Romania from Bulgaria, the Danube dramatically emerged at Guigeni in all its majesty, the empress of Balkan rivers with its mighty reach and banks[8] of towering woods. Its sudden appearance announced the beginning of the Northern Dobrodgea where the landscape changes into rolling, undulating grasslands impressed with winding valleys. Crows crisscrossed the parched fields of burnt sienna and raw umber under a cloudless sky, angry that the fields were now empty of food and that autumn had stripped the foliage from their lofty summer haunts, revealing their cantankerous private lives to the world. In a final proclamation of their existence, the hills surge up to over a thousand feet at Ciolpan and then, as if in abject surrender, they fall away and vanish completely into the flat watery horizons of the Black Sea.

Like Romania's other rivers, the etymology behind the name Danube is complex. In German *Donau*, in Hungarian *Duna*, in Serbo-Croat *Dunav*, in Bulgarian *Dunava* and in Romanian *Dunărea*, there is an indisputable commonality of title, yet all sorts of origins have been proposed by Romanian scholars—Iranian, Celtic, Thracian, Dacian and Cuman. Both the Greeks and Romans called it *Danubius* but why the Greeks called it *Istros* downstream from the Iron Gates remains a mystery unless of course that's as far as the Greeks thought it went. Some wordsmiths would say that it might well stem from the Avestic *danu* 'fluid, mist, dew', a language that belongs to the

---

[8]   *Luncas* in Romanian means 'woods on the water's edge'.

16

Iranian group of the Indo-Iranian branch of the Indo-European family of languages. My hunch is that since the Danube starts in the Black Forest, the chances are that its nomenclature originated there and flowed downstream with the once gurgling spring water.

I had come in search of the Lipovans, whose story starts in Russia in the seventeenth century. In 1656, the Russian Church service was changed on the orders of Patriarch Nikon of Moscow for mistakes had crept in over the centuries, mainly due to mistranslations and corruptions of the original Greek texts as they mutated into Church Slavonic. For instance, the Russians made the sign of the cross with two fingers rather than three as the Greeks did; the spelling and pronunciation of Jesus was at variance as was shaving of beards and the number of Alleluias uttered before the Gospel. Those who disagreed with the changes were excommunicated and later persecuted; Nikon himself, Patriarch of Great, Little and White Russia fell foul of Tsar Alexis in 1658. Alexis's eventual successor, Joseph II, confirmed Nikon's reforms and thus heralded the beginnings of the *Raskolniki*, the dissenters, and in particular the *Starovierstsi* or Old Believers. By the end of the eighteenth century, there were at least ten different sects, one of which was the Lipovans who had migrated to the area around the River Prut and the Danube Delta rather than commit suicide by self-immolation.

My three clues to their existence in the Delta were with one exception very out of date. A photograph of a 'Russian in Tulcea' taken by Queen Marie on her journey down the Danube in 1904 and her description[9] of them as 'peaceful, fair-haired giants, their type never changes. They are everywhere easily recognizable with their blue eyes, their honey-coloured beards and scarlet blouses that can be seen in all places, bobbing about like giant poppies in their flat, black boats'; Sacheverell Sitwell's reference to Lipovan fishermen in *Roumanian Journey* in 1938—he called them 'sea cossacks', frequently red-bearded; and encouragingly, a statistic published on the internet that the Romanian government officially recognize a minority of 'Russians/Lipovans of 0.2 per cent'. In addition, I had

---

[9]   Queen Marie of Romania: *The Country that I Love*

read that Lipovans do not shave and wear shoulder length hair and furthermore, they had a reputation as being prodigious consumers of alcohol.

On the South-western shore of Lake Razim or alternatively on the North-western shore of Lake Golovitsa—both lakes merge here—lies the eighteenth century fishing village of Jurilovca. With its flowerbeds of bright chrysanthemums and avenues of neatly pollarded lime trees, it is a prosperous little town with a working fish factory at the port and a fleet of high-prow Delta fishing boats, which uncannily resemble North American Indian canoes. Although its 'architecture, costumes, and customs' had been billed as 'of Lipovan tradition', my problem was that there was no one to be seen in the streets except a group of old ladies huddled together in the doorway of the church. Then my luck changed for into sight limped an elderly bearded man, wearing a jaunty Bob Dylan cap. Tapping out a route with his stick, he slowly and methodically approached the solitary bench in the town square, next to a blue building with a Cyrillic sign and a fishing boat incorporated into a small pond in front of its entrance.

"Lipovan Centre", he announced with pride after he had recovered from his exertions.

"Are you are a Lipovan too?" I asked.

"Yes and there are 3,000 like me here in Jurilovca." I mused where they could all be at three in the afternoon.

"And the beard?"

"Oh, yes, I have always worn one; it's part of our tradition."

My new acquaintance was called Ivan Vidineyo, aged seventy-eight and the only surviving member of his family of five brothers and four sisters. He had spent his life as a merchant seaman on commercial fishing boats and like many sailors, told me of his fond memories of Gibraltar and Halifax, Nova Scotia, those far off nautical capitals of his former fishing world. Slowly, exhausted by his walk and my abysmal Russian, Ivan began to doze off and I left my source on the subject of Lipovans gently snoozing in the warm autumnal sun.

The next village along the shoreline of Lake Razim is Enisala, an old Thracian settlement, later on the greatest Dacian necropolis in

Dobrodgea, and then a Roman camp. As one comes over the brow of the hill, the Byzantine fortress of Heracleia rebuilt by the Genoese in the thirteenth century lies in splendid defiant isolation on a small mount overlooking the lake. The combination of the similarity of Enisala to a Crusader castle and the appearance of a shepherd slowly driving his flock through a great field of stubble surrounding the bleached castle walls produced a strange affinity with the Holy Land.

When the Genoese remodelled and restored the castle, the waves of the Black sea still lapped the sandy shore beneath its walls. In those days, the lakes and lagoons of the Delta did not exist in their present form and for the Genoese, Enisala was key to the protection of the Danube river trade route. It is extraordinary to think that in the late Middle Ages the Genoese controlled the whole of the Black Sea and hence the trading routes to and from China, for the flow of goods from China to Europe did not follow a single 'silk road'. From their original base in Galata in Constantinople — their tower can been seen to this day — the Genoese had built up export markets in wine, oil, woollens, silks, skins, furs, corn and slaves, amassing a fortune in the process, yet most of it was spent on war, first against the Pisans and then against the Venetians. By the end of the fourteenth century, the Genoese were exhausted and their colonies in the East slipping away.

After the fall of Constantinople in 1453, the Genoese managed to obtain a favourable deal from the victorious Mehmet II and for a moment it looked as if their pre-eminent maritime trading position could be maintained. They had unfortunately overlooked the fact that the great fortress of Rumeli Hisari, which the Sultan had started to build before his attack, now controlled the Bosphurus and thus the hundreds of Italian ships that sailed into and out of the Black Sea. So their monopoly was at an end and twenty years later they left the Crimea, the centre of their Black sea colonies. Caffa (Crimea), the probable source of the Black Death in 1347 and in its day richer than Genoa itself, remained the main slave market for the Ottomans and Tartars and experienced brisk business for the next two hundred years.

The Turks called Babadag, a town on the shore of a lake of the same name, 'the Father of the Mountains'. As to why, there is no obvious reason: although the land is hilly, it is certainly not mountainous. Apart from hosting a great annual picnic each 15 June in the lime tree forest outside the town, Babadag could make a useful base for exploring Lake Rosca, with its geese, egrets, storks and Europe's largest pelican colony—depending on the time of year. In my case, in late October, the pelicans had departed, leaving me only with Sitwell's magical description: 'Far away, white cities gleamed and sparkled upon the horizon. It was the Orient of white domes and minarets; or it was the deception of a cool mirage in this reverberant heat. And then the truth came. These were white pelicans, towns of white pelicans camped upon the islands.'

The gateway to the Danube Delta is the bustling city and port of Tulcea, situated on the Tulcea channel which splits into the Sulina channel in the centre of the Delta and the Sfântu Gheorghe channel in the South. This was the ancient *Castrum Aegyssus* founded by the Greeks in the third century B.C. and later conquered by the Romans. At one time in the seventeenth century, Tulcea was best known for its numerous windmills; indeed Kurt Heilscher, the famous German ethnographic photographer, captured these *mori de vânt* with their huge ten-pole propellers driven by triangular cotton sails in his 1928 book on Romania. There was no sign of them as I drove through the suburbs at twilight in search of the Delta Nature Resort which I eventually located at the end of an unmade road a few miles past Samova to the West of Tulcea.

Set into the hillside below the vineyards of Movila Săpăta, this eco-resort is the brainchild of an eminent Indian businessman, Mr Diwaker Singh. Faced in muted tope-coloured clapper board, the main 'mother ship' hotel building and its thirty cabins remain stealthily landscaped, almost invisible until one stumbles across the wattle fence marking the outer edge of the Resort. This compatibility with the countryside is at the heart of the environmental thinking behind the Resort, explained Virgil Munteanu, its Chief Operating Officer.

Formerly the governor of the Danube Delta Biosphere Reserve Authority, Virgil is passionately committed to the task of conserving the flora and fauna, which gives the Delta both its importance and uniqueness in the natural world. An archetypal gentle giant, he tells a story of how he kept a sick swan in his office when he was governor; it nested in his filing cabinet and soon became the focal point of interest over and above national and local politics! Yet, when the call to arms arrived, he was a formidable opponent when he rallied worldwide support against Ukrainian plans to build a new canal in the Delta which threatened the entire environment.

"We have 95 per cent of the world's population of Red-breasted Geese visit us here—over 60,000 arrive in December from Siberia. But that's not so many compared to the two million birds we have in the winter!" His enthusiasm and knowledge was infectious. "There are seventy-five species of fresh water fish and 150 of marine fish."

"And sturgeons?" I asked, thinking of cavair—*ikra* and *paijusnaya* (the caul).

"There is a ten-year ban on catching them—in contrast to the nineteenth century when they were caught as far up the river as Vienna!"

Virgil, who studied for his PhD in Environmental education at Cheltenham in the mid-1990s, is now the international representative of the Danube Delta Biosphere Reserve Authority and its foremost champion in high places. With the detritus of ten countries and four capitals accumulating uninvited in the Delta, there were few occasions for humour. "We must be the only beneficiary of an economic downturn," mused Virgil. "In the 1990s, the quality of the water commensurately improved as the Romanian economy went into decline. The reed beds naturally filter the water but the metallic contents are impervious to this process—only industrial slowdown produces less metal pollution."

I asked him about the Lipovans.

"You will meet one tomorrow, Alan, I promise."
Hoping that I was now on a winning streak, I ventured:
"..and an Aromanian?"

This enquiry was prompted by another minority shown on the Romanian website, although in this instance no percentage was shown. The name *Aroman* is derived like Romanian directly from the Latin *Romanus* or 'Roman'; adding an 'a' in front of a consonant is a feature of the Aromanian language. There are several conflicting theories about the origins of the Aromanians: they were either Latinized (Latin-speaking) Greeks, who may have been Roman mercenaries, or a branch of the Daco-Romanian descendants of Roman colonists and soldiers or possibly descendants of Thracians and Illyrians.

Scattered over a wide area including Greece, Macedonia, Bulgaria, Albania and Serbia, the Aromanians settled in the Romanian lands after the Turkish occupation of their homelands, and a further influx arrived after the First World War when the Romanian government offered land and incentives to settle in the newly acquired Southern Dobrodgea province. Today there are estimated to be between 25,000 and 50,000 Aromanians in Romania.

Virgil considered my request carefully before cautiously replying: "Problem here for you is that there are no Aromanian communities. They are completely integrated with Romanians. Maybe they have small cultural identity but otherwise the same as all of us. Very well part of Romanian society. So, sorry, no Aromanians for you....."

To mitigate the disappointment which must have fallen across my face like a long evening shadow, he added: "....but the Lipovans — you will really like."

Next morning on the quayside at Tulcea, I waited for the Delta Nature Resort speedboat to hove into view. After a while I became conscious of a scraping noise coming from the other side of the pontoon I was standing on. To kill time, I wandered across to see what was going on and that is how I met Sacha Ivanov and his speedboat. He was busily cleaning the deck, muttering to himself as

Old ...

... New

LIPOVANS

From the trap ...

... to the pot

River traffic

DANUBE DELTA

Mile 23—Lipovan 'Des Res'

he picked small silver flakes off the transom seat. It transpired that the previous occupants had used the boat for a fishing trip and left behind a malodorous and unsightly confetti of fish scales.

"Why they bother?" chuckled Sacha. "Full moon now; pike lose their teeth. Must wait for wax moon before you fish." He held out his arm like a hairy banister rail for me to grip while I lowered myself into the boat, a streamlined four-seater with a massive 90 HP outboard engine.

I took stock of my skipper cum guide for the next two days. Built like a squat wrestler, with short cropped grey hair, a ruddy face and cool blue eyes trailing a cat's cradle of smile lines behind them, Sacha sported the latest line in Chanel sunglasses for Men. I admired them: "Chanel, very smart."

He grinned at me. "Yes, we go to Black Sea by canal."

The engine roared into life and we sped off into the centre of the river, at this point called the Bratul Tulcea, the southern of the two branches that the Danube splits itself into at Patlageanca. Initially our route followed the course of the wide river, banks lined with elegant stands of trees, their roots exposed like arboreal veins by the ebb and flow of flood waters. After the Mile 36 marker post, we turned North along a waterway dotted with little clumps of anglers on either bank, camped between the willow trees whose naked roots were matted with webs of vegetation like the tangled hair of ancient shipwrecked survivors.

Sacha told me that he spent the last twenty years as a commercial fisherman, but now aged forty-three this was his new job. "I like very much," he beamed.

As we passed by boats full of villagers who had been out collecting wood, silently rowing along the labyrinthine canals, he explained to me the origin of the term Lipovan. "Lipa is Russian tree for making icons. So we are called Lipovans."

As an afterthought, he added: "Czar hung the Old Believers up by their beards on trees and the wolves ate them."

"What is name of this tree in English?" I asked.

"Lipa tree."

I nodded sagely and only learnt later that the липа tree is a lime tree. Turning East into a smaller channel, we entered cormorant country, easily distinguishable by the naked branches of the treetops, excorticated by the bile vomited by these gluttonous birds. Grey herons and white egrets flew lazily past. Sacha suddenly tooted his horn and shouted to a man cleaning a net on the muddy bank.

Like a Master of Ceremonies at a civic reception, Sacha turned towards me and announced in stentorian tones: "My good friend, Laurence. He is my neighbour!"

We disembarked on the mud flats and I was ceremoniously introduced to Laurence and his two companions, who were the sole inhabitants of an island secreted in the middle of this green wet muddy world. Their old camp, sited in a clearing hacked out of the undergrowth, had been swept away by the devastating floods of last April; in its place, they had built a small hut with mud walls and a reed roof, home for the three of them and two dogs for a week at a time. Inside the hut stood a large communal bed, a table and a small stove concocted out of an oil drum.

Laurence was the leader of this little band of piscine hunters. Fishing these waters since the age of twelve, he is now twenty-seven and married with a small child. Every other week he spends here, catching pike and pike-perch through an ancient and elaborate system of nets and traps. He had done rather well when I saw him, with a catch of twenty fat pike. With the exception of the closed season which lasts from 15 April to 15 June, this piscine existence is a relentless struggle for survival.

As we made our way back to the boat, Sacha exclaimed: "The fishermen are poor men. You know one is Turk? All world is here in Delta—Italians, Greeks, Macedonians, Russians, Polish, Hungarian, Jews, German, Romanians and Ukrainians."

He considered this statement like a wine taster about to pronounce judgment and then added: "I like this job very much. Very, very perfect."

After restarting the engine, as we reversed slowly into midstream, Sacha declared with an expansive wave of his arm: "I know everyone, fishermen, families, everyone…!" At this moment, I knew I had met

Sacha before, on the well-thumbed pages of *The Wind in the Willows* for surely he was the very personification of Ratty.

The shallow entrance to Lac Nebunu appeared on our left; a hushed, sepulchral pond where the birds were eerily silent and strange frogs of constantly changing colours chastised us with their guttural croaks. Unregulated canal building has resulted in the silting of this lake for Sacha remembers it when he was young as the home of giant catfish, with some specimens reaching 300 kilos. Stories abounded that their diet consisted of large birds and small children. As we went further into the remote recesses of the Delta, I began to feel that I was trespassing on a watery surface that belonged to birds, not men; my very presence was a malfeasance.

On the Sontea Canal, heckled by diving gulls, we passed by a river cruiser, its decks packed with jolly anglers. Somehow Sacha managed to foul one of their lines and after much hollering from its surprised and increasingly distressed owner, he recovered the errant fishing rod and returned it to the bereft angler minus its valuable spinning reel. Perversely, since it was clear to me that the whole incident had been of Sacha's making, the angler lobbed two cans of beer into the speedboat as a thank you for saving his rod!

Baclanestii Mari, according to Sacha, meant Cormorant Lake in Russian. We stopped on it to examine a fish trap which consisted of two long nets, one attached to the bank, which met in a three trap 'Talian' set up. The purpose of the nets was to direct the fish into the trap complex and in this instance judging from the dozens of dead perch the ruse had succeeded. A shot suddenly rang out.

"Hunting something," muttered Sacha disapprovingly. We then noticed a dead swan floating in the water about fifty meters away. With several deprecatory tut-tuts accompanied by a slow shaking of his head, Sacha confided in me his verdict: "Many problems for he who shot swan. Possible stay in jail five years."

"But we don't know it was shot. Maybe it died of bird flu?"

"No, definitely shot. One gun allowed to shoot five birds a day—geese, pheasant, duck. On this I feed my family for one week. No swans."

More shots echoed across the stillness of the lake. Sacha shrugged and opened the throttle to full power, whisking me in a green and brown blur towards a village called Mile 23. The roots and combed weeds reminded me of a cargo of wigs, false beards and eyebrows washed ashore.

Sacha kept up his commentary, ad-libbing as we hurtled through the narrow canals like a chase in a James Bond film. "One big rat!" he shouted, as a coypu-sized creature sensibly dived beneath the boat to avoid imminent decapitation. "Marsh harrier will catch rat," he voiced vengefully.

'Toot, toot' went the horn. "This is my cousin", Sacha shouted above the roar of the wind as he waved to a man on a boat heading in the opposite direction. "Look, he catching a big pike."

The long, low houses of Mile 23 came into view but we sped past and only slowed down when we reached the junction of the Danurea Veche and Bratul Sulina. Sacha proudly pointed to an obelisk that marked the completion of the realignment of the channel in 1894, a massive construction and engineering achievement orchestrated by an Englishman, Sir Charles Hartley. For some reason, the engraved script on the obelisk only mentioned the name of King Carol I!

We stopped for lunch at a village house in Crisan. Our hostess produced *mămăligă*[10] and soup, catfish, pike-perch with garlic sauce, apple strudel, all served with tuica and home-made white wine. With its predominantly Romanian and Ukrainian population, Crisan did not measure up to Sacha's Lipovan standards and so we returned to Mile 23, which he assured me was a proper Lipovan village. A typical fishing settlement located on the "Old Danube", the village is laid out along the side of the river, a straggle of reed-roofed blue and white painted single storey houses masked by tall reed fences. Many have a wooden motive of three cockerel tails stencilled in their eaves. In summer, colourful gardens of flowers and vegetables, orchards of plum, quince and pear trees, and small one-man vineyards, enlivened by Golden orioles nesting in the fruit trees and mating sladder-frogs, mellow this bleak and remote human habitat.

---

[10] Mashed cornmeal, a staple food of the Romanian country diet.

As we walked down the dusty road along the riverbank, I pointed out the salted pike hanging in the gardens. Sacha quickly responded: "Yes, good fishermen but they do two things too much. One, drink too much vodka. Two, sing too many songs about grandfathers catching plenty of fish." Our way was blocked by an impromptu barbecue on the tow path; three large men in track suits were grilling freshly caught fish prepared by a small man with a beard, who was busily de-scaling perch on a work bench.

"Lipovan", announced Sacha and he started to converse with him in Russian.

"This villager is drunk", he pronounced, like a doctor giving a fatal diagnosis. "They are giving him a glass of white wine for every fish he cleans."

A horse amiably ambled over, intent on joining in the party. By now it was getting dark and we left the warm glow of the charcoal grill enveloped in an alcoholic haze behind us as we fearlessly sped along the darkened waterways back to Tulcea. The temperature dropped, the air grew chill and despite being wrapped up in a camouflaged Russian parka, I could feel my bones beginning to freeze. To my horror, we shot past the city and just as I was about to remonstrate with Sacha, he cut the engine and we drifting silently in the darkness.

"This is where Sulina meets big river. Very important place I show you." The problem was that by now it was pitch black. After graciously thanking Sacha for this 'special moment in time', he got the hint and returned to the quayside in Tulcea, where we agreed the time of our meeting the next day.

In the pre-war years, there was another Russian sect found in the Delta, the *Skoptzis*. Among the various *Raskolniki* which included such exotic groups as the *Kylsti* (flagellants) who according to one chronicler 'hold secret meetings[11], sing wild stirring hymns, dress in white and jump and dance and whirl', *Bezbrachniki* (free lovers), *Stranniki* (wanderers), *Molchalniki* (mutes), *Molokani* (milk drinkers) and *Dukhobors* (spirit wrestlers), the Skoptzis were famous for practicing self castration. Believing that Christ never died but

---

[11]   Known as *radeniye*.

wandered constantly across the earth in different forms including that of Czar Peter III, the uncouth and debauched husband of Catherine the Great who had been detained in 1672 in a villa at Ropscha near St Petersburg, allowed only his violin, negro servant and favourite dog before being strangled by Alexis Orlov, the Empress's proxy murderer, the Skoptzis advocated chastity. Who can blame them?

Citing *Matthew 19:12—"and there be eunuchs which have made themselves eunuchs for the kingdom of heaven's sake"*- and *Luke 23:29—"blessed are the barren, and the wombs that never bare"*, the Skoptzis took these texts to their logical extreme. The greater number of Skoptzis submitted to the 'first purification', which required that they remove their own testicles and scrotum with razors, pieces of glass or even a bit of sharpened bone. These initiates were said to have given up the 'keys of hell' but to retain the 'keys to the Abyss'. Those who removed their penis as well were awarded the honour of 'Bearers of the Imperial Seal' and were considered 'worthy of mounting white horses'. Female members of this sect did not remove their ovaries, but mutilated their external genitalia and nipples. The highest degree of feminine participation was the complete amputation of the breasts.

There are no signs of the Skoptzis today.

Early next morning, I walked along a ridge of vineyards behind the Delta Nature Resort, putting up a cock pheasant and crossing paths with a large dog fox, a *vulpoi mare*, returning to his earth. The Ukraine lies only a few miles to the North beyond the reed banks, a relatively new border in the greater historical scheme of national boundaries in these parts. It was, after all, only in 1938 that Sacherverell Sitwell travelled around this area, visiting Ismail, Valkov and the monastery at Petropavlosk, in those days all part of Romania.

Sacha was waiting for me at the little jetty below the Resort, this time at the helm of a twin-hulled shallow-bottomed boat with a pedestrian Five HP engine. No longer at the controls of his speedboat, it was altogether a more restrained and less exuberant Sacha who piloted me out into the watery wilderness, observed only by grebes. He pointed out the islands of reeds tethered like barges to the side of the channel. "In spring, with big water, they move, sometimes one kilometre."

After navigating down increasingly shallow and narrow channels, many no more than woody claustrophobic watery tunnels, occasionally stopping to inspect fish traps whose waterproof hoops of *korn* (a mountain shrub with tasty olive-like berries) remain undetected by the catfish, we emerged into the open water of Lac Saon, a large circular lake aptly named from the Turkish word for circle. On the far hills, I could just make out the white onion cupolas of *Cocosh* Monastery—translated by Sacha as "husband chicken"—and in the middle distance the spire of Saon Monastery, our lunchtime destination.

In contrast to the record flood levels of the spring, the water level was now at a record low, making disembarking a challenge. After three attempts to beach the boat at the monastery, each one involving running it aground several meters from the shore, Sacha spotted the rickety remnants of a jetty and we managed to clamber ashore without wading knee deep through the oozing mud. Making our way through an orchard with plum trees festooned with fishing nets, we reached the little blue and white wooden church built by the Russians in 1846. The barrel-vaulted narthex led the eye to a triconch of apses which were illuminated by four windows set high in the wooden octagonal tower, allowing light to flood in like spotlights on the silver–faced panels of the iconostasis. Sacha bought ten candles, all of the thin variety in memory of the dead. His eyes filled with tears as he murmured, "so many I know now dead."

The monastery of Saon is a self-contained community of thirty-five nuns and two priests. It boasts a small menagerie of two ostriches, chickens and turkeys, whole colonies of cats and dogs and a cage full of pheasants, apparently caught in traps and donated to the sisters by hunters in exchange for redemption. "Nothing from shop", explained Sacha, "everything grown, reared or caught." Lunch took place in the refectory with its newly painted walls crammed with saints and prophets, a splendid rendering of the traditional painting of the Last Supper and two full-length portraits of contemporary bishops. A young nun brought in plates of sheep's cheese, quails eggs, sausages, stuffed peppers and pork and then turning to the icon of Christ on the wall, she addressed her Grace to Him. We sat down and Sacha, who had been rather muted all morning, found himself at the head of the table and began to hold forth.

"When sailor, me vodka champion and arm wrestling champion. Also businessman. As engineer, I have cupboard in engine room. Fill with vodka very cheap: I sell in Angola fifty millilitres for five US dollars." He smiled at the thought of his past riches.

Then he continued in a confessional tone: "They catch Sacha and tell him he is a bad example to Romania. Very embarrassing."

From the shores of Africa, he took us to the West coast of Scotland which reminded him of 'paradise' for the sheep there were pure white and there was plenty of water in the hills. Maybe it was the fixative eyes of the saints observing him from the walls or a thought creeping in from the side but suddenly he became maudlin. "Sacha very poor today; under Ceausescu, we could all go on holiday but old structure has collapsed. My son is at school two hundred miles away; I cannot afford to visit him".

A little ray of golden light borrowed from the halos of the saints shone in his eyes. "But after ten days I miss fishing, so freedom is better in that you have a choice. It's better if you have your life how you want."

This philosophical twist to his conversation cheered him immensely and he beamed at a portrait of St. Nicholas. "I have two Saints days. On 6 December, Romanians celebrate St Nicholas; on 19 December Russians do! So I have two parties!"

The journey back took us through a labyrinth of still, svelte reeds, their spear-tipped leaves occasionally catching the breeze, and fluttering like Chinese battle flags before kow-towing in dulcet waves before the imperial wind. The Greeks called these reeds *phragmites*, the name for a fence. There are moments when closed in by these dense ranks of *phragmites communis* and *australis*, one could be forgiven for imagining one is on an expedition up some jungle river in Sarawak. Emerging back in to the open water, a kingfisher heralded our arrival and flashed past the bow, a turquoise tracer bullet in the twilight. On either side of the boat, moorhens frantically flip-flopped and skedaddled across the surface of the water in half-hearted attempts to get airborne, more a display of whimsical intent than determination to succeed.

Sacha was not very good at farewells; nor am I. He gave me a prolonged bear hug, wished me well and told me to look him up next time I was in the Delta.

"If not here, then I'll be fishing on the canal. You know where to find me." With a wave, he headed off up the road into the night, hands in pockets, shoulders slumped, more Russian than Romanian, a true Lipovan.

CHAPTER TWO

POLISH COSSACKS AND SZÉKELYS

To the West of Somova, in the direction of the Danubian city of Galaţi, lies the hinterland of the Danube Delta, bordered to the South by the Macin Mountains and to the East by their smaller neighbours, the Niculitel Hills, and to the North by two vast Ukrainian lagoons, Lacu Cahul and Lacul Ialpug. Between them, the land clings to its existence thanks to a series of dykes and causeways. Half way to Galaţi, the town of Isaccea forlornly looks across the river at its former possessions now in the Ukraine. This small town of humble houses has an extraordinary historical pedigree, mainly founded on its location as one of the few fordable crossings on the river. King Darius I of Persia defeated the Scythians here in 514 BC as he marched North; the Romans called it Noviodunum and made it the base for their Lower Danube fleet and the headquarters of their *Iovia Legio*; the Byzantines followed suit and elevated it to an Episcopal see; the Genoese built the port of Vicina nearby; the Ottomans and Principalities fought over it; the Russians besieged it and it finally came into the Romanian fold in 1878. No one could accuse Isaccea of irrelevance in the past but now it is a sleepy place, astride a river than no longer has a fleet, its former trade routes bypassed by modern transport networks.

The rain, driven by a ferocious East wind, lashed down on the featureless landscape, obliterating in anarchic brown smudges what little evidence of human activity there was to be seen in the late autumnal cycle. There are no bridges here; ferries to the cities of Braila and Galaţi provide the only link from the Delta to what seems the mainland of Romania. The bold orange road on my map that confidently connected Smardan to Braila was either a figment of the geographer's imagination or a printing error. Fortunately I had checked with Virgil before I left and now stood on the quayside at Zaclau/I.C.Bratianu/Movlieni, watching the wind whip up three-foot high waves and waiting for the ferry stockpiled with heavy trucks and buses to scurry and slew its way across like a crab heading for its burrow in a thunderstorm. In the pouring rain, no city would have looked inviting but Galaţi with its vast steelworks and forests of cranes looked more inhospitable than most. The unloading and loading of the ferry was choreographed chaos, at times relying more on divine intervention than the competencies of the crew, who, swathed in yellow oilskins, stood around chatting in stark contrast to the miserable bunches of rain-sodden passengers huddled beneath the bridge. Everyone puffed furiously on damp cigarettes.

I had come to Galaţi in search of Mazepa's tomb in Saint George's Monastery to see what, if anything, remained of this strange monument to a legendary seventeenth century Polish adventurer who became a Cossack *hetman*.[12] Born the son of a Polish gentleman in Bielo-Tzerko in the central Ukraine in 1644, young Stefan Mazepa was supposedly caught *en flagrant délit d'adultère* with a Madame Falbowska by her husband, a nobleman in whose house he was staying. There is a school of thought that attributes this story to a smear campaign orchestrated by a rival called Jan Pasek, a fellow page whom Mazepa had crossed swords with at the court of King Kazimierz after reporting him for treachery. On Pasek's release, the two quarrelled in public in an altercation that ended with them slapping each other's faces.

A dab hand with the pen, Pasek's revenge was to publish a libellous account of a fictitious affair that ended with this humiliating scene:

---

[12]   Chief of a Cossack clan.

"...After stripping him naked, they placed him on his own unsaddled horse's back, with his face to the tail and feet to the horse's head. Then they tied his hands behind his back and his feet under the horse's belly, shouted at, struck with whips, tore the blinkers off, and fired a few shots over the fleet-footed horse. The panicked steed galloped homeward as if it were rabid. And the way was through dense woods, thickets of hawthorn, hazelnut, buckhorn, and briar, down barely visible trails... A rider usually has to bend down, holding the reins in hand, and bypass dangerous places. Sometimes a tree branch would hit him on the head and rip his clothes. You can thus imagine the injuries the naked horseman must have received, for the swift, frightened and hurt horse was galloping wildly and at random until it galloped out of the forest... Reaching his home, the wounded Mazepa began to call his guards. At first the latter could not recognize him. Then they finally let their exhausted and frozen master in. He was barely able to speak."

The plot has striking similarities with the Greek myth of Hippolytus—meaning 'Loose horse'! He had spurned the love of his stepmother, Phaedra, who in revenge accused him of rape. As punishment, the gullible Theseus put a curse on him. Bound to his chariot, the innocent Hippolytus was killed when a sea monster startled his galloping horses. This legend was used in a tragedy by Euripides (484-404 BC) and later by the Roman author, Seneca, in his *Pheadra* and the French playwright Racine.

Voltaire takes up the story in his 1731 *Life of Charles XII*: 'On the discovery of an intrigue with the wife of a Polish nobleman, the latter had him tied, stark naked, to a wild horse, and set him free in that state. The horse, which had been brought from Ukrania, returned to its own country, carrying Mazepa.' The French writer André Dorville repeated the story in 1764, this time embellishing it with the name of the beautiful Countess de Bra-, the scene as the Chateau Bielas-tok and Mazepa being caught by an elderly Count[13] en flagrant at the Countess's feet. When his mount finally came to a halt in the Ukraine, Mazepa was welcomed by the Cossacks and eventually became their

---

[13] Possibly Count Jan Zagorowski and his young wife, Elena Kowalewska.

Hetman. He spent the rest of his life fighting for Tsar Peter the Great until his last years when he turned against him and sided with the Swedes; he committed suicide by taking poison rather than surrender to the Russians after the fall of Bender.

The truth was more prosaic. Educated by the Jesuits in Warsaw, Stefan joined the Krakow court of King Jan Kazimierz (Casimir) and was sent to study in Holland. In 1656-59 he learned gunnery in Deventer and visited Germany, Italy, France, and the Low Countries. At the age of nineteen, he was sent as an envoy to the Polish-ruled Cossacks on the West bank of the Dnieper, the river that dissects modern day Ukraine, and by 1669 had entered the service of Hetman Doroshenko of the West bank, initially as a squadron commander in the Hetman's Guard, and later as chancellor. In 1674, he was captured by the Zaporozhians and handed over as a spy to Ivan Samoylovych, the Cossack Hetman of the East bank. He convinced him that he was of more use alive than dead and after becoming Ivan's assistant, he successfully plotted to remove him from office and became Hetman himself in 1687 and a stalwart supporter of Peter the Great in his wars against the Ottomans and Crimean tartarate and initially the Great Northern war against Sweden and Poland.

Mazepa's love life had stabilised in 1669 when he married Anna Fridrikiewicz, the widow of a Colonel and the daughter of a Colonel, Semen Polovets, who brought with her much of her father's regimental property. Soldiering in those days could be immensely profitable. Anna died in 1702 and two years later, just before his seventieth birthday, Mazepa asked Colonel Kochubey for the hand of his daughter, Motrya, who also happened to be the Hetman's god-daughter. The problem was that she was sixteen.

Throwing caution to the Steppe winds, Mazepa put pen to paper:

"My dear heart, my darling little rose,
I suffer in my whole being at the thought that you are far from me; I cannot see any more your eyes and your white face. I kiss and embrace you tenderly."

Then,

"My well-beloved heart,
You know how I love you, with all my heart, like a madman. Your
Grace, I have never loved any one in the world this way. It would be
my happiness and joy to see you come to live in my house."

Alas for Mazepa his overtures were rebuffed, his love for Motrya unrequited and the Kochubeys' fury unabated; they never forgave him. The following year, he found a new girlfriend in Princess Anna Dolska, the widow of the Grand Marshal of Lithuania. At least this time the object of his desire was in her fifties. However, her tendency to dabble in politics and to buy and sell information made her far from dependable and she may well have played a part in Mazepa's fateful decision of October 1708, when he decided to throw his lot in with the young Charles XII of Sweden who was marching towards the Ukraine on his way to join battle with the Tsar. Why he chose to betray Peter is unclear. Maybe he had had enough of fighting far-off wars that only benefited Russia; maybe he was impressed by the young Swede's invincibility to date. But it was an ill-judged decision because the following June the Swedish-Cossack army was comprehensively beaten at the Battle of Poltava. The wounded Swedish King and the old Hetman fled to Ottoman-held Bender (in today's Moldava) and from there to the little village of Varnitsa, where, three months later, his head supposedly resting on a saddlebag stuffed full with looted diamonds, the fickle Mazepa died. The story of his interment is as dramatic as that of his life.

The funeral of His Most Serene Highness, Ivan Mazepa, Hetman of the Zaporozhian Host, was held on 4 October 1709 at Bender in Moldavia. Heading the procession was the greatest soldier of the day, Charles XII, followed by representatives of France, The Porte,[14] the Crimean Khanate, Poland, Wallachia and of course the Prince of Moldavia; all paid homage to the man who had defied the Tsar and his territorial ambitions. How come then he was buried in Galaţi?

---

[14] The name used by Western European governments to describe the political entity of the Ottoman state.

In 1710, his tomb in Bender was desecrated by Ottoman troops, so his relatives obtained a *firman* (an Ottoman decree) that granted them permission to take his remains to the Holy Land. On the way to Jerusalem, passing through Galați, they found out that the St. Gheorghe Monastery was subject (like almost all other monasteries in the Danubian Principalities at that time) to the Orthodox monastery of the Church of the Holy Sepulchre. It was therefore permissible to consider the monastery as the equivalent of the Holy Land and so they built a crypt under the church where they interred his remains, thereby complying with the decree and the wishes of his fellow Cossacks. The funeral stone was decorated with Polish and Cossack symbols and with his own escutcheon; one of whose symbols was the one-headed Ukrainian eagle. So far, so good.

Two years later, a detachment of Tartar soldiers opened it up in search of Mazepa's treasure; not a coin was to be found. Then, in the early 1800s, the family of a noble man, the Boyar Deretchi Basa, decided to bury him in the Monastery church. Digging around, they uncovered the crypt of Mazepa, but not knowing who he was, they placed the boyar beside him, pretending that Mazepa's crypt belonged to their own old and noble family. Seven years later, the family reopened the tomb and fulfilled the Orthodox commemoration ceremony, but they were not allowed to put the bones back in the crypt, due to a new law that forbade burials inside churches. So both Mazepa and the boyar were buried nearby the church and the family used the occasion to carve a new tombstone imitating the original one: the sculptor not knowing the significance of the one-headed eagle carved a two-headed Austrian eagle on the gleaming new white marble plate! This 'new' tombstone was apparently last seen in 1860; the original ended up in the collection of Prince Mihai Ghica, the brother of the Wallachian ruler Prince Ghica (1830) but has since vanished.

Having condemned Mazepa as a traitor, Peter ordered the Russian and Ukrainian churches to anathematize him. Thereafter, both Imperial and Soviet historians did their utmost to vilify poor Mazepa. Unwittingly, they created a potent symbol of Ukrainian independence,

Mazepa on his way to Ukraine

MAZEPA

... arriving

... to become Hetman

Zăbala

SZÉKELY MANOR HOUSES

Turia

a task initially and mischievously started by Lord Byron in his epic poem about Mazepa's ride.

> *Away, away, my steed and I,*
> *Upon the pinions of the wind,*
> *All human dwellings left behind;*
> *We sped like meteors through the sky,*

Figuratively Byron had also been strapped to a horse by English society in punishment for his affair with his half-sister Augusta Leigh. Byron started his 869 line epic poem in Venice in April 1817 and finished it in September two years later; its completion was interrupted by the composition of *Childe Harold* and no doubt by Byron's busy sex life for he bragged he had 'over 250 women' in Venice in one year.

Pushkin followed Byron's *Mazepa* with his epic poem *Poltava* in 1829—he had changed the name from Mazepa at the insistence of his publisher, a decision he later regretted. He had been fascinated by the story of Mazepa after reading the Decembrist Kondratii Ryleev's *Andrei Voinarovsky*, a poem about Mazepa's nephew who had been kidnapped en route to Sweden by agents of Peter in 1716 and imprisoned in the Peter and Paul Fortress before being exiled to Yakutsk in far-off Siberia. Such was Pushkin's fascination with Mazepa that he sought out the Hetman's grave at Charles XII's camp at Varnitsa. More concerned with the political aspects of the story, how in his quest for power Mazepa had compromised loyalty with cunning and ruthlessness and how this later came to destroy him, the poem was caned by the critics.

Then Victor Hugo, inspired by Byron, reworked the story in *Les Orientales* in 1828:

> *Ils vont. Dans les vallons comme un orage ils passent,*
> *Comme ces ouragans qui dans les monts s'entassent,*
> *Comme un globe de feu;*
> *Puis déjà ne sont plus qu'un point noir dans la brume,*
> *Puis s'effacent dans l'air comme un flocon d'écume*
> *Au vaste océan bleu.*

The poets Alfred de Vigny and Charles-Augustin Sainte-Beuve came up with similar offerings, more in remembrance of Byron than Mazepa but the Paris art scene took the theme of *equus eroticus* to heart, starting with a lithograph by Théodore Géricault in 1823. Horace Vernet, best known as a military painter and Orientalist, produced his dramatic canvas, *Mazeppa and the Wolves*, in 1826; a naked youth bound by a thick rope to a white stallion, spine on spine, head on head, alarmingly surveys a snarling pack of wolves surrounding him on all sides. He followed this with a second, blatant homo-erotic painting of Mazepa lying stretched out in a cruciform on the back of a horse, which is struggling to climb out of a river onto the bank. Nude, bound, head on the horse's neck, thighs spread, 'eminently violable and open to every intrusion', the young man stares at the night sky, more dead than alive. Did Vernet use a corpse as a model like Géricault's studies for *The Raft of Medusa*? Eugène Delacroix got round to painting a rather tame watercolour of the horse-bound Mazepa and last in line was Louis Boulanger—his sister was having a fling with Delacroix at the time—with a grand canvas, *Supplice de Mazeppa*, which depicts Mazepa being attached to a stallion by a gang of burly servants, all stripped to the waist, while the cuckolded nobleman looks on impassively.

On the musical scene, Liszt in turn was inspired by Victor Hugo and the result was Etude No. 4 in D minor; characterized by one reviewer as a display of Liszt's 'graphic violence', the six minute composition is of such extraordinary difficulty that many pianists would rather be strapped to Mazepa's horse. Finally, Tchaikovsky, inspired by Pushkin, composed the opera *Mazeppa* which was premiered at the Bolshoi in 1884.

While I was daydreaming about the exploits of Mazepa, the captain of the ferry had decided it was too rough to cross, so we remained hitched to the bank, unable to disembark for the next two hours, a time penalty that sadly prevented me from finding the monastery for I had to be in Transylvania that evening.

However, when I returned to England, there was a letter waiting for me from a friend in Bucharest who had been conducting some background research on Mazepa:

'Galaţi was a strategic point at the end of World War Two and the communists defaced not only the tomb of Mazepa but also the culture and identity of the population in that area. Therefore, a whole quarter of Galaţi is called Mazepa, but nobody knows who the man really was—some sort of outlaw? Nearby in Braila lived the famous 'Terente', the Romanian Cassanova of the late nineteenth century. They still keep his bollocks in the medical museum in Bucharest.

In fact, the whole St Gheorghe monastery was surprisingly demolished well before 'big C' started his demolishing opera. Torn to pieces in 1962 and plunged into the Danube. Then apartment blocks built over the place. Unfortunately, the tombstone of Mazepa was not rescued, as they did later in other similar cases, taking the artworks and historical monuments to the museums.

In 2004, a monument representing the hetman Mazepa was installed in the Libertatii Parc in Galaţi, on the spot of a former Muslim cemetery. At the ceremony attended the governors of the Ukrainian districts of Odesa and Cahul, local authorities from Galaţi and the chief hetman of Ukraine with his Cossack troopers, General Ivan Bilas.'

Tecuci, Mărăşeşti and Pancia appeared as grey ghost towns in the torrential gloom as I headed towards the 4,500 foot Mestercanului Pass which crosses the Vrancea mountains to the South of Oneşti. These sleepy towns by the Siret river were the Romanian equivalent of Ypres and Passchendale, for it was here in August 1917 that the Germans launched a major offensive against a joint Russian-Romanian army; by September, the Romanian 1st Army had lost 610 officers and 26,800 NCOs and soldiers, while the German 9th Army had lost about 47,000.

In 1933, an English traveller passing through Mărăşeşti spied the memorial to the battle on a little hill beyond the town and recorded his visit thus: 'In summer the sea of corn swept up to its doors, now only the furrowed earth billowed to the horizon. The building was circular and low-domed. In the centre was an altar enclosed in a small room. Off the corridor, which encircled it, were thirteen rooms, about ten feet long and four wide, each with a window looking over the plains. In the walls were recesses built in the shape of coffins standing on end, the stone lids stood askew revealing shelves on which were rows of broken skulls. In one room stood a flag leaning by the window, a cold breeze blew through the iron grille rustling the dry crown of bay leaves with a sound like the whispering of spirits. There was a smell of death. I was glad to leave it.' That memorial was replaced in 1938 by the Mausoleum for Heroes, a huge dome in the monumental style of Lutyens.

As I began the descent down the twisting mountain track, the pine trees providentially parted and there laid out below was the *Háromszék*, the vast, fertile oval-shaped valley of the Székelys and one of the loveliest in Transylvania. Great beams of white light pierced through gaps in the slowly disintegrating cloud cover, eerily pinpointing the town of Târgu Secuiesc to the West. John Paget passed through it in 1850, describing the whole district as 'a gently undulating plain, covered with the richest crops, dotted over with flourishing villages, watered by the meandering Aluta, and bounded on two sides by the most beautiful chains of mountains it is possible to conceive'. A few miles from there lay my destination, the Mikes Estates at Zăbala.

Nine hundred years ago, when the young Hungarian kingdom pondered how to defend its Eastern frontier which followed the mountain tops and passes of the Carpathian mountains, this very track would probably have been used by wild Petcheneg Turkic tribesmen as they conducted their incursive probes into Transylvania in search of sustenance, women and booty. They were one of the main reasons why King Bela recruited the Saxons to colonise the *Siebenbergen* (Southern Transylvania) and then allowed the Teutonic Knights to establish themselves in Brasov. His strategy worked and before long, groups of 'friendly' Petchenegs had been settled by the Hungarian kings in several parts of Transylvania, for example in the region of

Baraolt. Indeed, from 1213, Petcheneg soldiers are shown on the rolls of the Hungarian army and a document from 1224 refers to the *silva Blachorum et Bissenorum* in South-eastern Transylvania.

Towards the end of the eleventh century, the Petcheneg threat had been superseded by the Cumans, another warlike Turkic people. They dominated Moldavia and the Wallachian plain and like the Petchenegs, raided deep into Transylvania, fighting against the Hungarians and the newly arrived German colonists. It must have been evident to them that the advantages of life as a farmer outweighed that of a nomadic Steppe warrior for soon groups of them settled down in the Hungarian kingdom, mostly on the rich land between the Danube and the Tisza. The Cumans thus became Christians at the beginning of the thirteenth century and in 1227, a diocese was organized for them in the valley of the Milcov near Craiova. Although the Cuman language is closely related to Turkish, which was of course widely used in the Romanian Principalities in the seventeenth and eighteenth centuries, it is exciting that some Cuman words have survived: *beci* 'cellar', *toi* 'climax', *scrum* 'ash' and place names such as Caracal (from Cuman *kara* 'black', and *kala* 'fortification, castle') and Teleormanu (from Cuman *teli* 'wild', and *orman* 'forest').

My hosts at Zăbala were the Mikes family and I left the subject of Petchenegs and Cumans to one side as they were from an altogether more illustrious Székelys family and I did not want to get involved in a dispute about who arrived first. The fanciful version of the origin of the Székelys goes like this. When the semi-nomadic tribes who lived between the Caucasian and Ural mountains moved West in the eighth and ninth centuries, their vanguard crossed the Eastern Carpathians and found itself on a rich fertile plain in Eastern Transylvania. There, Omedzur, son of Attila the Hun, ordered his 3,000 warriors to halt and thus the Székelys arrived in today's Csik county. They settled down under the leadership of their *rabobans* to await the arrival of the main body of Huns en route for today's

Hungary; their horses were so numerous that their hoof prints could been seen at night mapping out the Milky Way or 'The Road of Hosts' as the Huns called it. That's the traditional version of the arrival of the Székelys, what the famous Eastern European historian Hugh Seton-Watson dismissively described as *arrière-pensées*. He maintained that it was only in the first decades of the twelfth century that Kings Koloman and Ladislav began to settle Magyar colonists in the East of Transylvania,[15] 'whom an ancient but almost certainly erroneous tradition, lasting till our own day, regarded as descendants of Attila and his Huns'. From 1437 onwards, the Székelys along with the Hungarians and Saxons formed their own *universitas*. Like the Saxons, they were organised into seven, later eight, seats or *Sedes* (Szék) under their own *comes* or count, holding their lands direct from the King.

Where the Székelys differed from the Magyars was they were all technically 'noble' and therefore exempt from taxation except the payment of an ox[16] on the occasion of a coronation, marriage or birth of a crown prince. However, there was a quid pro quo military trade-off with the *primores* or captains providing three to five horses, the *primipili* a sole horsemen and the *pixidarii* foot soldiers. Another difference was that they held their land in common and thus no great feudal estates were created. Ironically, this admirable egalitarian structure was to prove a financial restraint in the centuries to come and no Székelys family amassed the equivalent of the great estates of the Magyar nobility.

Living in the remote South-eastern corner of Transylvania, the Székelys were left to their own devices and one can see today on their gates carvings of God's tree with the sun and half moon motifs of the Székelys coat of arms. They had their own dance, the *csürdöngölő*, and their own pottery at Vargyas. Unfortunately they lost their tax-free status together with their immunity from confiscation of land in

---

[15] The confusion may stem from the fact that even in the late Middle Ages, the Székelys used a runic alphabet of which out of the 37 characters, 21 were ancient Turkic, 3 ancient Greek and 3 Slavic, the remainder Finno-Ungric.

[16] For a *ökörsütés* or ox-roast.

the sixteenth century; many were reduced to conditions of serfdom and their lands apportioned out by Princely grant. What saved the Székelys from oblivion was their reputation for military prowess. One apocryphal story goes that when King Stephen of Hungary gave his daughter in marriage to a young Scotsman (of royal blood, of course), the bride was accompanied on her return to Edinburgh by a hundred Székelys soldiers. What we do know is that they became the Habsburg Frontier Guard under Joseph II and produced more than their fair share of generals right through to the Second World War.

The Mikes family date back to fourteenth century and are mentioned by Baron Apor in his memoir *Metamorphosis Transylvaniae* (1783) as providing the *föispán* or Lord Lieutenant of Szolnok county in the person of Count Mihály Mikes and the same Mihály was Captain of the *szeks* of Sepsi, Kezd, Orbo and Miklosvar. Their most famous ancestor was Kelemen Mikes, who was born in the village of Zágon just to the east of Brasov in 1690. The house does not exist anymore but in the garden one can still see the oak trees planted by his father, Pal Mikes, on the birth of his son. Sadly, Pal was arrested by the Austrians for treason and subsequently executed, leaving young Kelemen to be brought up by a step-father who prudently arranged for his conversion to Roman Catholicism. Educated at Cluj by the Jesuits, in 1707 Kelemen entered the service of Ferenc Rákóczi II, Prince of Transylvania, and followed him throughout the tumultuous years of the Hungarian uprising against their hated Habsburg overlords.

After the Treaty of Szatmar in 1711 when the rebels laid down their arms, Kelemen accompanied his master into exile, eventually ending up in Turkey where he resignedly wrote in August 1718: 'If I must stay here, it's goodbye to the wedding dance.' After the death of the Prince in 1735, Kelemen was sent by his Ottoman hosts to Iasi in Moldavia, where he found 'the inhabitants are like wild animals'. He managed to extricate himself from the Moldavians and returned to Turkey via Bucharest, where he lived out the rest of his life in Tekirdag among the other Hungarian exiles until he died of the plague in 1761 after forty-eight years in exile from his beloved Transylvania.

Kelemen's enduring legacy was his book *Letters from Turkey* which described life in exile and the topics which dominated it in a series of letters to a fictitious aunt. The letters were found among his effects and were first published in 1794; they have been a best seller ever since.

The story of the current generation of the family is also one of exile. Katerina, a gracious and elegant woman now in her early sixties, lived at Zăbala with her mother and grandmother; both her parents were Mikes for 'there were seven branches to choose from'. In 1949, they were evicted by the Communists—their crime was to be well-born and property owners—and the following year, her mother was sent to a labour camp[17] in the Northern Dobrodgea. After eighteen months of forced labour in rice fields, housed with dozens of other prisoners in a flimsy wooden hut, the authorities sent her to Cluj; Katerina joined her mother eight years later and then managed to obtain an exit visa to Austria where she started a new life in exile at the age of 16.

Forty two years later, Katerina returned to Zăbala with her two grown-up sons, Gregor and Alexander Roy Chowdury, to reclaim their family property. Much had changed. The manor house—Kastély Mikes—had been used as a children's home (sixty employees and five children) and the imposing guest house, built by her great-grandfather in 1895, had been utilised in 1998 as a hospital for fifty psychiatric patients. When they had been evicted that dark night back in 1949, the Mikes family members had been allowed one small case each; today there was nothing remaining of the contents of their houses.

We had dinner in the little Swiss chalet that a great-grandmother had bought at the Paris Exhibition of 1889 and re-erected in the beech woods behind the Kastély. Gregor, the elder brother, is a natural entertainer, spinning stories laced with wry humour, wicked charm and self-deprecation, all ending with a flashing white smile,

---

[17] The Romanian Socialist Republic set up eleven large and several smaller concentration camps in the marshes of the Danube delta. 78 per cent of the prisoners were Hungarians, who, in many cases, were interned together with their families and children.

21ˢᵗ C Székelys (Mikes)

18ᵗʰ C Székelys (Csoma)

SZÉKELYS

Mihail the Shepherd today and yesterday

Csoma's memorial (Darjeeling)

Buffalo boss

TRANSYLVANIA (1)

The Bonny Ploughmen

Sachsiz: Citadel on the hill and Church in the Valley

TRANSYLVANIA (2)

Sighisoara High street

Sinners ...

LAST JUDGMENT

... heading for the River of Fire

an arched eyebrow and a throw-away languorous shake of a mop of curly dark hair.

"You know, Alan, I think I'm quite lucky to be here," opined Gregor. I concurred, thinking how nice it would be to have a castle in Transylvania.

"When the asylum was in the old guest house, I used to go and talk to the inmates, mainly old people, all sad and depressed — except one old man, who had managed to have himself admitted instead of his wife. He ate her food, slept in her bed and was always smiling! I made quite good friends with a younger guy. He was always coming up to me for a chat and was pretty well informed about most things. Then one day he let slip that he had cut up his father with a axe a couple of years before."

He paused long enough for me to work out a variety of solutions to his predicament, the most viable being to run all the way to Bucharest and hope the friendly inmate was not following. Then he continued:

"For some reason, he left the next day. You see, I am lucky to be here!"

In contrast, Alexander, a wise head on young shoulders and equally charming and considerate as Gregor, comments on matters of importance and gravity as a foil to his brother's irrepressible levity. The role of Gregor's beautiful wife, Zsolna, blonde and blue-eyed like the Byzantine Empress Helena of Hungary, is to preside over the two of them like a political chat-show hostess, thus ensuring that the audience, in this case me, heard both the funny and serious side of every topic.

The talk was all about the future, how the estate could be made financially self-sufficient though it was clear that there would be no way to restore it to its heyday in the late nineteenth century when the family had transformed themselves from modest landowners to proprietors of a major forest products business complete with railways and overhead cableways. Katerina's ninety-five-year-old aunt, who nearly became engaged to King Zog of Albania, can dimly recall this pre-First World War era, pronouncing it 'very busy'.

"You wrote to me about meeting a *Csángó*," said Gregor at the end of dinner. "Well, we can do better than that for we have a Csángó museum in the village donated by Professor Pozsony Ferenc of Cluj University. It is in the garden of his family home."

I was fascinated by this minority since the jury appeared to be out as to whether they really existed today. Csángó is the official designation as well as the popular name for Roman Catholic Hungarians living in Moldavia, the word deriving from the verb *csang/csáng*, to wander or ramble. The original Csángós had settled in Moldavia as part of the Hungarian border defences, possibly just after the Mongol invasions of 1241–1242. Their medieval culture had apparently survived to a remarkable extent with some villages boasting more than thirty different folk dances. Among their musical instruments, there are such ancient pieces as the bagpipe (Balkan and Hungarian versions), lute, trump and the peasant flute with six holes, but they also use the violin, piano accordion and drum.

In May 2001, the EU committee on Culture, Science and Education after meeting representatives from the Csángós recommended that the Committee of Ministers encourage Romania to ratify and implement the European Charter of Regional or Minority Languages and to support the Csángós in various ways such as the possibility of education in the mother tongue; an option for Roman Catholic services in the Csángó language in Csángó villages churches and the possibility for the Csángós to sing the hymns in their own mother tongue; specific programmes for the promotion of Csángó culture; an information campaign about the Csángó culture in Romania; the unique linguistic and ethnographical features of the Csángós to be appropriately recorded; the economic revival of the area, for example through the establishment of small and medium enterprises in Csángó villages.

The response of the Romanian authorities was somewhat nonplussed. As regards numbers, they pointed out that in the January 1992 census, 2,062 people described themselves as Csángós of which 1,352 were in Moldavia. This number should be seen in the context of the total population recorded for the historical province of Moldavia—3,751,783, of whom 3,691,420 were Romanian, 5,895 Magyar, 5,940 German and Polish and 47,194 other nationalities. Furthermore, it should be noted that the census recognised the right of every individual freely to declare his or her ethnic, linguistic and religious origins.

In respect of the request to provide education in the Csángó language, the authorities pointed to a number of difficulties, particularly the fact that the Csángó language is not a written language, but is handed down orally from one generation to the next. Consequently, there are neither textbooks nor any trained teaching staff. Furthermore, the small number of pupils would considerably increase the costs of teaching, which it would be difficult for Romania to meet in the economic conditions facing the country.

To find the facts which lay behind this impasse I went to meet Istvan Kinde, a student of the Professor, who was caretaking the Csángó museum. His quarters were in a cosy wooden building sandwiched between the museum and an old village house, which contained a collection of Zăbala memorabilia. Here he studied for his PhD, sleeping in the loft and showing the occasional visitor around.

"There are few distractions here, so you should be able to write your treatise undisturbed", I ventured. Istvan nodded rather glumly, so I quickly got him onto the subject of Csángós.

"There were three waves. The first in the reign of Andreas II in the thirteenth century went to protect the Hungarian Kingdom against the Cumans, Turks and Tartars—you know it was the Hungarians and Saxons who founded Moldavia's cities? Their descendants live around Roman. The second wave, in the fourteenth and fifteenth centuries, settled in the area of Bacau, places like Gioseni. They included some Hussites who had fled to Moldavia from Bohemia and translated the Bible into Hungarian."

"Protestant Csángó?" I interjected.

"Yes but they were re-catholicized in the nineteenth century." I sensed he felt this would have been a serious oversight if left unchecked.

He continued: "Finally, the third wave in 1764. These were Székelys Csángós—you know *Szűcs* is Hungarian word for tailor?—who fled eastwards after the Habsburgs had attacked them at the infamous meeting at Miercurea Ciuc. They created their own villages near the Hungarian border, places like Pustiana and Cleja."

Istvan was referring to the events surrounding the formation of the Székelys border regiment ordered by Maria Theresa in 1762. Ostensibly for the defence of the Eastern frontiers, the real Imperial agenda was to deploy Székelys regiments in the western wars of the Habsburgs. The Székelys protested against foreign military service, their German commanders and the fact that they could not regain their ancient freedom in exchange for their service. In response, on 5 January 1764, Austrian troops attacked the village of Madéfalva (Siculeni) and killed over 200 of its inhabitants. This atrocity is still remembered as the Terror of Madéfalva, or *Siculicidium.*

"How many Csángós would you estimate there are today?"

"About 65,000 is realistic number for those families in Moldavia with Hungarian language." He paused for a moment to reconsider his estimate. "Many of course are in Italy. Four buses leave Bacau every day for one Italian village!"

As to the Csángó language, Istvan explained that they spoke a mixture of Romanian, Middle Ages Hungarian and their own words. In the 1950s, a hundred Hungarian schools were founded in the Csángó regions of Moldavia but the authorities conscripted Transylvanian teachers who became homesick and drowned their sorrows in drink: the schools closed in 1959.

In 1990, a Csángó Society was founded in Bacau to promote their cause. "Csángó identity," explained Istvan, "is expressed primarily through religion—they are devout Catholics; then through the traditional village clothes, each village having its own distinct decorations and colours; then through language but of course Romanian is the common language that links all Csángó groups. Then there are the adopted cultures, the dance being 'round' like the Romanian—the Renaissance style of dancing couples never made it across the Carpathians—and the national dress similar to Romanian. They used to produce their own pottery but there is only one working potter left."

Istvan then booted up his computer and showed me his gallery of pictures of Csángó village life. Most of the houses seemed to be lived in by single old people, who eked out a desperately poor existence, rummaging for bits and pieces along the banks of the River Siret, stripped bare to its shingle foundations.

"There doesn't seem to be much future for the young", I observed.

"No, that's why they are in Italy. But there are still some around; many of the Csángó girls come and work in the Székelysfold in the summer. I think really to look for Transylvanian husbands."

"So you may be in luck?"

"First I must finish my treatise!"

Although I hadn't actually met a Csángó other than Istvan, I was now certainly much better informed about them and headed towards Gregor's next recommendation, the village of Chiuruş about ten kilometres South of Zăbala. Here apparently was a Tibetan museum. It turned out that the village was the birthplace of Alexander Csoma de Körös, who, according to the displays of maps and books in the window of a small house by the bus stop, had spent three years in a freezing monastery cell in Tibet compiling the first English-Tibetan dictionary. After a lot of toing and froing to find the key holder, including the recruitment of a large gypsy man whom I put in charge of the search, I managed to gain entrance to the museum and this is Csoma's incredible story.

Born in 1784, Csoma showed signs of wanderlust from an early age; his cousin Joseph Csoma recalled he was 'like a swallow is impelled on a distant journey when the autumn arrives,' and added 'as boys, we could never compete with him in walking, because when he happened to reach the top of a hill, that did not satisfy him, but wished to know what was beyond it, and beyond that again, and thus he often trotted on for immense distances.' Despite his tendency to wander off Csoma was a conscientious student; at the age of fifteen he entered the *Bethlenianum*, a then-famous Protestant school in Aiud, where fired up by the growing sense of Hungarian national consciousness, he vowed to track down the origins of the Hungarian people believed to be somewhere in far off Asia.

Fluent in Latin, Greek, Hebrew, German, French, Romanian and Turkish, he won a scholarship to Göttingen University in Germany, where in addition to studying English, he learnt Arabic after being told about "certain Arabic manuscripts which must contain very important information regarding the history of the Middle Ages and of the origins of the Hungarian nation when still in Asia".

His studies completed, Csoma was ready to embark on his quest and set off from Chiuruş in February 1820. Count Teleki happened to encounter him on the road soon after his departure and noted that he was 'clad in a thin yellow nankeen dress, with a stick in his hand and a small bundle'. The curious Count enquired: "Where are you going, M. Körösi?" To which Csoma replied, "I am going to Asia in search of our relatives."

Csoma's route was circuitous. After nine months studying Slavic languages in Croatia he headed for Bucharest, where he hoped to polish up his Turkish. His plan to progress to Constantinople, where he intended to turn North to Odesa and hence to Moscow, was thwarted by an outbreak of the plague and so instead he took a ship to Alexandria, where he hoped to bone up on his Arabic. Again an outbreak of plague intervened and his ship, after several weeks of cruising round the Eastern Mediterranean looking for a plague-free port, finally landed at Latakia in Syria. From here, he departed on foot to Aleppo and then on to Mosul, somewhere along the way switching to Asiatic dress. After rafting down the Tigris to Baghdad, he joined a caravan to Tehran, where, befriended by the British consul, Henry Willock, he spent the next four months studying Persian.

Now operating under the *nom d'occasione*, 'Sikander Beg'[18], Csoma pushed on down the Silk Road and reached Bokhara, where he found captured Russian soldiers still being sold as slaves in the market

---

[18] Possibly a pun on Iskander Beg, the famous sixteenth century governor of Montenegro. *Beg* is the same as Turkish *Bey* for chieftain or governor.

place. Hurrying on, he arrived in Kabul on January 6, 1822. Intent on his quest to reach the Tarim Basin, land of the Uighurs and putative home of the Hungarian people, Csoma left Kabul after only thirteen days and by mid-March 1822 had reached Lahore. Travelling via Amritsar and Srinagar, on June 9 he became one of the first Europeans to reach Leh, the main city of Ladakh. However, he discovered that the road to the city of Yarkhand (now Shache), on the Southern edge of the Tarim Basin was 'very difficult, expensive, and dangerous for a Christian'. So he stopped. Perhaps he had run out of money, perhaps he was exhausted and uncertain but he turned round and headed back to Srinagar.

In a story like this, one has to occasionally pause and take stock. The young boy from the small Székely village of Chiuruş is now thirty-eight and fluent in at least thirteen languages. He has sailed, walked and rafted his way from Transylvania to Tibet without a companion and with virtually no money. However, this was just the beginning.

In the town of Dras, half way back along the road to Srinagar, Csoma met up with a Mr William Moorcroft[19], the Veterinarian Superintendent of the East India Company's Stud, who was on his way to Leh to source Turcoman breeding stock for the Company's stables and also to gather commercial and military intelligence of interest to the British. At a loose end, Csoma decided to turn around and accompany his newfound friend, a decision that was to change the course of his life.

On arrival in Leh, Moorcroft came into possession of a letter, which an alleged Russian agent had been carrying to Ranjit Singh, the Sikh ruler of Punjab and Kashmir. Written in Russian and signed by Count Nesselrode in St. Petersburg, the letter aroused intense curiosity in Moorcroft, who suspected some Russian mischief was afoot in the Karakorams. Csoma had no trouble translating the letter into English and also prepared a translation into Latin that was forwarded to Calcutta (Moorcroft having assumed that Latin would thwart the agents of Ranjit Singh should the missive fall into their hands). It now

---

[19]   William Moorcroft: *Travels in the Himalayan Provinces of Hindustan and the Panjab; in Ladakh and Kashmir; in Peshawar, Kabul, Kunduz and Bokhara; from 1819 to 1825*

dawned on Moorcroft that his Hungarian companion had considerable potential as an intelligence officer and he outlined a proposal for him—how about compiling an English-Tibetan dictionary? The British in India were at that time intensely interested in Tibet. In 1774 George Bogle, the first Englishman (or rather Scotsman to give the hardy Glaswegian his correct attribution) to reach the country, had spent five months as the Panchen Lama's guest at Tashilhunpo monastery in Shigatse, and in 1783 Samuel Turner[20] was the first European to reach Lhasa since the Austrian Jesuit John Grueber in 1661. But little progress had been made in establishing trade or diplomatic relations due to the fact that there was an almost complete ignorance of the Tibetan language. The only existing Tibetan dictionary was a compilation by a Capuchin friar entitled *Alphabetum Tibetanum*, which had been published in Rome in 1762. Encouraged and sponsored by Moorcroft, Csoma returned to Srinagar to scope the project and after five months aided by a Tibetan who also spoke Persian, a language in which Csoma was also proficient thanks to his friendship with the British consul in Tehran, the newly recruited Székelys spy decided they must start from scratch.

Consequently, Moorcroft proposed that Csoma prepare his own Tibetan dictionary. 'As well in pursuance of original plans of his *own for the development of some obscure points of Asiatic and of European history*,' Moorcroft wrote to his superiors (his italics), 'Mr. Csoma will endeavour to remain in Tibet until he shall have become the master of the language of that country, and be completely acquainted with the subjects its literature contains, which is likely, on many accounts, to prove interesting to the European world.'

With funds from the Asiatic Society of Bengal and from Moorcroft himself Csoma returned to Leh in May of 1823 and from there retired to the monastery of Yangla near Zanskar, where he devoted the next sixteen months to intense study of the language. His chief instructor was a lama named Bandé Sangs-rgyas-phun-tshogs, who in

---

[20] Turner was a Captain in the East India Company who was sent to Tibet by Warren Hastings together with the surveyor Samuel Davis and naturalist Robert Saunders to strengthen the relations which were established by George Bogle.

addition to being the chief physician of Ladakh, had spent six years travelling in Nepal, Bhutan, and Tibet, and made an apt teacher.

Csoma would spent the next eleven years involved in one way or another with Tibetan studies. In 1825 the government of India put their imprimatur on his activities and granted him a modest monthly stipend of fifty rupees; in return he promised to produce a Tibetan dictionary, a grammar, and short accounts of Tibetan literature and history. He returned to Zanskar in August of 1825 only to find that the lama who had helped him previously had lost interest in the collaboration. He was, however, able to amass a huge collection of Tibetan manuscripts, which he brought back to government headquarters near Simla. From 1827 to 1830 he retired to a cottage in the village of Kanum on the River Sutlej in Upper Bashahr where he again immersed himself in the study of Tibetan language and Buddhist texts, aided here by one Sans-rgyas-phun-tshogs, a lama from the nearby monastery.

Dr J.G. Gerard,[21] who came to Kanum to vaccinate the locals against smallpox, left a telling portrayal of the Hungarian scholar's life: 'The cold is very intense and all last winter he sat at his desk wrapped up in woollens from head to foot, and from morning to night, without an interval of recreation or warmth, except that of his frugal meals, which are one universal routine of greasy tea.' Although the area abounded with grapes, apricots, and other fruits, Csoma would not eat them, holding to the 'prudent conviction that they could not make him any happier'. Gerard also met the lama assisting Csoma, a man of 'great erudition,' who 'exhibits a singular union of learning, modesty, and greasy habits; and Mr Csoma in this last respect vies with his learned companion.'

According to Gerard, Csoma clearly did not consider his Tibetan studies an end in themselves, but simply as a stepping stone into Central Asia, the putative home of the Hungarian people. His next goal, he confided to Gerard, was to reach Shigatse and Lhasa, where he wanted to peruse monastery libraries for information about the ancestors of the Hungarians and take up the study of Mongolian

---

[21] Brother of Captain Alexander Gerard, a 'surveyor' with 13th Bengal Infantry: both were British spies.

language, which he believed he could learn from lamas in those cities. For, as Gerard noted, in his own italics, *'his great aim and unceasing anxiety is to get access to Mongolia'* where he believed he would finally find the clues he needed to piece together the ancient history of the Hungarian people.

His work in Kanum finally completed, Csoma returned to Calcutta in 1830 where he started to prepare his Tibetan dictionary and grammar for publication, the latter finally published in 1835. He now asked the government for permission to remain for three years in India 'for the purpose of improving myself in Sanskrit and in the different dialects; and, if Government will not object, to furnish me with a passport in duplicate, one in English and one in Persian, that I may visit the North-western parts of India'. The passports were duly granted and Csoma absorbed himself in the study of Sanskrit, Mahratta and Bengali languages. By the beginning of 1838 Csoma was back in Calcutta. Here he took a room in the Asia Society's building and began work as the Society's librarian.

All the while, despite his apparent diffidence, Csoma had still not lost sight of Lhasa and East Turkestan, the land of the Uighurs. He was fifty-seven years old at the beginning of 1842 and he must have realized that if he ever wanted to reach these increasingly elusive goals, he had to start soon. In a letter to the secretary of the Society dated 9 February 1842 Csoma announced that he was about to 'leave Calcutta for a period to make a tour in Central Asia' and perhaps with a presentiment that this long-postponed trip would be his last, he included what in effect was his will, leaving all his belongings to the Society, 'in the case of my death on my intended journey'.

The date when he left Calcutta is unknown, but he reached Darjeeling, in the foothills of the Himalayas, on 24 March, apparently travelling on foot. By 6 April Csoma was ill with fever and by 9 April, according to his doctor, 'he was confused and slightly delirious, his countenance was sunken, anxious, and yellow, and altogether his state was bad and dangerous'. He finally died at 5 a.m. on 11 April, 'without a groan or a struggle'. The final effects of this extraordinary traveller from Chiuruş consisted of 'four boxes of books and paper, the suit of blue clothes he always wore, and in which he died, a few sheets, and one cooking pot'. He was buried in Darjeeling, where a suitable monument was eventually erected over his grave by a Hungarian Count. The inscription on it read:

"A poor and deserted Magyar, with no funds or applause yet driven by a patriotic resolve and perseverance... sought to find the cradle of the Magyars, but came to be overwhelmed by his pains. You, our land's mighty and rich, should follow the example of this orphan-boy and be faithful Magyars not in words but in actions, inspired not by empty display but by a devotional fervor."

The burly gypsy, who had helped me find the key holder to the museum, was patiently waiting outside the door as I emerged, a large hat held open in his hands for a tip. He seemed insulted by the size of my offering and remained rooted to the spot. I cheerily waved goodbye, he angrily shook his hat and we parted inimically.

My next meeting was with Katerina in Covasda where she had promised to show me the village 'leather' shop after I had spotted some fox pelts dangling over the banisters in the chalet and inquired into their provenance. In fact, it turned out to be a small fellmonger and tannery situated in a neat row of houses by the river. Inside lay piles of skins, some with fur, some with wool, mostly sheep, lamb, goat and fox but there were a few I did not recognise—Pine-marten, Beech-marten, civet? The all-in-one fellmonger-tanner-fashion-designer cleaned, cured and dyed the skins and then made them into made-to-measure garments like jackets, coats and waistcoats, judging by those on display all to a very high standard. "We also do repairs", announced the proprietor's son, pointing at some well-worn farmers' leather jerkins. As we left, I spotted a pile of Astrakhan wool hats but like the ugly sisters and Cinderella's slipper could not find one to fit me, which was a shame since the days were getting colder and I planned to spend that evening in the forest.

Alexander Mikes, himself a bear-like figure of a man, had asked me to go bear watching in the beech woods of the Bodocului Mountains, about an hours drive to the North. We rendezvoused with his forester, Ioani, at a small farmhouse by the road beyond Balvanyos, where we were also joined by the State Forester, an older man with a cigarette permanently on the go. Squeezing into a minute Japanese 4 x 4, we headed up a steep track through beech trees reddened by the setting sun, crossing silent glades surrounded by sentinel birch trees until we reached a clearing at the far end of which was a small wooden hut built on stilts. This was to be our hide for the next two hours and somewhat of a gas chamber as well for the two foresters chain-smoked a particularly vile Romanian untipped cigarette called Carpati, producing an acrid fog increasingly difficult to see through let alone to breath in.

The elder forester heaved a sack of broken Easter eggs onto his shoulder and dispensed its contents into three troughs about seventy meters away from the hide. He returned, pulling up the ladder behind him, and we settled down to wait. Before long, a large male dark brown bear appeared and tucked into the chocolate, quickly followed by three fearless grey-coloured cubs watched over by a very nervous mother who shuffled about indecisively on the edge of the wood. Two foxes with magnificent white tipped tails joined in the performance but once darkness had fallen, the foresters turned on a spotlight and the ursine cast quickly left the forest stage. Not for long as it turned out; they were all back within twenty minutes, together with two new young male members of the troupe. Eventually the chocolate ran out, the bears left and I was released into the pure night air, spluttering and coughing my way down the ladder.

The next day was All Souls Day, a holiday in the village. Fortunately, Mihail, the Mikes's shepherd, had not taken the day off and I found him with his little flock of twenty or so on the edge of the park. Now seventy, Mihail had been tending sheep since he was twelve years old and there was little he didn't know about life as a

Transylvanian shepherd. I asked him whether he minded if I tested him on the meaning of some Albanian words, an exercise I was longing to undertake to prove the theory that shepherds are the glue which have held the Balkans together since time immemorial. Putting both his hands on top of his cherry wood stick, he placed his chin on them and nodded for me to begin.

"Ba?"

"Baci (milk)." Oh dear, in Albanian it means the shepherd in charge of the sheepfold.

"Baigë?"

"Baleg (dung)." Identical.

"Berr?"

"Bar" (the interjection with which the shepherd urges on his sheep.) but Mihail added, "that's an old word."

"Shut?"

"Ciut (hornless)." Identical.

"Shtrungë?"

"Strung (milking place)." This was a bit more specific than the Albanian meaning of sheepfold.

"Shkardë?"

"Zgard (dog collar)." Identical.

I was confident about the last one. "Flojere?"

"Fluier (small whistle pipe or shepherd's flute)." A sure winner.

Of the twenty-five words on my list supposedly common in meaning to both Albanian and Romanian shepherds, Mihail had recognised fourteen which went someway to proving that Balkan shepherds have much more in common than their often-warring nation states. Long live the shepherds!

There is a charming Székelys story about a shepherd and a young woman of noble birth. Once upon a time, a great lord had a very beautiful younger sister. One day a young lord from Hungary presented himself as a suitor, became engaged to her and the day for the wedding was fixed; however near the lord's house was a large hayfield where the lord kept his sheep and the young shepherd who looked after them would play his pipe as he shut them up in the fold at dusk. The beautiful sister often looked out of her window and listened to the young Romanian piping and had secretly fallen madly in love with him. Neither her widowed father nor brother knew of this. The day before the wedding, the guests arrived from all over Transylvania; alas, the bride was nowhere to be found. Her embarrassed father duly wined and dined them and her suitor returned home without a bride. Some years later, her brother was going through the forest and saw from his carriage a Romanian couple watching their sheep. Although barefoot and wearing a long skirt of broadcloth, he recognised the woman as his sister and sent a servant to implore her to return home. She sent word back that she would surely never leave her shepherd, that if she had loved him once she would love him until death. She later gave birth to a son whom her brother took into his own household, obtained noble rank for him and found him a well-born wife. Thus ends this tale of humble kindness.

Throughout the day, a procession of couples and families carrying great bunches of magnificent yellow and pink chrysanthemums made their way down the village street towards the graveyard which lay behind the Roman Catholic church. When dusk finally fell, hundreds of candles flickered mysteriously among the gravestones revealing reverent family groups standing like shadowy statues in eerie yellow patches of light; the only movement was an occasional child running hither and thither, oblivious to the solemnity of the occasion, probably more scared than mischievous. The darkness of death met the Light of Life on this cold October evening.

I walked back through the moonlit park, navigating my way to the Swiss chalet by the silhouette of the *Kastély* against the rising moon. Probably starting as a fortified single-storied manor house in the fourteenth century when the Mikes had been given a charter to hold a market in the village, the design of the Kastély had evolved over the centuries; an old print in the village museum showed a seventeenth century Renaissance two-storied building with an open porch surmounted by a Palladian loggia and with a vast roof like a shepherd's hat made out of tiles. Later in 1867, Benedek Mikes had added mansard windows to create a third floor in the old attic and clumsily plonked a second loggia on top of the existing one; neither modification improved the look of the original façade.

As the moon flitted between the swaying canopies of the dark beech woods, the old Romanian incantation came to mind:

O luminous moon, luminous moon, come and take away the spell and the desolation, and the hatred from the world...and drive it away to wild mountains and forests; and us and our children and those who shall be born unto us thereafter, leave us clean and pure like refined gold and like the sun that shines brilliantly in the skies.

On a chirpier note, the lovely verse of the Elizabethan Englishman Francis Beaumont introduced a skip to my step through the dewy meadow that led up to the chalet, albeit booby trapped with giant molehills and littered with ominous signs of rummaging wild boar:

Shake off your heavy trance,
And leap into a dance
Such as no mortals used to tread:
Fit only for Apollo
To play to, for the moon to lead,
And all the stars to follow.

Surely a sentiment that any right-minded Székelys would embrace.

CHAPTER THREE

BARONS AND BUFFALOES

I left Zăbala on a miserable day, taking the rain-swept road to Târgu Secuiesc, a neat market town relatively unchanged since its last spruce up in 1890. It has still managed to retain its medieval layout of the early 1400s for its covered alleyways that lead off from the square into 'inner yards' like spokes from a wheel hub were once the commercial arteries of the guilds—tanners, bootmakers, potters, joiners, butchers and hatters to name but a few.

In the sodden fields, families of cabbage pickers were busy at work, bending, picking, straightening, lobbing in a never-ending rhythmic cycle. An invisible gear seemed to ensure that the green orbs never collided in mid-air as they plummeted into the carts from all directions. In the cold drizzle, all colour had drained from the world save for these white flecked green comets hurling through space.

The little town of Turia lies about five miles North-east of Târgu Secuiesc on a river of the same name. At the end of the village, surrounded by a wall of wooden sheds is the family home of the Apor family. In 1736, Baron Petar Apor of Turia wrote a memoir, bemoaning the changes in Transylvania from 'the wealth of its simple modest times to the penury of its present haughty, extravagant and demented estate'. In effect the *Metamorphosis Transylvaniae* is an anti-Austrian polemic written by what we would call 'a grumpy old man', a epithet that the good Baron would probably not dispute. Born in 1676 at the family home in Turia, Petar's father died of the plague soon after his birth and he was brought up by his uncle, Count István Apor, at one time the Treasurer of Transylvania. Educated by the Jesuits at Cluj, he graduated to the Royal Hungarian University at Trnava where he had studied law and philosophy. His career however was put on hold by a two-year spell in prison on suspicion of being involved in Prince Ferenc Rákóczi II's *kuruc* rebellion against the Habsburgs. He went on to become Chief Justice of the Háromszék and föispán of Küküllô County, two significant but not major appointments, a fact he was rather conscious of.

There were many Austrian bees buzzing around in the Baron's *shako*, none more irksome than the proliferation of titles that resulted from the Habsburg takeover of Transylvania in 1687; anyone who had supported the Austrians was either ennobled or promoted from Baron to Count. The Apors, who had arrived with the first wave of Székelys in the thirteenth century, felt devalued for 'in olden times counts and barons came from very ancient stock'. Now 'so many of us are counts and barons that, if we conducted our counties and baronages as did the Hungarians of old, the whole of Transylvania would not be enough for us to live up to our titles.'

Eating and drinking habits had also changed for the worse. The drink at breakfast was called *aquavita* and men also drank a 'good, delicate, bitter-sweet vermouth ....considered healthy as there were no such weak stomachs as people have today'. Lemon juice and butter were never used in cooking and meal times were 'not in the French fashion': lunch was served on wooden plates at 10 a.m., dinner at 6 p.m. and it was a case of bring-your-own-knife— spoons were communal. It was unheard of to ask for a *glas wein* (glass of wine) since wine was served in two-handled unglazed red pitchers and passed around for swigging. Contrary to modern taste, old wine was the drink of coachmen and grooms. The Baron railed against the introduction of French fashion—'it is not the emperor's taxation that has brought hardship upon Transylvania, but the vain adornment of your wives and daughters'. As to men's fashion, '(in my day) long hair was very rare indeed...it was unheard of for it to be bound at the back with a ribbon or cord like a horse's tail as is the fashion nowadays and even less for it to be worn in a net.'

The current Baron, Czaba, has seen far more drastic changes in his lifetime than his fulminating fractious ancestor but on the several occasions when I have met him, he had not once complained of his lot; indeed, he is that most unusual person, a 'cheerful old man'. I had arrived unannounced and asked the farm manager as to the Baron's whereabouts. A short call on a mobile phone delivered up the eighty-six-year-old Baron ten minutes later, coasting serenely into the farmyard on his bicycle, straight-backed as if riding a thoroughbred horse. Clad from head to foot in the latest weatherproof gear, Czaba had been about his business on the farm and in the village, impervious to the foul weather that raged about him.

Such octogenarian hardiness comes as no surprise to those who know the Baron's story. Summarily evicted from Turia in 1949, Czaba and his family were sent to Blaj, where they were not allowed to work or leave the town. These edicts lasted until 1964. The authorities had wanted to send him to work on the infamous Black Sea canal and he spent forty days in a Securitate prison awaiting his fate; his training as an agricultural engineer saved him for the state needed him alive. But his sister's husband, a Banffy, was imprisoned for seven years.

After 1989, there were opportunities to leave but the Baron's determination not to abandon his homeland is echoed in Sandor Remenyik's poem *Eredj ha tudsz!*—Leave if you can.

> *Home I shall remain,*
> *darkly croaking, like a winter crow on a dead poplar tree.*
> *I know not yet*
> *Whether I shall ever find a quiet corner*
> *But I shall stay at home.*

Greeting me warmly, he confided in a quiet voice: "There have been some exciting discoveries in the manor house." Turia *conac*[22] is a single storey fifteenth century building built over cellars, with mansard windows later inset in its ample loft. A late nineteenth century neo-classical enclosed porch and loggia topped with a triangular pediment had been added rather incongruously to the façade as was the fashion in those days. Some years ago, murals of flowers, swallows and saints had been discovered in a small room off the main reception room and the great supporting lateral beams in the loft were found to be decorated in the tradition of coffered ceilings but in this instance without cross spars, suggesting that the roof had once been exposed to the rooms below. But the magnitude of the new discovery dwarfed these: under its white washed walls, the dining room had been hiding an artistic secret—it was in fact decorated with a riot of floral designs of roses, vines, acanthus leaves and pomegranates, all in muted pastel colours. On the wooden panels, which flanked the window seats in the recesses of the thick defensive outer walls, were now revealed pictures of pretty girls with lace ruffs on their wrists and saucy smiles on their faces.

Bidding the Baron fond farewell, my route from Turia took me through the bear-watching country of Balvanyos down into the Olt valley and then across the hills to Baraolt, where the wild Petchenegs had first settled. Over 400 miles long, the Olt river is one of the five great rivers that have defined the history of Transylvania; the others are the Mureş, the Tisa, the Bistriţa and the Someş. With the exception of the Tisa, which historically has delineated the Northern border, the others all breach the mighty walls of the Carpathian Mountains, none more dramatically than the Olt which over millions of years has opened up a gap through the once impenetrable 6,000 foot Southern mountains between Sibiu and Râmnicu Valcea. The Romans called it *Alutus*, the Saxons *Alt* and the Hungarians and Romanians, for once in agreement on the same name, *Olt*, the 'o' probably being a Slavonic change.

---

[22]   An unfortified manor house; a *culă* is fortified. A *kuria* in Hungarian can be either.

In the beech woods above Baraolt, a file of gypsies was making its way slowly up the steep slopes of the snow-covered hills, searching for brushwood and small logs to heap on to their handcarts, already piled high. I wondered how far they had come for there were no villages or hamlets within miles except the empty huts of the charcoal burners on the top of the Chingii Pass. On the other side of the pass lie the twin valleys of the Homorodul Mic (little) and Homorodul Mare (big) rivers, which in late spring are sensationally covered in deep-pile quilts of wild flowers.

The distinguished botanist John Akeroyd has compiled a list[23] of the wild flowers that paint these spring and summer grasslands—

'wiry grasses dominate the sward, together with a fabulous array of yellow, pink and purple legumes...– Sainfoin, dwarf brooms, Dyer's Greenweed, and numerous clovers, vetches and milk-vetches. White ox-eye Daisy and frothy panicles of Dropwort dot the grassland, along with the yellow of tall Lady's Bedstraw and massed Hay Rattle, and the crimson heads of Charterhouse Pink, (putatively) known in Transylvania as "Blood of the Holy Virgin"'.

'Steeper slopes, belts of scrub dominated by blackthorn, privet and wild pear interspersed with open grassland, can best be described as 'Transylvanian wood-steppe'. Here lurk floral gems such as the Red Viper's-bugloss, Soldier Orchid and Purple Viper's-grass.'

'Perhaps the choicest plants thrive on the hottest and driest south-facing slopes. Here the flora is distinctly steppic—sparse greyish tussocky grasses, purplish vetches such as Montpellier Milk-vetch, and three denizens of the '*Pontic-Sarmatian*' steppes of Ukraine, handsome Yellow Flax, blue-flowered Hairy Flax and Nodding Sage, the latter with tall bowed violet spikes. Liliaceous plants such as Branched St Bernard's Lily, Wild Asparagus and Tassel-hyacinth add an exotic or Mediterranean feel.'

But in the late autumn only the parched ochre stalks of harvested maize remained, the last stragglers of nature's summer bounty, and any

---

[23] From Plant Talk Issue 30, October 2002. Also see '*The Historic Countryside of the Saxon Villages of Southern Transylvania*' by John Akeroyd, Fundatia Adept, Romania (ISBN 973004533X).

hint of regeneration lay dormant, cached in the rows of deep brown crevasses left by the ploughman. The landscape was now deserted as if some terrible host of invaders had just swept through, destroying all before it. No sowers, no hoers, no harvesters, no ploughmen were to be seen, only the occasional shepherd and his flock far away on the distant blue hillsides.

The two Homorodual rivers meet at Rupea, a bustling market town overlooked by a fortress, the Cetatea din Rupea, which straddles the pimply basalt hill to the North of the town. Originally called *castrum Kuholm* or prominent rock, it was built in the early 13th century by the Teutonic Knights and formed part of a series of fortresses, including Brasov, Feldiora (the Knights' headquarters), and Râsnov. The Order of Teutonic Knights—*Deutsche Ritterorden*—had been founded by the merchants of Lubeck and Bremen in 1120s to provide a hospital for German pilgrims in Jerusalem. Alas, it disappeared following the fall of the city in 1187 but when the Third Crusade arrived two years later, including a large number of Germans, it was re-established outside Acre. Alongside the Knights of St John and the Knights Templar, the Order became a military organization in 1198 and then, by Imperial Act, the Grand Master and his successors were granted membership of the Imperial Court in 1214 and sat in the Imperial Diet with the rank of Prince, a meteoric ascent into the European political firmament. Brains and brawn carried the day.

In 1211, the Grand Master, Hermann Von Salza, started negotiations with the Hungarian King, Andreas the Second, for a permanent home in Transylvania for the Order, numbering at that time about a hundred Knights. Andreas had two big problems: Transylvania's four key South-eastern mountain passes—Oitoz, Buzău, Predeal and Bran—were proving impossible to defend against the marauding Cumans and those same passes were key Crusader routes from the North into the Balkans and Levant. Furthermore, Andreas was under pressure from the Pope to put in a personal appearance on the Fifth Crusade.

Related by marriage to the Teutonic nobility — Andreas's first wife Gertrude was from the Bavarian family of Andechs-Meran — the King was at first well disposed towards the Knights and reached an initial agreement with them, virtually ceding the sovereignty of the Brasov area or *Burzenland* to them in exchange for its defence. This triggered a rebellion by some of his magnates who first assassinated the hapless Gertrude in the royal palace in 1213 and then dictated the terms of his second marriage, this time to Yolanthe Courtenay, whose family was firmly opposed to the Teutonic Knights; indeed her father, Peter the Second, became the Latin Emperor in 1217.

At first, the presence of the Order appeared to solve Andreas's problems. The King himself passed a desultory year in 1217 in the Lebanon on a half-hearted crusade where he spent much of his time collecting gory relics — he returned home with the heads of St Stephen and St Margaret, the right hands of St Thomas and St Bartholomew, one of the water-jugs used at the marriage feast at Canaa and part of Aaron's rod. But on his return, he discovered that the Knights had built stone forts instead of the agreed wooden designs — one can still see the ruins of the *bergfestungs* (mountain fortresses) at Feldioara and Codlea — and, furthermore, had dared to issue their own coinage. As far as Andreas was concerned, these activities were tantamount to the establishment of a separate, independent state and after a bloody fight, his army summarily ejected the Order in 1225.

Undeterred by this failed experiment of statehood, the Deutsche Ritterorden regrouped in the dramatic mountain fortress of Montfort from 1230 to 1271 and then relocated to the city of Acre until its capture by the Saracens in 1291 when it moved to Venice, its long time ally. In 1309, the Knights established themselves in the great gothic fortress of Marienberg (Malbork) in Prussia where they remained until 1457, despite being bankrupted following their disastrous defeat at Tannenberg in 1410, when nearly 100,000 men were killed. The Order then moved to the fortress city of Konigsburg and finally to Mergentheim in Franconia where it was dissolved by Napoleon in 1809. Today the Order has reverted to its original function of providing care to the needy, just like its English peer, the Knights Hospitallers of St John.

The remote Saxon village of Viscri lies about 10 miles to the west of Rupea, approached down an unmade road that winds through small valleys staked with gaunt steel poles of long-abandoned hop gardens. My village friends, Roman and Annette, were busy cooking red cabbage in a vast pot. Other than the purchase of a house by the Prince of Wales, their main news concerned the new and uncharacteristic militancy of gypsies when being filmed on camcorders. The background to this was a $30 million federal law suit brought against the makers of the film *Borat* by gypsies from the village of Glod. Their US attorneys claim that the film depicted them (and other villagers) as 'rapists, abortionists, prostitutes, thieves, racists, bigots, simpletons and boors'. Although Glod is on the other side of the Carpathians, the gypsy jungle drums had been highly efficient and now the word had gone round Transylvania that all filming should be paid for, no matter the status of the hapless camera person!

Over the hill to the North of Viscri is another Saxon settlement called Mesendorf (*dorf* is German for village) dating back to 1322; in 1966, there were 656 Saxons here but by 1995, only 29 remained, a result of the mass emigration to Germany of the early 1990s. If Robert Browning in his *Tale of the Pied Piper* did not quite understand how the Saxons came here:

> *In Transylvania there's a tribe,*
> *Of alien people who ascribe*
> *The outlandish ways and dress,*
> *On which their neighbours lay such stress*
> *To their fathers and mothers having risen,*
> *Out of some subterranean prison*
> *Into which they had been trepanned,*
> *Long time ago, in a mighty band,*
> *Out of Hamelin town in Brunswick land,*
> *But how or why they don't understand.*

There is no mystery how they left. It was in response to Chancellor Kohl's declaration that the doors to Germany were open to all those of German descent.

I had come here to visit a new enterprise backed by British investors: water buffalo farming. There were no native buffalo in Romania; they came from South Asia via Turkey and Bulgaria in the Middle Ages and were kept by the Saxon farmers for their milk — twice as fatty as cow's — their meat, and for ploughing and pulling carts. In a typical village of 200 or so households, there used to be several hundred head but numbers have fallen sharply, first under communism and later with the departure of many Saxons to Germany. A few farmers still rear buffalo and produce buffalo products, but the relative difficulty of milking them, and the lack of bulls (once the numbers fell, the villages no longer kept their own bulls) meant that many villages that have had reared buffalo for hundreds of years now had none at all.

Transylvanian Natural Products is determined to reverse this trend and has established a herd of 400 buffaloes. Remarkably tough animals, they can survive most of the year outdoors but need to be housed during the snows, which can last from December through to March. Indeed, it was snowing on the day of my visit and so I was able to inspect the animals in their new sheds. With their great horns and impassive black faces, one wonders what is going through their minds, especially in the light of tales of cunning homicidal attacks on hunters in the African bush. I asked Cosmina Carluga, the office manager, whether they were as docile as they looked.

"Buffalo are like people; they are temperamental only if changes introduced. If everything is same, they are very nice and well-behaved."

"We had visit from Prince Charles in May," volunteered Kalin, Cosmina's husband, who is overseeing the building programme.

"Yes, and a picnic too," continued Cosmina, "everything organic."

"Including the *ţuica*?" I ventured, referring to the nippy 40 per cent spirit that accompanies most Romanian repasts.

"No *ţuica*. It was business picnic." Nothing like being put firmly in one's place.

Currently, the Mesendorf milk is being sold in bulk but plans are afoot to add value through a processing plant in Rupea, allowing Transylvanian organic yoghurts and Mozzarella cheeses to be sold throughout Europe.

When the Saxons first arrived in Transylvania, they built fortified churches—*kirchenburgen*—in which the whole village could take shelter from the bloodthirsty assortment of marauders and brigands, later Turks and Tartars, who would look in uninvited. It was only in 1776 that the last Tartar raid took place. These fortress churches were usually sited in the centre of the village, sometimes on the edge, always on a piece of raised ground to give the defenders the advantage of height. But on the way to Sighisoara from Mesendorf, in the village of Saschiz (*Keisd* in German, probably from Hungarian '*kez*' for hand, signifying protection), this arrangement had been scrapped in 1347 in favour of a stand-alone castle[24] built high up on a hill above the village —*Die Keisder Burg*—combined with a church with a fortified choir and knave erected in the village centre with a single outer wall and a defensive belfry—a *glockenturm*—just outside its perimeter. Always a large village, there were 1,435 people here in 1786 and 2,308 in 1966, these refuge arrangements had obviously worked and Saschiz was known throughout the region for its decoratively painted furniture and *Keisder Krüge*, hand painted mugs and pitchers.

After asking directions from the newly opened Tourist Information office[25] in the centre of the village, I set off up a track that zigzagged its way up the hillside to the North and then disappeared down a sunken road into the beech woods. The snow began to intensify, building up a treacherous white layer on top of the autumnal carpet of unrotted leaves. Clinging for dear life from one branch to another, I swung, slipped and scrambled my way up to the walls of the citadel (*cetatea*), avoiding the precipitous chasms below me until, finally finding a gap in the curtain wall, I entered the keep or *wohnturm* on

---

[24] *Burg*, although describing a fortification, equates more to the idea of a 'refuge'.

[25] This is sponsored by Fundatia ADEPT, an organization founded by Nat Page and Jim Turnbull, which brings together Romanian and wider European expertise to carry out conservation and rural development projects including responsible rural tourism.

all fours. Here there was an open space about the size of a football field, surrounded by a stone wall at least ten meters high with signs of a long vanished wooden vigil way. Four watchtowers—*wächterturm* -stood at each corner and above the entrance, there were the remains of several other towers—a school tower (*schulturm*), pastor's tower (*pfarrturm*), gate tower (*torturm*), and an armoury (*pulverturm*). Somewhere under the snow-covered mounds of rubble was a well going down 300 foot. The snow drifted relentlessly across the enclosure, total silence prevailed. A thick white veil masked the village below, the houses only identifiable by the shapes of their newly iced roofs against the darkening background of the storm.

Charles Boner, an English traveller, had come here in 1865 and asked a villager about the *burg* where I was now standing. He was told 'we Saxons went away from home to enjoy our liberties and to be where there were no feudal lords. No, that is a burg of the burgesses: they built it; here they took refuge in case of attack, with their corn and valuables; here still the corn is kept, lest, when the families are at work in the fields, fire should break out and destroy it all.'

I reached the medieval town of Sighisoara as darkness fell. The snow had not let up and had been augmented by a bitter wind that blew it into every crevice of ones clothing. *Schässburg* to the Saxons, Sighisoara is a small fortified town on the side of a hill overlooking the Târnava Mare river; surrounded by a defensive wall divided into sections by thirteen towers originally financed and manned by the town guilds—jewellers, rope makers, butchers, furriers, weavers, tailors, shoemakers, locksmiths, fishermen, coopers, ironsmiths, tanners and tinners—with the exception of some nineteenth century buildings, the town remains almost pristine.

Founded by Saxons in the mid twelfth century, Sighisoara was first documented in 1280 as *Castrum Sex*—Castle Number Six—and known as the Rothenburg[26] of Transylvania. The records of 1585 reveal the pecking order of the town officials by salary: the school rector thirty Gulden a year (and loaned seventy-five Gulden); the

---

[26] Rothenburg ob der Tauber is a Bavarian town known for its well-preserved medieval buildings. In the Middle Ages, it was an Imperial Free City.

church organist and town trumpeter each thirty-four Gulden; four civil servants each twenty-four Gulden; the master of the baths twelve Gulden; and the town midwife three Gulden. One draws ones own conclusions about civic priorities in those days!

One of the town's most famous features is the 300 steps that once connected the lower town to the *Bergschule* on the top of the hill. The last 175 steps known as the *Schülertreppe* were built in 1642 and are encapsulated in timber like a giant wooden caterpillar. Situated at the bottom of these steps is Teo's cellar, which he proudly advertises thus: "Wine and brandy making is a long tradition in our family. The brandy, which is a home made local drink, contains only healthy and natural ingredients and is stored in cask, which gives its distinctive golden-yellow colour." The brandy he is referring to is called *ţuică* in Romanian and the double-distilled version is known as *palinka*. Every village has its own still[27] and although the ingredient may well be 'healthy and natural', the after-effects can be dire if too much is imbibed. Palinka can contain anything from 50 to 80 per cent alcohol. For the next half hour, I sampled Teo's libations of plum, apple and pear liqueurs, trying casks of varying ages. The colour soon lost its golden-yellow 'distinctiveness' as the whole cellar became a pleasant, mellow blur and I left swaddled in an invisible cloak of warmth and well-being, utterly impervious to the snow and ice that lay in wait for me on the cobbled streets.

After a snug night in a beautifully restored medieval town house overlooking the Piaţa Cetatii, it was time to leave Transylvania and head for Bucovina in Northern Moldavia. It was an ambitious journey to undertake in the snowbound conditions but in Romania one can generally be assured of finding shelter in a village and hamlet, so the risks of spending a night out in the snow are much reduced. The road to Sovata was clear but the 4,000 foot Bucin Pass across the Gurghiu Mountains made for heavy going and after sliding most of the way

---

[27]   EU Regulations will probably kill off this ancient tradition.

down the hill past several cars that had skidded off the road, I was relieved to reach the market town of Gheorgheni on the upper reaches of the Mureş river.

Called *Gyergyószentmiklós* in Hungarian after two saints (*Gyergyó* is a district of the Székelysfold, its name possibly derived from Saint George, whose story was brought to these parts by the Crusaders returning from the Levant; *Szentmiklós* meaning Saint Nicholas) this town is the furthest East Hungarian community in Transylvania. In 1910, the Hungarian population was 96 per cent; today it is 88 per cent, nearly all Roman Catholics as befits the Székelys tradition. They are deeply rooted here and as one ethnographer put it, 'the history of Gheorgheni is the history of the struggle with the forest'. What do people do here? According to the mayor, 'jobs like agriculture, shepherding, wood processing and mining, out of which come the domestic occupations: pottery, being representative the centres of Corund and Dăneşti, wood carving, shingling, painting the wood furniture, texturing, spinning, embroidery, sewing in geometrical and floral adornment, knitting straws and wattle, egg-painting.'

At the end of the seventeenth century, several Armenian families left Moldavia because of political in-fighting and harsh Ottoman rule and settled down near the passes of the Eastern Carpathians; within a few years, they had boosted the industrial and commercial life of the whole Giurgeu basin and Gheorgheni in particular. Such was their prosperity that they built a pretty Baroque church, distinguished by an incongruous Renaissance-style gate.

The Rubin Hotel has occupied a corner of the main square for two hundred years. I asked for a glass of wine.

"I know you want a glass of wine but what colour—red or white?" the waitress retorted.

"White, please."

"Are you sure you want white?" she gruffly inquired.

"Yes, please," I replied, beginning to feel unnerved. "…if that's OK with you."

"No problem. If you want white, I will bring you white. Anything else?"

"No thanks."

"Are you sure?"

"Yes."

"So, you are sure." She walked off to deal with a table full of elderly ladies, leaving me perplexed. Had I missed something out? The wine when it finally arrived was excellent. On the wall of the bar was a poster-size black and white panoramic photograph of the town square, Liberty Square, taken on a sunny day in 1926— the whole town had turned out to watch bands, dancers, acrobats and soldiers all parade through the square. I wondered whether this was akin to *Ezer Székely Leány Nap* (The Day of A Thousand Székely Girls) which takes place on *Sarlós Boldogasszony* (Visitation of Our Lady Day) on the Şumuleu Ciuc Saddle.

Later when I paid the bill, my previously terse waitress smiled shyly and confessed that English was her favourite language and she loved to practice with 'real' English people. She told me how much she enjoyed our conversation and I suggested that she approach the hotel manager to take charge of their marketing material displayed in the entrance. Its opening paragraph read: 'In the centre of Gheorgheni Rubin Hotel awaits it's dear customers with 18 rooms with two and three beds, as well as 4 apartments furnished after the highest standards in two of these hidromassage bath tubes are waiting to comfort our customers.'

Beyond Gheorgeni, over the 5,000 foot Pângăraţi pass through the Curmaturii Mountains, the road descends into some of the most dramatic and wild landscape to be found anywhere in Europe; this is the Bicaz Gorge *(Cheile Bicazului)* which starts at the *Trei Fantani*, the brook of the Three Cracks. The winding channel carved by the ceaseless torrents of the Bicaz river through a 1,000 foot-high wall of limestone crags continues for over three miles. At one point called 'the Gate of Hell' the vertiginous rocky columns almost embrace each other, creating a habitat for the aptly named wallcreeper, a rock-climbing, long-billed nuthatch known to the Chinese more poetically as a rock flower, and for chamois, those sure-footed mountain goats, who spend their lives defying gravity. Descending to 'Hell's Porch' through the narrowest point of the gorge nicknamed 'Hell's Throat', I stopped to inspect a house aptly named 'Hell's Villa'. It needs an artist like the nineteenth century German Romantic painter, Caspar David Friedrich, his *Rocky Ravine* comes to mind, to convey the drama of this landscape and to reveal the spiritual effect it has on those who travel through it, experiencing the contrast of shadow and light, of night and day, indeed of heaven and hell.

The gorge is more of a passageway than a pass which prevented the Sultan's or the Habsburg Emperor's armies from pouring through it to lay waste to Transylvania or Moldavia. The road was only built at the turn of nineteenth century. For mountaineers, the towering flanks have a strange attraction, none more than the 'Stone of the Shrine', a vertical wall of rock that rises up a sheer 1,000 foot. First climbed in 1934, the record to beat today is that of Zoltan Keresztes, who climbed it barefoot and in full Székely dress, a black cloth hat, shirt made of cloth with cuff and close collar, waistcoat braided with black, grey, white, red and blue designs, trousers of white cloth tied on the leg and a black cloth jacket; he dispensed with the black boots with soft-tops. Beat that.

Chapter Four

AUROCHS AND MOONS

The Bicaz river, after forcing itself through the narrow confines of the gorge, joins forces with a much larger river, the Bistriţa—a Slavic word for crystal clear[28]—which starts way up in the North of Romania, its springs scattered around the Prislop Pass and the 7,000 foot Mount Ineu. The two meet at the town of Bicaz, once a small mountain village with a sleepy customs post on the Austro-Hungarian and Romanian border where the main activity was rafting on the Bistriţa river. By tradition, the tree trunks were linked together, forming a raft or *pluta*; a helmsman or *plutaş* would then steer the raft downstream to the wood processing facilities at Piatra Neamt. Sadly all this came to an end in the 1950s when the river was dammed in order to provide power for one of the largest cement plants in Romania. Fortunately for the job prospects of the inhabitants of Bicaz the plant is still functioning under the new and reinvigorated ownership of Heidelberg Cement.

I was now in the old Romanian Principality of Moldavia, easily confused with the newly independent former USSR republic of

---

[28] Consequently there a many rivers of this name throughout the Balkans and Russia.

Moldova. Since they were once one and the same, it is worth revisiting their early history. After the Hungarians had conquered Transylvania in the eleventh century, they recruited the Saxons to populate it and defend its eastern passes in the Carpathian Mountains; beyond this natural barrier lay the open spaces of the steppe from where the Mongols launched their murderous invasion in 1241, nearly destroying the entire Hungarian kingdom. As a result, the Hungarians consolidated their grip on their eastern frontier by enforcing the power and influence of the crown; hardly surprising that in 1349 the maverick Voivode Bogdan, exasperated by a life under King Louis the Great, crossed the Carpathians and settled in *Terra Moldovana*, well out of reach of the Hungarians.

Wasting little time, Bogdan adopted the ox head or auroch and a star as his coat of arms and minted his own coinage in neighbouring Poland; soon markets appeared in Baia, Câmpulung and Rădăuţi and in 1374 the Patriarch of Ochrid[29] consecrated the first bishopric in Suceava. Taking a leaf out of the Hungarian book of governance, the Prince, known as Hospodar from the Slavonic *Gospodar* or Lord, had absolute powers over his Boyars or nobles. His council was purely advisory.

Borders in those days were somewhat ill-defined since the Prince did not have the resources to police and defend them but a rough estimate shows the eastern boundary of Moldavia following the Dnister river (now running through Central Ukraine), the southern one from just West of Odesa to Buzau, the western one from the Carpathians North to Chernivtsi (now in Ukraine) and then back across to the Dnister river. Today, within these boundaries, lie the Romanian province of Moldavia, the independent state of Moldava, and the Ukrainian lands along the Danube including Bilhorod and, in the north, Procutia.[30]

The problem that came to dominate Moldavian politics for the next four hundred years was Turkey. Nineteen years before Bogdan

---

[29]   A Hellenised see in Macedonia
[30]   The area of the Ukraine on the North and North-east of Moldavia. Formerly a province of Poland.

first crossed the mountains, Bulgaria had come under attack from the Ottomans. In 1371 the regional power of Greater Serbia went into decline after the battle of Marica River, a disaster compounded by the victory of Sultan Murad 1 at Kosovo eighteen years later. Ominously Sultan Bayezid invaded Wallachia, Moldavia's neighbour, in 1391. Attempts by the Hungarians to alleviate the situation came to nothing when a crusade led by King Sigismund was crushingly defeated at Nicopolis in 1396. Ironically, it was the Mongols who saved the day in 1402; the great Tamerlane captured Bayezid and the acquisitive Ottoman war machine temporarily went into abeyance.

In 1417, Moldavia's neighbouring principality, Wallachia, stated to pay an annual tribute of 3,000 ducats to the Porte but it was Hungary that the Turks really wanted. Sultan Murad invaded Transylvania and was only stopped by the military genius of one man, János Hunyady, a Wallachian by birth and the only person claimed today by both the Hungarians and Romanians[31] as a national hero. This brilliant soldier checked the Turks at Belgrade in 1441, defeated them at Alba Julia the next year and the following year scored a resounding victory at Nis that led to a ten-year peace treaty. Foolishly, the young King Wadislaw of Hungary broke the treaty and was killed on an ill-judged campaign at the battle of Varna in November 1444; however his death did result in the election of Hunyady as regent for the infant Ladislas and once again Hungary went on the counter-offensive, attacking the Ottomans in Wallachia and Serbia.

Another towering figure emerged at this point, this time a young Turk, Sultan Mehmet II. After capturing Constantinople in 1453, he pushed west to Belgrade when the great Hunyady confronted him. It was a sad day in August 1456, when this 'Athlete of Christ' died of the plague, leaving his son, Matthias Corvinus, in charge. Now it was the turn of Moldavia to produce an outstanding leader, Stephen the Great or *Stefan cel Mare*.

---

[31]   Known to the Romanians as Ion Hunyadi or Huniade; also referred to as John Corvinus and as Johann Corvin von Hunniad, Prince of Siebenburgen.

It is hard to describe the awe and reverence that Stefan is still held in Romania today[32]; the English equivalent of Stefan merges the legendary exploits of Elizabeth I, Essex, Cecil, Raleigh and Drake into one person, producing a national hero of massive stature. He was by the standard of his time — and I would venture of any time — a character genuinely worthy of the extravagant accolades bestowed on him by history.

Grandson of Alexander the Good, Stefan owed his accession to disgruntled boyars after Peter Aron, his younger brother, had murdered their father, Bogan II, and to the support of the infamous Wallachian leader, Vlad Dracul, who was in search of a solid ally against the Turks. It was an unpropitious moment for after the fall of Constantinople, Moldavia stood exposed to the new Ottoman super power. It could not rely on Hungary, for Matthias was looking West towards Bohemia and Austria for new conquests; it could not rely on Casimir of Poland, who was embroiled in the Baltic and Lithuania; nor could it rely on Ivan of Moscow, who faced the ever persistent Tartar threat. The obvious solution for its new ruler was to pay a tribute to the Porte and enjoy a quiet life. This was not to be the way of Stefan.

First, he set about organising an army of 50,000 men, recruited from all over Moldavia; equipped only with padded jackets and home-made weapons, this was no hi-tech force but it could mobilise and disperse in a week. Then he created a series of massive stone fortresses, either reconstructed or built anew, at Suceava, Hotin, Soroica, Orhei, Cetatea Alba, Crăciuna, Neamţ and Roman. All were capable of withstanding artillery fire and long sieges. In 1465, he captured the Danube fort of Chilia, an action that provoked King Matthias of Hungary, who wanted his Eastern neighbour to be weak, to attack him in November 1467. Stefan shrewdly withdrew his forces from the line of advance and lured Matthias to Baia where on 14 December, in a daring night attack, he cut the Hungarian army to pieces. Moldavia was never again troubled by Hungary. Despite this resounding victory, Stefan was peeved by some of the battlefield

---

[32] In 2006, the public voted Stefan the 'greatest Romanian of all time' in a Televiziurea Română poll.

deficiencies he had noticed among his boyars—he beheaded twenty and impaled forty.

Meanwhile, the Ottomans had completed the conquest of Serbia and Bosnia and in 1470 were poised for an all-out attack on Hungary. Radu the Handsome, the new Prince of Wallachia, was in no way minded to stop them. Stefan, knowing that Moldavia was also on the Ottoman shopping list, acted decisively. In 1473 he replaced Radu with his own nominee and waited. This infuriated the great Mehmet II who sent Stefan a note to the effect that he was to surrender Chilia immediately and pay an annual tribute to the Porte. Stefan refused.

So, in the summer of 1474, a powerful Ottoman army under the Grand Vizir Suleiman the Eunuch, together with Besarab of Wallachia (the very man Stefan had replaced Radu with) attacked Moldavia. Once more, Stefan showed himself a master of strategy; he withdrew the population northwards, denying all supplies to the enemy and rendering roads impassable. On 10 January 1475, Stefan attacked the Ottomans at Vaslui and inflicted a crushing defeat on them—four high-ranking pashas were killed and 100 flags captured. As the historian, Hugh Seton Watson, wrote: 'So, the country that was modestly set up, little over a century before, at the foot of the Eastern Carpathians, got an unexpected international status.'

Stefan now turned to the West for help in 'cutting off the pagan's right hand'. He wrote: '*I have pursued the enemies of Christendom, I defeated them, crushed them down and by our sword they perished.*' He warned that the Sultan would soon come '*with all his might against us to subjugate Moldavia, the gate of the Christian world that God so far has protected. If this gate, which is our country, is lost—God forbid! —then the entire Christian world will be in great peril.*' Pope Sixtus IV, genuinely moved by this appeal, addressed Stefan as *athleta Christi*[33], a title previously bestowed on Janos Hunyadi when he raised the siege of Belgrad. But no help came.

Mehmet, incensed by the defeat at Vaslui, personally took charge of a new invasion in 1476. With his Northern flank threatened by the Tartars who were in league with the Ottomans, Stefan found

---

[33] "Verus Christianae fidei athleta"

himself overstretched and was defeated at Răsboeini in July. He fled to Poland but with cholera in its ranks and no supplies to live on, the Ottoman Army was forced to fall back. With the timely arrival of a Hungarian army, this time friendly, Stefan returning post-haste from Poland was able to harass the Turks back across the Danube. Mehmet considerately left Stefan alone after this.

On Mehmet's death in 1481, Stefan once again went into Wallachia and took control of it in order to create a buffer against the Turks. In 1484, the new Sultan Bayezid II seized Chilia and Cetatea Alba, the two great fortresses and trading posts which both protected Stefan's Danube flank and contributed handsomely to his exchequer. This was a blow for what had once been dubbed the Tartar road, the trade route which linked Poland to the Black Sea, had become a prosperous Moldavian commercial artery and these two fortresses its critical transport terminals. A year later, the Turks plundered and burnt Suceava although Stefan, with the help of Casimir of Poland, defeated them at Cătlăbuga as they retired south. It was more of the same in 1486 with Stefan once more prevailing, this time at Scheia to the North of Roman.

The rest of his reign was a constant tussle with the Porte, not helped by the intrigues of Poland and Hungary muddying the political waters. A Polish-Turkish peace was concluded in 1489, leaving Stefan with little choice other than to open peace negotiations himself and to finally pay tribute to the Porte. A last attempt in 1500-1502 was made to retake Cetatea Alba and Chilia—the loss of the latter had always stuck in Stefan's throat since he had employed over 800 masons and 17,000 labourers to build it in 1479—but it came to nought. Two years before his death in 1504, Stefan told the Venetian envoy: 'I am surrounded on all sides by enemies and have fought thirty-six battles since I was lord of this country, of these won thirty-four and lost two.' He was indeed a true champion of sixteenth century Christendom.

The historian, Miron Costin, summed Stefan up with Romanian perspicacity: 'acute of judgment, sober, not proud, but a stubborn defender of his rights, in war always on the spot, well versed in military science, generally favoured by victory, never depressed by misfortune:

ever expecting a better turn to affairs. The Moldavians think of him in political respects, with that veneration with which one holds a saint in religious honour'. On 21 June 1992, the Romanian church sanctified Stefan; magnanimously, his sword pilfered by the Turks in 1538, was loaned by the Topkapi Museum in Istanbul for the occasion.

Stefan's heirs struggled to maintain Moldavia's independence. His son, Bogdan the One Eyed, succeeded him and almost immediately had to do a deal with the Porte. In return for complete autonomy, respect for Christianity, non-interference with Princely elections, and an undertaking that no mosques were built and no Turks land ownership, Bogdan parted with 4,000 ducats, forty broodmares and forty falcons per annum. Alas such treaties were more honoured in breach than observance and Bogdan was killed fighting the Tartar allies of the Ottomans in 1517.

Turkish eyes as always were still on Hungary and on 26 August 1526, Sultan Suleiman comprehensively defeated King Louis at Mohacs; the dead included the young King, five bishops, many nobles and around 50,000 soldiers. Soon after, in 1527, Petru Rares, an illegitimate son of Stefan, was elected to the Moldavian throne. He found himself in the midst of a complex intrigue between Sultan Suleiman, Ludovico Gritti the Sultan's Venetian agent, Janos Zápolyai the Ottoman Sultan's puppet king of the conquered Hungarian lands, and Ferdinand Habsburg of Austria, the object of the Ottoman's fury.

Petru had certainly inherited his father's ruthlessness but lacked his moral authority and is rather unfondly remembered by history as a compulsive and scheming opportunist. With Zápolyai and Ferdinand at loggerheads, Petru took the opportunity to seize part of Transylvania in 1529 (including Cetatea de Baltă, the Rodna silver mines and the Székely district). The next year, after threatening to roast its inhabitants, he sequestered the Saxon town of Bistriţa. One will never know whether his newly extended western flank was tenable in the long term—probably not—but it was foolhardy in the extreme for Petru two years later to try and wrest Procutia from Poland. He was soundly defeated at Obertyn despite having made treaties with the Russians and Tartars.

Petru's political career was characterised by intrigue on a Byzantine scale. Here is a sample. Gritti, the Sultan's agent, arrived in Moldavia in 1534 to do a deal with Petru: Gritti wanted Transylvania (probably for his own family) and hence needed Petru's acquiescence which was duly given. With this undertaking in the bag, Gritti went on to Transylvania where he foolishly murdered the envoy of Zápolyai. All hell broke loose and Gritti rushed back to Petru. Far from safe conduct as had been previously agreed, Petru handed him over to the Hungarians who promptly executed him. Gritti's two sons were sent to Iasi in Moldavia where they were beheaded—on the orders of Petru.

This meant war with the Porte was inevitable, so Petru dashed off to negotiate a treaty with Ferdinand. He played the 'salvation of all Christendom' card rather well: Ferdinand assigned him three fortresses, Bistriţa and 6,000 ducats a year. Unbeknown to Petru, Zápolyai had intercepted his correspondence to Ferdinand and sent it to the Sultan. The result? In 1538, the Ottomans over-ran Moldavia and Petru found himself spending a year in one of Zápolyai's prisons. In his absence, the Porte placed Petru's nephew, Stefan the Locust, on the Moldavian throne. This hapless youth was killed by discontented boyars and suddenly Petru's star was back in the ascendancy for Zápolyai, his gaoler, died in 1540, an opportunity which enabled him to escape and present himself bold as brass to the Sultan as the best man for the job of Prince of Moldavia.

With a mesmerising mixture of abject pleading, mouth-watering presents and non-stop flattery, Petru succeeded in persuading the Sultan to reinstall him on the Moldavian throne and returned in 1540, triumphant but poorer. The new terms were onerous: a standing bodyguard of 500 muscle-bound Ottomans, tribute raised from 4,000 to 12,000 ducats per annum and his son to be held hostage in Constantinople. The wily Petru died in 1546, by now an irrelevance to the Porte after the fall of Buda in 1541. His son, Ilias, the hostage, had by then become a Muslim and after a few years on the Moldavian throne decided that the job offer of Pasha of Silistria was more conducive to his ambitions, so he was succeeded by his younger son,

Stefan, who died of debauchery after a reign of only eighteen months. In 1592, Alexander the Bad, the last descendant of Stefan, was hanged in public in Istanbul; Stefan's dynasty had disappeared in less than a hundred years on account of its own ineptitude and the political efficacy of its enemies.

The story of Stefan and Petru Rares may seem a long introduction to Moldavia but it is the very foundation of the history of this former Principality and the source of its collective pride that was so successfully grafted on to the new Romanian state, The United Provinces, in the mid-nineteenth century. Their legacy was not just political for between the two of them they left behind a tradition of building, painting and the decorative arts that all come together in the spectacular and enduring heritage of Moldavia's painted churches and monasteries to which I was now heading.

It was that time of year when both villagers and town dwellers were laying in supplies of wood for the winter. Judging by the varied activities along the side of the road, there seemed to be a number of different ways of ordering. The bulk order comprised an entire beech tree minus its branches. The recipient presumably required a large chainsaw, several axes and a great deal of time, enthusiasm, energy and expertise as was the case for the next type of order, which consisted of large sections of tree. Beech boughs and branches could be ordered separately but still a hefty chainsaw was required. Then there were large logs which needed splitting by axes, logs for stacking only and off-cuts from the sawmill, the last two dealt with by handsaws. The final category comes under 'bits and pieces from the wood', usually collected by hand and lugged all the way back to the hearth. These various loads were delivered to the front door by lorry, pickup, horse-and-cart and handcart. Once I saw two oxen dragging four lengthy pine trees down the village street and on another occasion spotted a mixed load consisting of a pig in a poke and several lengths of timber, bumping along together on the back of a cart. Sawing takes place wherever the load is dropped, which is more often than not in the middle of the street.

The road led up through the hills to Târgu Neamţ and then followed the course of the river Moldova North-west to Gura Humorului, all along the way overlooked by the brooding ridges of the Carpathians. I reached Voroneţ at dusk, just as the village was changing from its day to night routine. The air was full of richly scented smoke identifying the type of wood burning in the stoves, here beech, there pine. Horse and carts rattled by in the gloaming, heading for the farmsteads, which were still hives of activity. Inside the barns I could see the farmers stacking hay and packing maize stalks, illuminated in pools of yellow light like a scene from a Caravaggio painting. Each yard smelt pungently of pigs and cows; only the sheep were still out on the hills.

During the day, it is easy to walk past a village pub in Romania and be unaware of its function for it often looks like a small shed attached to the side of an ordinary house without the paraphernalia of pub signs and garishly branded umbrellas which identify its English counterpart. At night, however, it is easier to find because of the luminescent chinks and muffled hubbub percolating onto the street and on this particular evening the sound of a shepherd's pipe. There were four customers in the parlour, two youths—one of whom had a broken nose and macabre impression in the centre of his forehead probably caused by a blunt instrument such as a hammer—a little old man wearing an astrakhan hat with matching fur on his face and a nattily suited middle-aged man, who turned out to be his son. Delighted at the unexpected appearance of a stranger, the old man resumed his pipe playing *vivace*, much to the annoyance of Ovidiu, the Adams-family look-alike youth, who told him to desist, an order that provoked outrage from the buxom barmaid and she gave short shift. The piper finally stopped when his suave son told him to shut up and sit down. There was an expectant pause, which I took as my cue to order drinks all round. *Vorona* was the preferred tipple, an odourless and colourless schnapps tasting of very little. Then the concert resumed and I left before the altercations started up again.

A full moon rose in a vee-shaped indentation on the spiked crest of the Carpathians, trying to shine with the strength of its brother the sun and light up the dark forests below it. Such moments are poignantly captured by the Romany poet, Luminiţa Mihai Cioabă[34]:

> *Don't forget your name gypsy child*
> *because only in your hair does the moon*
> *sprinkle the brilliance of stars*
> *to teach you*
> *of the beginning*
> *the love from far beyond*
> *the sky.*

A strange pale orange glow fell across the beech canopy; I longed to see its effect on the painted church of St. George at Voroneţ monastery just down the road but it was firmly locked for the night, protected by high walls and vigilant dogs.

The beauty of these painted churches is breathtaking; scattered like brightly decorated boxes around Moldavia, they are perfectly positioned in relation to the folds of the fields and slopes of the woods surrounding them. A Romanian art critic surmised that the secret of these painted churches was threefold: the harmony between the churches and their natural setting, the harmony between their architecture and frescoes and the harmony between their colours and the light.

When Stefan the Great sanctioned the construction of his first church at Pătrăuţi in 1487, his requirement was simple. The form and layout should meet the needs of the Orthodox Church and thus the organisation of the interior needed to be linked to the Byzantine tradition of a rectangular plan with a triconch or three apses at the eastern end. In the Orthodox design, the eastern apse containing the altar and sanctuary is separated from the nave or *naos* by the

---

[34] Luminita Mihai Cioabă: *Don't Forget Your Name Gypsy Child* (translated by Adam Sorkin)

iconostasis, a pictorial 'wall', behind which mass is celebrated. The *naos* leads to the *pronaos* or narthex and in the larger churches, this design is extended into *exonarthex* or porch, which either can be open as at Humor and Moldoviţa or closed like at Voroneţ. A tomb room, usually containing the graves of the founder of the church and his family, is often situated in monastery churches between the naos and pronaos.

If the ground plans were Greco-Byzantine, stemming back to the days when Constantine had first settled in the Greek trading city of Byzantion in 330 AD, the elevation, building techniques and stone ornament used in their execution were contemporary Gothic, a style that had originated in France and then spread throughout Western Europe during the twelfth century. Gothic architecture was all about arcuated form, pointed arches and windows, thrust and counterthrust. Whilst the little painted church of Pătrăuţi begs no comparison with the mighty cathedrals of Trier or Bourges or Cologne, the very form of its hewn stone buttresses, its portals and window frames, the interplay of arcades and recesses are all indicative of Gothic and Romanesque influences imported from Poland and Transylvania, countries with excellent links to the West, which bordered on fifteenth century Moldavia.

What was uniquely Moldavian in concept and execution was the system of vaulting used to support the drum and octagonal tower above the naos, which resulted in the 'broken roof' form. The geometric problem facing the architects was how to reduce the rectangular plan of the naos to a square. By throwing two equidistant sets of two or even three arches along the shorter sides of the rectangle, they created the critical square design; on top of it was another arrangement of four arches, this time at forty five degrees i.e. the base of the pillars sat on the apex of the arch beneath it. On top of that was the square base of the drum, again at forty five degrees. Thus the weight was perfectly distributed, no one arch being exposed to more than a single load. In later years, buttresses on the outside walls provided additional strength.

Little is known about the Master Builders who were responsible for the design and construction of these Moldavian churches. Certainly no strangers to church architecture, the challenge for them was to use stone, not wood, and the associated problems of weight and stress. Building materials were not a problem for there was an ample supply of stone at the quarries at Vama, situated at the epicentre of the building region, and the surrounding forests offered a selection of the finest timbers. What is for sure is that they were kept busy by Stefan, for, between 1487 and 1504, almost thirty churches and monasteries were erected by the Prince and his Boyars. Legend would later have it that for every victory over Moldavia's enemies, there was a church erected in celebration of its salvation.

To understand the interior paintings and external frescoes of the painted churches, one has to return to the origins of Christian art, which is still found in the iconography of the Orthodox churches. As John of Damascus (676-749 AD) wrote in his treatise *On Icons:* 'The icon is a song of triumph, and a revelation, and an enduring monument to the victory of the saints and the disgrace of the demons' More recently Bishop Timothy Ware put it like this[35]: 'The Tradition of the Church is expressed not only through words, not only through the actions and gestures used in worship, but also through art—through the line and colour of the Holy icon. An icon is not simply a religious picture designed to arouse appropriate emotions in the beholder; it is one of the ways whereby God is revealed to us. Through icons, the Orthodox Christian receives a vision of the spiritual world' John Julius Norwich writes in his Short History of Byzantium 'The instructions given to the painters and mosaicists of Byzantium were simple enough: "to represent the spirit of God". It was a formidable challenge, and one which Western artists seldom even attempted; again and again, however, in the churches and monasteries of the Christian East, we see the task triumphantly accomplished.'

As Sacherverell Sitwell noted[36], 'the conception of a painted church is purely Byzantine in its origins. Byzantium entered most strongly into the history and oral tradition of the race who built these churches....As an idea, the painted church belongs to that category

[35]   Timothy Ware: *The Orthodox Church*, Penguin 1997
[36]   *Romanian Journey*

in the imagination of the Byzantines that caused them to gild the tree trunks in their gardens and to spray gold and colours upon the plumage of the pigeons'. Byzantine art had flourished for over a thousand years (from 330 to 1453) across a huge region, today comprising Turkey, the Balkans, the Middle East, Georgia and parts of Italy. The natural heir to the technical traditions of the classical world, for instance the icon was the direct descendant of classical portraiture, Byzantium was at the very centre of the first centuries of Christian art and when the envoys of Vladimir of Russia came away from Constantinople, they breathlessly reported to the Tsar: 'We knew not whether we were in heaven or on earth.'

There were strict rules to be observed in Byzantine ecclesiastical art, for mosaics and wall paintings had to obey certain laws, including a 'hierarchy of precedence', where an image had to occupy a specific place either as a symbol or decoration or sometimes as a function. Indeed at the Seventh Ecumenical Synod in 787 AD, it was stated 'art belongs to the painter, but the disposition of it is the prerogative of the venerable Holy fathers'. Thus the positioning of the frescoes, which decorate both the outside and inside of Moldavian churches, was not in the gift of the artist. The entire building expressed the organization—both horizontally and vertically—of the Orthodox church: the upper part of the church, including the vaults, symbolized a stone heaven, the triumphant 'divine church'; the lower part, the walls, represented the 'fighting church' with paintings of biblical legends and soldier saints.

So although there was no question of unbridled originality in the later Renaissance or Modern sense, this did not result in stagnation for within the restrictions imposed on him, the artist was able to retain his individuality through his use of line, the agitation he invested in his subjects' eyes, the combination of colours he chose and the style of draperies he applied to the figures. Furthermore there were plenty of design motives for the artists to play with for Byzantine ornament was a tantalizing compote of Roman, Syrian and Persian influences, the latter supplying a range of traditional Iranian motives like tulips, chrysanthemums, pomegranates, vines and acanthus leaves.

Why paint the entire outside of church? No one is quite sure of the answer. The idea of covering facades with coloured lime plaster is very old indeed, dating back to the seventh century BC in Greece. In the Middle Ages, exterior mural paintings flourished in Italy, Germany and France as well as in the Balkan Peninsular. Next door to Moldavia in Transylvania, there are many remnants of exterior frescos. However, these were all isolated images, placed on the main façade and around the entrances.

Nowhere had the complete exterior of a church been covered in religious paintings. It may well have been that Stefan and Petru Rares wanted to make the teachings of the Bible accessible to all as a way of binding the interests of Church and State together. The churches were too small for everyone to fit inside and as farmers were in any case used to standing around in market places and chatting, wall paintings were the best means of educating and informing them. After all, the great St Basil had directly referred to painting as 'the Bible of the illiterate' — 'what the word transmits through the ear...painting silently shows through the image.'

Then there was the propaganda value of the external paintings, representing the triumph of good over evil, and more explicitly the victory of Christianity over Islam. Were they the medieval equivalent of political advertising on outdoor poster sites? Certainly, their cumulative effect was a direct appeal to save Moldavia from disaster through inspiring its people with confidence in ultimate victory. Perhaps the answer is a combination of both, together with an extraordinary spiritual vision for it is only the latter that can explain the perfect juxtaposition of church, woods and fields, the harmony of the colours of the frescoes with those of the landscape and the ever-changing light and the brilliance of the compositions.

But back to Voroneţ. The next morning I walked up the valley, past the pub of the night before, and there at the end of the road lay Voroneţ monastery, founded by Stefan the Great in 1488 and painted in 1534-

35 in the reign of Petru Rares. The West wall of the naos shows Stefan and Lady Maria as the votives, the 'offerors to God', together with their two daughters and son, Bogdan III. The intercessor is that popular military saint, St George.

All of the externally painted churches share certain 'themes' — The Heavenly Hierarchy or The Prayer of All Saints[37], The Tree of Jesse, The Akathistos Hymn and The Last Judgment — but it would be a disservice to lump them all together. In the case of Voroneţ therefore I have chosen its finest exterior frescos, The Last Judgment on the West wall and the Tree of Jesse on the South wall as outstanding examples of Moldavian church art.

The idea of a Last Judgment first appears in Ecclesiastes: "I said in mine heart, God shall judge the righteous and the wicked; for there is a time there for every purpose and for every work" (*Ecclesiastes 3:17*). After the ninth and tenth centuries the depiction of The Last Judgment, this time based on the Book of Revelations, became one of the important themes of European painting and was often displayed on the inside of the western wall of churches. Early works include the Last Judgment in Sant'Angelo in Formis, in the Santa Maria Assunta on the Venetian island of Torcello, and on the cupola of the Baptistery in Florence. They are all divided into a series of independent horizontal compartments for the iconographic tradition still exerted considerable influence in Italy.

In Byzantium, when the scholar Theodore Metrochites restored the ruins of Chora (Kariye) in 1312, the Last Judgment follows this traditional compartmental style. Novelty does appear in the form of a snail carried by an angel that represents Paradise. At around the same time, Giotto started his Last Judgment on the interior of the West wall of the Scrovegni Chapel in Padua (1306), where the panels and divisions have begun to disappear but the rigid scheme of painting figures on different scales graded according to their importance still remains true to Byzantium. In the lower portion of the painting, to one side of the huge wooden cross, are groups of saints and the blessed, while to the other are the demons and those who have been

---

From Jesse's rod ...

JESSE'S TREE

... sprung a "tree"

sung standing up ...

AKATHISTOS HYMN

... while Constantinople held out

Procession of Saints ...   *... and its bishops*

SAINTS ETC

Ladder of St. John climactus

Father Cleopa in the tradition of Moldavian hermits

FOUR FACES OF FAITH

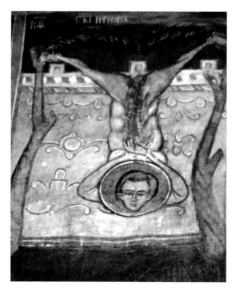

Painful death or ....   *... uncomfortable life (Stylite)*

condemned to hell. Above them, as if on the edge of a heavenly stage, the twelve apostles sit on their thrones. Higher up still, on either side of the windows, eight choirs of angels are visible, while the ninth choir floats in the centre, holding the mandora with the majestic figure of Christ, the judge. Four of the angels sound the fanfare toward the four quarters of the globe, proclaiming the arrival of Judgment Day. The front ranks of angels carry crusading standards and are dressed in helmets and armour as they lead forth Christ's heavenly armies.

Compare this with the West wall of Voroneţ nearly two hundred years later and there are very few changes. Indeed it could be argued that Giotto's version was more 'modern'. There can be no better example of the forces of conservatism at work in Byzantine art than this Last Judgment, for nowhere in the Moldavian painted churches of the 1530s and 1540s can be seen the dramatic, writhing naked bodies of Lochner (1435), Van der Weyden (1450) and Memling (1472), the vigorous, muscular devils of Signorelli (1499), the bizarre sinful world of Hieronymus Bosch (1510) and the grandiose treatments of the theme by Durer (1511) and Michelangelo (1536). It wasn't that the Moldavians knew nothing of torture and how to arrange for their enemies the most excruciating and agonising exits from life —they were expert and prolific dealers in death. It was simply that they would have considered depicting such graphic and anatomical images of torture and death as vulgar, worldly and altogether missing the critical Byzantine point—art belonged to heaven, not to earth. As Timothy Ware[38] summarized, 'for behind all the shortcomings of Byzantium can always be discerned the great vision by which the Byzantines were inspired: to establish here on earth a living image of God's government in heaven.'

Placed on the Western walls of the churches, except at Arbore and Râşca where it is on the South wall, the painting of this theme of the blessed and the damned is necessarily symmetrical. Starting on the top registers with the Gate of Heaven and the bust of the Ancient of Days, with angels wrapped in rolls and zodiacal signs signifying the end of earthly life for mankind, the painting unfolds

---

[38]   Timothy Ware: *The Orthodox Church*, Penguin 1997

to the Diesis, with Christ as Judge and the Virgin and John the Baptist alongside Him. The *Psychostasia* or weighing of souls and of sins by the Archangel Michael follows directly underneath, and then two camps bisect the picture—on the one side, the righteous, who include the prophets, hierarchs, martyrs and true believers, are invited by St Paul to form a long line at the Gates of Heaven where St Peter awaits them with Abraham, Isaac and Jacob; on the other, the sinners—the proscribed enemies of Christianity of the time, identified by their dress as Jews, Turks, Tartars, Armenians and even Franciscan Friars—await their fate under the supervision of Moses. The division between Good and Evil is marked by the River of Fire—"Then shall He say to those on the left hand, the curse of God is upon you, go from My sight into everlasting fire" (*Matthew 25:41*). The death of the righteous man and the death of the sinner in the River of Fire are symbolised by the resurrection of the dead, especially those drowned or devoured by wild beasts. Introduced in *Corinthians 1:52*—"….for the trumpet shall sound, and the dead shall be raised incorruptible, and we shall be changed", the text for these dead is: "And the sea gave up the dead which were in it; and the death and hell delivered up the dead which were in them; and they were judged every man according to their works. And death and hell were cast into the lake of fire. And this is the second death" (*Revelations 20:13-14*).

On the West Wall of Voroneţ, the Last Judgment more or less follows this traditional sequence but variations include the twelve disciples seated on benches studded in colourful mosaics; among the unbelievers lurks a Black Angel, a devil symbolising a heretic, for heresy was viewed as far more dangerous than any overt denial of Christianity; St Peter, holding the keys to Heaven, is followed by St John, St Constantine and St Helena and others; and King David is shown playing the *cobza*, a medieval Moldavian instrument, not the traditional harp of the Old Testament. Who said Byzantine artists were restricted?

Moving literally a few yards, past the little Gothic entrance of the church, one finds an entirely different display, this time the Tree of Jesse. In religious art, the formal tree, with a thick stem and branches growing upwards like palms and terminating in buds, was popular throughout Asiatic countries, originating in Iran and commonplace in early Georgian and Armenian churches. In Greek mythology, Adonis, whose mother the gods had changed into a myrrh tree, came into the world when the tree was split asunder.

The symbol of a tree in Christian texts can be traced back to the Tree of Life and the Tree of Knowledge of Good and Evil in the Garden of Eden and also to texts in the Book of Psalms: "And he shall be like a tree planted by the rivers of water, that bringeth forth his fruit in his season; his leaf also shall not wither; and whatever he doeth shall prosper"(*Psalms 1:3*); "the righteous will flourish like the palm tree: he shall grow like a cedar of Lebanon; those that be planted in the house of the Lord shall flourish in the courts of our God. They shall still bring forth fruit in old age; they shall be fat and flourishing" (*Psalms 92:12-14*). The Tree is also found at the end of Revelations: "In the midst of the street of it, and on either side of the river, was there the tree of life, which bare twelve manner of fruits, and yieldeth her fruit every month; and the leaves of the tree were for the healing of the nation" (*Revelations 22:2*).

It was relatively late in the twelfth century, when the specific image of the Tree of Jesse first appeared in Western Christian art: mosaic fragments of the image can still be seen in the Basilica of the Nativity[39] in Bethlehem. The returning knights and clerics of the First Crusade most likely brought it to Europe at the beginning of the thirteenth century. The Tree of Jesse is placed on the outside of the wall of either the funeral chamber or the Pronaos, the spaces that precede the Redemption and Incarnation in the naos. It is celebrated on the two Sundays before Christmas, the Sunday of the Holy Progenitors (Adam and Eve) and the Sunday of the Holy Fathers.

---

[39] The Basilica of the Nativity was built by the Emperor Justinian (527-565) on the site of an earlier Constantinian basilica.

Horizontally, there are usually seven registers to the Tree, possibly representing the seven columns of the Temple of Divine Wisdom of Solomon in the Book of Proverbs. The fourteen vertical lines or registers match the sacred number mentioned three times by Matthew—it occurs in his list of Christ's ancestors.

The Tree of Jesse symbolises the link between the Old and the New Testaments and is based on Isaiah's prophecy, proclaiming the descent of Mary and Jesus from Jesse, the father of King David. "And there shall come forth a rod out of the stem of Jesse and a branch shall grow out of his roots" (*Isaiah 11:1*). Whilst Jesse is a minor figure in the story of the Old Testament—his claim to fame is solely as the father of King David—he is also the critical link back to Abraham and Melchizedek, King of Salem, from whom Moses received a blessing.

Literally sprouting from Jesse's side come the stalk and branches of figures of the Judaic Kings and scenes announcing the birth of Christ. At Suceviţa, in a perpendicular line above Jesse, who lies prone on the lowest register, are pictures of Kings David, Solomon, Rehoboam, Josiah, Manasseh, and Iehonia, topped by a portrait of Saint Fecioara (The Virgin Mary) and, on the highest register, Christ.

There is a wonderful variety of pictorial effects used to 'decorate' the tree: for instance, at Voroneţ, leaves and flowers—tulips, bluebells, lotuses, bindweed or Our Lady's Lap or Swallow's Dress—are painted in profusion. A vine, a Mazdean symbol of life, is sometimes used as the linkage that reflects the unity between the body of the church and its Head, Christ. "I am the vine, ye are the branches: He that abideth in me, and I in Him, the same bringeth forth much fruit; for without me Ye can do nothing. If a man abide not in me, he is cast forth as a branch, and is withered" (*John 15:5-6*).

To understand this painting, it is important to note that the blood relatives of Christ are often interspersed with others who are not, for example John the Baptist, Isaiah, the three men in the fiery furnace and Daniel. The message for the beholder is that descent from Christ is a matter of grace, not blood, and the Law is founded on grace. Thus the rulers of fifteenth and sixteenth century Moldavia had a legitimate authority that stemmed from Christ. In fourteenth century Serbia, the ruler and his family inserted portraits of themselves into the Tree, a custom which the Moldavians wisely did not imitate since they were only too aware that the Ottomans had conquered Serbia in 1459.

The Tree is often underpinned with or flanked by the 'pagan' philosophers, adjudged by the Byzantines as forerunners of Christ on account of their powers of reason and sense of justice. In the Orthodox church in Constantinople, any debate about the Christian religion was argued not just on the word of the gospels, but also on the highest philosophical and theological levels. At the early sixteenth century court of Suceava, the tradition of Hellenistic learning, revived by the great scholar Photius in Constantinople in 858, was vibrant; most of the books were Church Slavonic[40] translations of Greek writings. It is worth recalling here that the New Testament was written in Greek and the writings of the Early Christian fathers—Athanasius, Basil, John Chrysostom, Isidore and Theodoret—were also in Greek.

Thus Greece is well represented under or alongside The Tree by Apollonios, Solon, Aristotle, Sophocles, Thucydides, Socrates, Pythagoras, Plato, Plutarch, Philo and Homer. The Empress Sibyl, a composite character drawn from sibylline prophetesses from across the Middle East, is given the prominence bestowed on her kind by the early Christians. From Egypt, there is King Thoulis, and from the Levant, Balaam, the non-Jewish prophet who foresaw a Messiah.

So while there is an obvious connection here with Byzantium and its strong Greek antecedents, there is also a much older reality which the early Christians recognised, summed up by St Augustine of Hippo, who wrote in the fourth century: 'The very thing we now call the Christian religion was not wanting among the ancients from the beginning of the human race, until Christ came in the flesh, after which the true religion which already existed, began to be called Christian.'

The official language of the Moldavian Church and Chancellery until the late seventeenth century.

If one looks at a Moldavian painted church for too long, one's visual senses slowly begin to dysfunction such is the sheer volume of information they are presented with and so I headed North west to Moldoviţa for a perspective of two different themes. This is very much the church of Petru Rares; he founded it in 1532 and commissioned the artist Toma of Suceava to paint it in 1537. Probably the very first fresco was that of Petru as the votive with his wife Helena and sons, Ilias and Stefan, in attendance.

The immediate glorious composition that greets one after passing under the gate tower is the Prayer of All Saints, emblazoned on the three apses. Symeon the New Theologian describes it thus: 'The saints in each generation, joined to those who have gone before, and filled like them with light, become a golden chain, in which each saint is a separate link, united to the next by faith, works, and love. So in the One God they form a single chain which cannot quickly be broken.'

For a people in an almost constant state of siege, the sight of this huge composition must have been reassuring in sixteenth century Moldavia. Gracefully marching in serried ranks towards the Most Holy Mother of God, the Saints represent a collective appeal to save Moldavia from the Ottoman scourge. This spectacular theme is always found on the outside of the three apses in varying amounts of registers[41]. Rows of angels, seraphs, prophets, apostles, saints, fathers of the early church, hermits, martyrs and bishops horizontally all lead to the centre of the Eastern apse which is the focal point for the Virgin, intercessor for the redemption of the world and for Christ, its Redeemer. On the vertical scale, the highest register, just below the roof, depicts angels or prophets and represents the Heavenly Church e.g. angels are heavenly messengers and agents of God. The lowest register, nearest the ground, usually depicting hermits and bishops, represents the Earthly Church. On the interior walls of these same apses is painted the story of the Passion.

The scale of this theme of All Saints meant it was an enormous undertaking for the artists. For instance, at Voroneţ, there were nearly

---

[41] At Humor for instance, there are six registers: angels, prophets, apostles and missionary saints, the great hierarchs, warrior and healing saints, and finally the pious ones.

250 paintings in the theme, of which 204 still survive. Each painting, each face and pose, had to be marginally different in its treatment but, at the same time, come within the strict Byzantine regulatory code. This is in marked contrast to the style of Tommaso da Modena (1325-79) who was commissioned by the Dominican monks of Treviso to paint a series of full-length portraits of the order's most famous saints on the walls of their charterhouse. His realistic observation of the character and individuality of St Albert the Great (1200-80) injects a human dimension to the subject which, nearly two hundred years later, was still taboo with the Eastern Church in Moldavia.

The sheer number of individual panels tends to overwhelm the eye but it is particularly interesting to look out for archimandrites clothed in long albs over which they wear the *sakkos* (tunics) decorated with black crosses or squares; seraphs who "were in attendance above him; each had six wings: with two they covered their faces, and with two they covered their feet, and with two they flew" (*Isaiah 6:2*); cherubims of which "every one had four faces apiece (a man, a cherub, a lion and an eagle), and every one four wings; and the likeness of the hands of a man was under their wings" (*Ezekiel 10:21*) and whose "whole body, and their backs, and their hands, and their wings, and the wheels, were full of eyes round about" (*Ezekiel 10:12*); stylites like St Simeon Stylites of Antioch, who lived for thirty-seven years on a series of pillars of varying heights, the last one being sixty feet high and a mere six feet across; and a selection of hairy, semi-clad hermits from the thickly forested hills of sixteenth century Moldavia.

The second great theme I selected to view at Moldoviţa was the Akathistos Hymn. Images used by iconographers and fresco artists often related to Hymns, the songs of praise sung in the early Christian churches. This Hymn, called Akathistos because it is sung standing up (Greek *akathistos*, of which the *a* is privative and the *kathizo* meaning to "sit"; i.e. not sitting) was most likely composed shortly after 626 AD, the year in which Constantinople was saved from a Persian attack.

According to legend, when the Avars and Persians combined forces to lay siege to Constantinople, the inhabitants implored the support of the Virgin whose icon they carried in procession around the streets of the city. Their prayers were answered. Fire and brimstone rained down from heaven on the besiegers, destroying their armies and setting fire to their ships. Completed by the Patriarch Sergius, the Akathistos hymn thus became a war hymn to the defence of Byzantium.

History records a less miraculous version of events. On 29 June 626, the armies of the Avars and Persians did indeed invest Constantinople in response to the attack on the Persian kingdom by the Byzantine Emperor, Heraclius. Eighty thousand troops together with giant siege engines battered away at the walls throughout July. Patriarch Sergius, the Bishop of Constantinople and head of the Eastern Christian Church, made a daily procession along the walls to inspire his terrified parishioners. Then, in early August, Byzantium's Greek allies destroyed a Persian naval force in the process of ferrying troops across the straights. Coupled with news of further defeats on the mainland and of new alliances against them, the besiegers packed up and left, bemused at their misfortune and demoralized by their failure. Constantinople may have had divine protection but as Dimitri Obolensky succinctly summarised[42]: 'The Empire had been saved by the land walls of Constantinople, its overwhelming naval superiority and the efficiency of its military intelligence.'

Linked to the Saturday of the fifth week in Lent, known as the Saturday of the Akathistos, the twenty-four *troparia* of the hymn (each beginning in turn with one of the letters of the Greek alphabet) celebrate the events of the life of the Virgin, from the miraculous Conception and the Annunciation to the flight to Egypt and other scenes of the Adoration of the Virgin. Alternate troparia are followed by panegyrics of the Mother of God, spoken by the Angel of the Annunciation, the Saints, the narrator and the crowd. Four times the *kontakion* of the Saviour of the City is sung: 'To thee, our defending general, the songs of victory! Thanksgiving, as having been saved from perils, I render to thee, I thy City, Mother of God.'

---

[42]   Obolensky: *The Byzantine Commonwealth*

George Enescu

Nicolae Grigorescu

THREE MOLDAVIAN SUPERSTARS

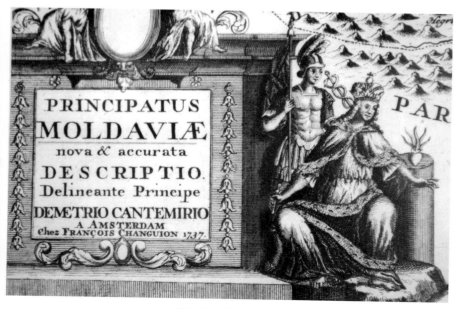

Dimitri Cantemir

Valeni Church

The 'houtsoul' verger

IN MOLDAVIA

A curious Last Judgment (right hand panel)

In iconography, the hymn is represented by twenty-four panels in either four or six registers, with the prophets often shown proffering their scrolls to the Mother of God in the one hand and with a symbol in the other. For example, Habakkuk holds a mountain, Ezekiel closed gates, Jeremiah a stone tablet, Jacob a ladder, Aaron his staff, Gideon a fleece, Moses a burning bush, Daniel a mountain, David an Ark, Balaam a star and Isaiah golden tongs. It helps to know your Bible really well when viewing this theme!

Studying the Moldoviţa frescoes in detail, we find on the upper tier the Burning Stake, the Annunciation (four episodes—the apparition of Gabriel, the doubt of Mary, the questions of Mary, the descent of the Holy Ghost), the Visitation, the Misdeeming thoughts of Joseph and the Nativity of Christ. On the second tier, the progress of the Magi, the adoration of the Magi, the departure of the Magi, Mary and Joseph presenting Jesus to the believers, the presentation in the temple, the Virgin worshipped by the pious people, the Virgin and the Rhetors, Trinity and the Virgin worshipped by angels. On the next tier, the adoration of the icon of the Virgin, Jesus crucified, Mary worshipped by virgins and the Virgin as bearer of light. And finally on the last tier, the enthroned Pantocrator worshipped by hierarchs, the descent to hell, the adoration of the Virgin as a living church (three scenes) and the glorification of the Virgin. It's a lot to take in.

Next to the Akathistos Hymn is often found the fresco of the Siege of Constantinople, showing the citadel of Byzantium, with a procession winding its way through the city, bearing the Mandylion and an Icon of the Hodegetria Virgin. At Humor, the Knight Toma of Suceava, dressed in the garb of a Moldavian boyar, leads an army out of the citadel to meet the enemy attack, a clear reference by the artist to the Ottoman threat to Suceava. And on the South Wall of Moldoviţa in 1537, it is the unending massed ranks of the Ottoman janissaries and spahis with their round, beardless faces who are depicted attacking the City in 1453, replacing the unsuccessful Persians of 626 AD. The commander of the citadel has clearly impaled a Moslem on the end of his lance. This historical sleight of hand merely served to offend the Porte and by 1541, the Persians were back on the wall at Arbore in deference to historical correctness[43]. As the political situation vis-a-vis the Ottomans continued to deteriorate, the 'siege' scene was dropped altogether.

In one scene of the Akathistos Hymn, the Virgin is shown holding her mantle open, under which huddles a group of saintly Episcopal figures. This refers to the second miraculous end to a siege of Constantinople, for in 860, when the Byzantine Emperor was away campaigning, a fleet of Russian ships appeared from nowhere and set fire to every village and monastery on the banks of the Sea of Marmara. The terrified inhabitants of Byzantium once again paraded on the walls of their city, this time holding on high their most precious relic, a piece of the Virgin's robe. Lo and behold, the Russians packed up and left. Such was the stuff of Byzantine victories and in this case, salvation.

One of the reasons I had come up to Moldoviţa was to find a *houtsoul* (also spelt *Hutsul*), whom Philip Thornton in *Icons and Oxen* (1939) had described thus:

> 'there were *houtsouls* dressed in white or red trousers stuffed into neat top boots. Their women were wearing plain wrap-round skirts over a white chemise and their hair done up in a typically Polish way. They braid the hair in two long plaits and then wind it round the head like a halo, and tie a brightly coloured handkerchief over the plaits to keep them free of dust. The *houtsouls* live principally on Polish territory north of the Roumanian frontier, but there are considerable numbers that have settled across the border. They keep very much to themselves in their own villages, speak a curious form of Polish and regard themselves as being quite different in every way from their Roumanian and other neighbours.'

---

[43]   The inscription by this fresco spells it out: "Emperor Chosroes rose against Constantinople in 6035 with Persian, Scythian and Libyan armies, under emperor Heraklios, when the Holy Virgin, by her prayers, brought a rain of lightnings and fire over the besiegers".

Another writer, the ethnographer and folklorist Bronisław Gustawicz[44], had noted:

'Their dress is generally short and tight-fitting, but light and warm, adapted to the sharp climate and difficult climbing among the mountains. The highlander puts on a short *gunia (hunia)* or overcoat of his own make over a collarless linen shirt, and in winter adds a small coat. His head is shaded with long hair, usually flowing down to the shoulders, and is covered with a round felt hat or cap, the style of which varies by region. He wears a wide belt of hard leather, fastened with a long row of large brass buckles, often embroidered in various colours. He wears pants with clasps, of coarse white fabric, the seams trimmed with coloured string, and on his feet are light, soft *kierpce* (moccasins), which he secures with straps wrapped tightly around his ankles. His bag, from which he is never separated, hangs from his shoulder on a strap generally adorned with tightly studded brass hobnails; in it he keeps supplies for the road and a short pipe, sometimes also a powder horn. A shotgun hanging from his other shoulder, and in his hand a small axe, which some highlander clans, for instance the *houtsoul*, can use with amazing skill, complete the picturesque dress of the highlander and gives his whole form an air of reckless freedom and impudence.

The highlander women also wear moccasins, or on rare occasions coloured saffian shoes, and wear overcoats and coats much like those of the men; the women cover their heads with scarves or white *peremitki* (Ukrainian term for "head-cloths"); the girls weave their hair into braids. In some clans, namely the Ruthenian highlanders, instead of pants the womenfolk use woollen aprons, which they tie around their hips, and they ride horses and smoke pipes like the men.

To cover the resulting significant cost of provisions, they are compelled to resort to various means of earning money, since the income from the animals in their barns does not always and everywhere suffice for their needs. So they work with picks, hammers, and wheelbarrows in mines and forges; they work with axes and saws in forests; they work

---

[44] Gustawicz (1852-1916) was a teacher at St. Anne's Gimnazjum in Kraków.

producing shingles and planks, matchsticks, dishes, wood furniture and ornamental hatchets; they guide rafts when the waters are high, at which they distinguish themselves by their skill and courage; they work at weaving; sometimes they even leave the mountains in masses and go down to the valleys to do mowing and harvesting; or to earn their bread more easily, they conduct transactions with small amounts of capital, as the Bojkos do, or fix up horse wagons and travel to far lands with knitting needles or *kobza* (a stringed musical instrument), as the highlanders of the western part of the mountains do. Thus need makes the highlanders more industrious and versatile than the people of the plains.'

What a wonderful introduction and no wonder I went in search of this tribe of Polish mountaineers, lost somewhere in the hinterland of Northern Romania. After pouring over various maps which showed the eighteen *houtsoul* villages left over from the eighteenth century migration, the upper reaches of the Moldova river looked promising for a 'find'. However, my way was blocked by a market in full swing, mainly stalls of boots, shoes and coats but also of pigs and foodstuffs, both in anonymous sacks. The market traders all seemed to have vans or cars whereas their customers had arrived either in a horse-and-cart or on foot. A plentiful supply of palinka was being dispensed at key points along the straggly rows of stall-holders; several men were much the worse for wear and scuffles intermittently erupted. I did wonder about the gypsy couple selling their three-piece suite—were they in dire debt? On asking them in a roundabout diplomatic fashion, I discovered that the proceeds were earmarked for a holiday that had already been paid for!

Following the Moldova river North along the rusty skeletal remains of a narrow-gauge single-track railway, the countryside assumed an alpine complexion, where wood was in such abundance that fields could be fenced with rough post and rails and houses decorated with ornate shingle tile facings. I stopped to inspect an abandoned farm, each outbuilding skilfully and, judging by the heart shaped motifs, lovingly fashioned out of the trees that grew on the nearby hillside.

The *Górale* as they are known in Poland, a generic name for people living in the mountains, are dispersed in a broad arc stretching from the Tatra mountains on the Polish-Slovakian border to Chernivtsi in the Ukraine. Akin to Scottish highlanders, these Ruthenian hillbillies form clans, such as the Bojkos and *houtsoul*. One clan goes by the name of Podhalans, which is derived from this simple question and answer: "Where are you from?"

"Z hal—from the mountain pastures!"

As Orthodox Christians, the Górale were not popular with the Catholic Habsburgs or the Communists; the Lemko clan was chased out of their mountain villages in 1947 and dispersed across Poland.

I was intrigued by the folklore and customs the Górale once shared and wondered whether any were still practiced. For example, abduction of a bride—*vykkradanja*—was permitted, with her consent, if the parents disapproved of the betrothal; alternatively, the groom could purchase a bride at one of the many Girl Fairs. Weddings would last three days and at one point, it was customary for the groom to wash his wife in the stream, an excuse for a water-fight between the village boys. On the birth of a child, great importance was attached to its first bath: to harden the child against the cold, a pair of goose legs were first dipped in the water. A live rooster was carried at the head of a funeral procession (later donated to the priest); to avoid the return of the dead, favourite personal possessions were either placed in the coffin or on top of the grave.

Their songs are all about mountain life:

At our place
At our place there is a green meadow
Boys love me because I am young
At our place, oh, how the meadow is raked,
I have broken five rakes to do it.

The Shepherd gave me cheese
The shepherd gave me some cheese
So that I would love him.

Even if it's a whole ball (of cheese)
I still won't give myself to him.

Oh shepherd, oh shepherd,
You're shivering with cold,
It's from the žentycja
That you drank last Friday.

Oh shepherd, oh shepherd,
How sweet was that žentycja,
And if your sheep perish,
You too will be hung.

Weather conditions for spying *houtsoul* were poor. The snow kept everyone indoors and it was only when I reached the village of Argel that I spied a lone figure slowly walking down a track which connected the little church to the main road. He turned out to be the verger and after a great deal of confusion about the nature of my quest, he turned around and took me back to his church, holding my arm in a vice-like grip. After an extrapolated, conducted tour—the actual church was minute—during which we inspected every icon and commented on every ornament, I managed to extract from him that he was a *houtsoul*. Pathetically, I called it a day. To get to grips with these scarce Romanian minorities, one needs to launch a major expedition, preferably in the summer months when, like rare birds, they might be seen venturing out of their carefully camouflaged nests.

Eight months later, I resolved to resume my *houtsoul* hunt, this time drawing up a detailed plan of discovery to avoid disappointment. A lady from Swansea called Svitlana with a deliciously seductive voice made arrangements for me to approach my quarry from the North, that is from the Ukraine as opposed to Romania, and so it was in early July that I set off from London, clutching a copy of an old FT article, '*All you need is L'viv*', and the programme of my made-in-

Wales 'Ukraine Ukrainian Carpathians Tour'—Svitlana, 'the shining one', had left me in no doubt where I was going.

Nothing is straightforward in the Western Ukraine as I found out as soon as I landed. L'viv, literally 'Lev's place' after its thirteenth century ruler Prince Lev, is pronounced 'L'vov' by Russians and 'L'view' by Ukrainians; no one says L'viv except tongue-tied tourists. To be greeted by torrential rain and a howling gale came as no surprise since I had read that the same Prince Lev had to move his castle in 1256 due to the strength of the wind. The city's origins lie in its position on the ancient Baltic/Black Sea trade route, a factor which explains the number of visitors who have either made it their home over the centuries—predominantly Poles, Armenians and Jews—or occupied it by force—Turks, Cossacks, Tartars, Swedes, Austrians, Russians (three times) and Germans. The result is a bustling modern city of nearly a million people that spreads out like concrete spaghetti from a spectacular sixteenth century market place, Rynok Square.

Rynok, like many other Central European city centres, owes its grandeur to the Italian architects and craftsmen who exported their Renaissance designs, persuading princes, bishops and merchants to build new houses adorned with decorated portals, ornamented facades and arcaded courtyards. Certainly Roberto Bandinelli, owner of the fastest postal service between Poland and Italy, couldn't resist and opted for a design of two dolphins above his new entrance at No 2; the owners of No 4 went for an all black facade and their neighbour, the Cretan merchant Konstantin Korniakt, treated himself to a magnificent triple-storied arcaded courtyard. It was this house that was later bought by the Sobieski family and served as a royal residence for King Jan III, the victor of the battle of Vienna in 1683. Jan's portrait and those of his wife and children hang on the walls of the L'viv History museum, the current occupant of the building; none of them could be described as handsome but the looks of their descendants improved, including the very pretty Maria Klementyna, the mother of Bonnie Prince Charlie. On the subject of Anglo-L'viv history, I should mention that King Volodimir (Vladimir) Monomachos (1053-1125) married Gytha, a daughter of Harold, the last Saxon King of England.

After a night at the George Hotel, a majestic pink edifice circa 1900 designed by the Viennese theatre and opera house specialists, Ferdinand Fellner and Hermann Helmer (not Mr Helmet as the guidebook would have one believe!)—the contract for the L'viv Opera went to the Polish architect Zigmund Gorgolevsky in 1900; he committed suicide after it sank half a metre and nearly collapsed—I rendezvoused with my expedition director, Ludmila Rudanets, her husband Igor, the expedition driver, and Ilona, my interpreter.

"How was the hotel?" asked Ludmila. "You know many famous artists have stayed there—Balzac, Liszt, Sartre, Ravel and, of course, Tolstoy."

I wondered whether she had been expecting a contemporary English literary celeb.

"I did read something about Tolstoy. Didn't he find a bell in his room to summon 'a female companion'?"

"Really?" Ludmila gave me an enquiring look.

"Apparently he mistook the word *kurtyna*, which meant Venetian blind in Polish, for the Russian for courtesan (куртизанка)."

"Oh, I think that Polish for Venetian blind is *Żaluzja*. *Kurtyna* means a theatre curtain".

It was time.to protect Tolstoy's reputation and I dropped the subject.

We headed East, passing through countryside reminiscent of Northern France with rolling fields crested with woods until we reached the Dniester river where Ludmila insisted that I inspected one Lubart of Lithuania's castle. Perched on a hill above the town of Halych, once the thirteenth century capital of this region, the castle is in a sorry state; only one of its five towers still stands together with a short length of wall. But the view across the river conjures up better days when traders heading to and from the Black Sea by road or river could be stopped and taxed. The name Halych may be the origin of the word Galicia and is most likely derived from the East Slavic for jackdaw or *halka*, which was apt since a pair was nesting in the eaves of the tower.

By late afternoon, after five hours of bone-crunching driving, we reached Kolomiya, which was to be my base for the next week.

Situated on the River Prut, the town is a typical Austrian-Hungarian creation of the late nineteenth century, a former farming village which proliferated after the arrival of the railway in the 1860s into streets of pale blue, lime green, yellow and pink town houses. A little market was underway with a long line of about fifty vendors offering tomatoes, cucumbers, potatoes, melons, raspberries, fraises du bois, mushrooms, garlic cloves, lettuces, apricots, cheese, spring onions, milk and eggs; curiously, they were all selling an identical range of products.

With a turbulent history rarely of their own making, Ukrainians are always keen to set the record straight, so as soon as we had debussed, Igor informed me that the name of the town was derived from the tenth century King Kolomar, whose own name probably came from the helmet-like or *sholomiya* shape of the hill on which he built his castle. Then, of course, since there had been a Roman Legion here, it could conceivably have come from the Latin word *colonia*. Certainly the Legio V Macedonica, which had been based at Turda in Transylvanian for two centuries, would have been deployed this far to the North East at one time or another. The Romans knew of the River Prut and called it *Pyretus*. And then there was another option — because the early traders came along dirt tracks, they had to clean their carts before entering the town in order to comply with civic regulations; hence *miya* to wash, *kolesa* wheels. I liked the last one and told Igor that as far as I was concerned that was the version I'd use.

The Hotel Pisanka in the town square defies its English name of 'peasant'. Under the firm and watchful direction of Ludmila's mother, Mrs Olga Rudanets, a highly qualified administrator who has the authority and presence of a director of a multinational company, it ticks over like a Parisian five star hotel. My room overlooked the square at one end of which was The Great Egg Museum, the scene of my first cultural induction the following morning. This time my tutor was Jaroslav, the curator of the largest collection of *pysanky* or painted eggs in the world. Peering at me intently through thick glasses, he started on the subject of spiders (pavoochok/павучок) which was confusing since I thought we were there to talk about eggs. Pointing at what looked to me like straw cages hanging down from the ceiling, Jaroslav explained that for Ukrainians, the spider was sacred for it had saved Mary and the infant Jesus from Herod's soldiers by weaving a web across the entrance to their hiding place.

Looking sternly at me, he pronounced, "If you find a spider, never kill it. Remove and place outside."

It seemed inopportune to ask about the *karakut* or Black Widow variety, which had recently killed an old woman in the southern Ukraine.

"We hang these straw webs up at Christmas time to catch the spirits of our dead relations. You can see them move when they collide into them."

"What a terrifying sight that must be." I ventured and was blithely ignored.

"Then we leave food out for them, some *kutya* which is a Christmas Eve mixture of cooked wheat, poppy seed and honey."

"Like *kolyvo* at their funeral feast?"

"*Kolyvo* does not have poppy seed," replied Jaroslav in a resigned voice.

I decided to force the pace. "Jaroslav, are these eggs, spiders, whatever, anything to do with *houtsouls*?"

He squinted at me for what seemed a long time and then resumed his talk. I soon realised that I was in the presence of the world expert on *pysanky* and after an hour of absorbing information on colours, symbols, codes, dyes, paints and *pysachoks*, I thanked Jaroslav profusely and reported in to Mrs Ocsana at the Kolomiya History Museum, who was waiting for me with her pointer. We got straight down to it, starting with some *houtsoul* signs carved in a beam above my head.

"Horns mean milk, wool and meat; the circle means the sun and animals represent health, wealth and life." She rapped her pointer on the beam.

"Now you see three Christs—this one fire, that one water and that one Tree of Life."

She'd lost me.

"Here is St Nicholas—he's good for marriage and children; here St Barbara, she's good luck for women and here's St George, he's lucky for animals." She paused before delivering the coup de grace. "*Houtsouls* were Christianised twice. First by Prague priests in 871, then by Greek Catholics in 955. So you see that combined with paganism, they have three traditions. You'll soon understand."

I nodded enthusiastically since I was indeed in trouble, first in linking the Prague priests to St Cyril and St Methodius on their mission from the Byzantine Empire to Greater Moravia in 863; and secondly in wondering whether the Greek Catholics were actually missionaries from Kiev after the conversion of Rus to Christianity by Prince Volodmir in 988.

We moved to the next exhibit, a cabinet containing a collection of small ornamental axes.

"The *Bartka* or Third Arm!" Mrs Olga exclaimed. Then for some inexplicable reason, she vociferously opined that *houtsoul* men considered their wives as servants—a disgraceful attitude—before continuing on the subject of axes.

"The men had to throw the axe in the air, jump up and catch it. If they dropped it, they were banned from parties for a whole month." She allowed herself a smile.

Cabinets of folk costumes followed and I only managed to extricate myself from Mrs Olga after being enticed into her office to watch a *pysanka* being painted by her friend. I am now the proud if reluctant owner of half-a-dozen painted eggshells. Her parting advice to me was to read up on the works of Baltazar Hacquet, a French doctor who had studied the *houtsoul* culture in the 1780s. I am still considering the uphill task of ploughing through *Hacquet's neueste physikalischpolitische Reisen in den Jahren 1788 und 1789 durch die dacischen und sarmatischen oder nördlichen Karpathe.*

Exhausted by my initial induction to all matters *houtsoul*, I decided to take the train to Chernivtsi for a break. I had always been intrigued by the city as it features in the writing of the remarkable Gregor Von Rezzori, a quintessential twentieth century Central European figure who managed in the space of his peripatetic life of eighty-four years to be an actor, screenwriter, artist, art critic, film producer, playwright, novelist, art collector and finally memoirist. In *The Snows of Yesteryear* (an abysmal translation of *Blumen im Schnee* or *Flowers in the Snow*), he recalls his childhood in Chernivtsi, at that time known as Czernowitz for it was then under Austrian rule.

"Czernowitz, where I was born, was the former capital of the former Duchy of Bukovina, an easterly region of Carpathian forestland in the foothills of the Tatra Mountains, ceded by the former Ottoman Empire to the former Imperial and Royal Austro-Hungarian realm as compensation for the latter's mediation in the Russo-Turkish war; the Bukovina was at first allocated to the former Kingdom of Galicia, but after 1848 it became one of the autonomous former crown lands of the House of Habsburg."

Noting that everything in this summary was 'former' i.e not in the present, not truly exisitng, Von Rezzori admits to investing his birthplace with an 'irreal quality'. Did Chernivtsi still exist in his 'mythic twilight'?

The train from Kolomiya slowly edged its way East, following the River Prut to the North of the Carpathians, whose distant tree-lined ridges were just visible above the swaying ears of wheat fields that almost brushed the sides of the train. Distant villages, marked by onion-domed churches, lay scattered on the far horizon; in the foreground, families scythed their hay fields with a relaxed precision, rationing their energy to last out the long day. Everyone on the train seemed to be selling something—chocolate bars, peanuts, bottled water, newspapers. At each station, red-capped officials herded their charges on and off the train unless there were no passengers in which case they stood smartly to attention.

I had arranged to stay with Igor Dzeman, the proprietor of the Koral Hotel. This establishment on the outskirts of the city turned out to be a blend between a car wash, sauna bath, billiards hall, restaurant and hotel or as Igor put it, 'five businesses, same place'. With such a plethora of facilities, one could have spent the whole weekend there but I continued on my Von Rezzori homage and made my way to the city centre. Until the 1780s, Chernivtsi was no more than a large village of some 200 families: it was its promotion to the status of capital of the Duchy of Bucovina in 1849 and the arrival of the railway in the 1860s that catapulted it into a city, an almost overnight transformation. In forty years, it became an unmistakable Austro-Hungarian provincial capital, designed by architects from Vienna and Prague. Fellner and Helmer accounted for the Theatre and the Czech architect Josef Hlavka designed both the fantastical Residence of the Bucovinian Metropolitans and the great red-bricked Armenian Cathedral. Subsequently, both have had their usuage changed: the former is now the University and the latter a concert hall.

After a longish uphill walk on a very hot and dusty afternoon, I presented myself at the entrance lodge to the University to be told in no uncertain terms that only students were allowed in—"It is exam time!" The officious porter furiously gesticulated when I requested entry to the museum, hollering that this instruction came from no less a personage that the Rector himself. I retreated to a safe distance to work out an alternative strategy. Somehow I needed to become an instant student, so I befriended two young men who were confidently approaching the University, explained my predicament and after they had had a few salty words with the outraged porter, they delivered me into the care of a charming French-speaking lady who was the curator of the Church of the Three Hierarchs. From thereon, it was a delight to be shown around this extraordinary building, described by the Ukrainian government in its submission to UNESCO as 'resembling a medieval castle. Its high brick walls are decorated with ceramics and carved stone. Straight towers, butt-ends and pointed ledges are trimmed with high merlons. Steep slopes of the roof are decked with the ornament of white, green, blue and brown glazed tiles. All of them give an impression of eternity, sublimity and festivity'. A Byzantine architectural fantasy summed it up for me.

The Romanians gained possession of Chernivtsi for a brief period between 1919 and 1940, renaming it Cernăuţi. Von Rezzori scathingly described this interlude as 'hardly more than a fresh costume change in a setting worthy of operetta....the whole transformation was given no greater weight that the one accorded the changing scenery at the municipal theatre between *Countess Maritza* and *The Gipsy Baron or The Beggar Student.*' One such scene change involved the dismantling of a large statue of the Empress Elizabeth, a more fulsome figure than that depicted by Winterhalter in his famous portrait, during which her head came off. The citizens of Chernivtsi remain indignant to this day about this act of vandalism and revere the decapitated remains of Her Imperial Highness. In the University's Marble Hall, there is even a chrome cast replica of the headless Sisi.

The character of Chernivtsi today is dictated by the 20,000 students who study diligently during the day and play loudly at night. Von Rezzori's 'slovenly, deeply backwoods, leadenly nostalgic character, heavy with empty longings, of the no-man's-land between the cultures of East and West' is an image of the past, although it is easy to imagine that less than a hundred years ago this city would have been viewed in Vienna as being on the edge of the civilised world, a Von Rezzori 'hodgepodge of Swabian Germans, Romanians, Poles, Jews, Prussians, Slovaks and Armenians'. For me, there was a reassuring resonance between the brightly coloured nineteenth century vine-covered facades in shady tree-lined streets and the quietly confident mood of the inhabitants as they unhurriedly went about their business, no doubt figuring out like Igor how to run 'five business, same place'.

My *houtsoul* search restarted the next day with a new addition to the team in the person of Mr Nicola, an expert geographer and *houtsoul* ethnologist par excellence. First stop was Kosiv, a village in the *houtsoul* heartlands on the banks of the River Rebaitsa ('full of fish'). A quick tour of the market revealed many *houtsouls* manning stalls selling carpets, ceramics, wood carvings, metal ornaments and various skins, all designed for the tourist industry. There is a story that the Emperor Franz-Josef was very taken by *houtsoul* craftsmanship and endowed several schools for carvers, weavers and potters; it must have been their descendants Nicola introduced me to in a run-down factory complex outside the town, where craftswomen silently glazed pots while others wove rugs on clattering hand-operated looms. We then stopped off at a small house in the village of Gorod ('town'!) to watch a shepherd's wife weave a thick woollen *lyshnick* or bedcover. Her husband was away in the high pastures or *polonyna* and would not come home until the Birthday of the Mother of God on 10 September. I asked Nicola whether we had time to visit a *polonyna* but they are situated in the remotest areas of the Ukrainian Carpathians, so we compromised with a visit to the Bucovitz Pass, a few miles south of Sokolivska, 'the village of falcons'.

From the Pass, we walked up onto a high ridge, through meadows crammed with wild flowers—heathers, columbines, bright magenta Betany, red clover, knapweed, pink Goat's-rue, wild Marjoram, Globeflowers, Blue Vetch, Perforate St John's-wort, Forget-me-nots, Kidney-vetch, Clustered Bellflowers. There was no sign of an Edelweiss, a *houtsoul* symbol of love, as this touching story recounts. Young Marichka fell in love with Olexa who was a shepherd on Hoverla mountain. Much as he loved spending time with her, he was rarely able to return home as he couldn't leave the sheep by themselves. So to keep in touch with Marichka, he would take his *trembita* (Carpathian horn) and signal her across the valley:

Hey, Marichka, white flower,
I will love you,
Until the sun warms,
And the moon shines.

Marichka would listen to the sound of his *trembita*, fall in love even more and wait for autumn when her beloved would come down off the mountain.

One morning, Marichka woke up and didn't hear the *trembita*. 'Something dreadful has happened to my Olexa', she thought and set off to climb the mountain. Little did she know that bandits had murdered him, cut him into pieces and thrown him to the ravens before making off with his sheep. Calling Olexa's name, she forced herself through prickly bushes, scaled precipitous cliffs and peered into every gorge and cave. Her beloved never answered and each time one of her tears touched the ground it turned into an Edelweiss. The little flower never wilted, neither did her love.

Nicola explained to me that, in the past, *houtsoul* men had been famous loggers, building rafts and bringing the timber down river. Part of that tradition had been the *houtsoul* horse or *houtsouliki*, a sure-footed, strong and hardy breed that was equally at home in the forests or high pasture. Once almost extinct, the breed has now been reintroduced and there are currently about 200, one of which I found myself riding in the next village.

Kosmach, billed as the capital of Hutsulshchyna, was a *houtsoul* epicentre, the name apparently referring to its men who were renowned for their slovenly unshaven appearance due to their demanding work schedule. With a two-day stubble, I immediately felt at home and leaving the car outside the village pub, Nicola and I mounted our sturdy horses and rode to the house where we were to be the guests of the widow Maria and her daughter Ocsana. It began to rain and by the time we reached the little wooden building set back from the track in a meadow speckled with pear and apple trees, our party was thoroughly drenched. Wet through, I was despatched with a pail to draw water from a spring at the bottom of a steep slope and re-enacted the story of Jack and Jill several times before finally making it back to the top. I found a bedraggled Nicola huddled over an outdoor fire, which he was coaxing into life; apparently, we were going to eat barbecued *shashlik* come rain or shine!

Maria, busy preparing dinner, casually asked me whether I had seen 'the viper' on my way to the well. It was out there in the morning, she said. This was definitely the moment to sample her *domashni vino*, the name for innocuous sounding home-made wine but in reality a full-blown *tuiça*. After several toasts, the third being 'To love' and the fourth 'To crazy love', an enormous meal was produced and our hostesses looked on benignly as we began to devour it. Maria went through the next day's programme.

"First, breakfast. Then museum. Then berry and mushroom picking in woods. The lunch. Then freetime. Then souvenirs. Then Ludmila, she come and get you."

Nicola nodded knowledgeably and I marvelled at his grasp of the *houtsoul* dialect.

A sculpturer

His saddle

HOUTSOULS (1)

His studio

Houtsoul house

HOUTSOULS (2)

Houtsoul pub

"What you are really hearing is Ukrainian spoken with a thick English West country accent! When I first came to the mountains thirty years ago, their language was composed of 40% old Ukrainian, 40% modern Ukrainian and 20% Polish, Hungarian, German and Romanian loan words. Today, modern Ukrainian prevails and the challenge is how to keep the old language alive."

Did Maria have any *houtsoul* stories about the moon, I enquired. She beamed at me, not unlike a full moon herself, and recounted the following.

"Cain and Abel make sacrifice to God. Abel is shepherd, so he chooses lamb." This was said with an approving look. "Cain, he bring fruits and vegetables from his garden. God pleased with Abel but not with Cain. This upset Cain who picks up rake and kills Abel." She waited for me to nod that I understood the story so far. I nodded. "Well, you see this story on full moon. Particularly the rake." On that note, Maria and Ocsana bade us goodnight and hurried off into the rain-sodden night to stay with neighbours.

The museum turned out to be a little wooden hut where the *opryshok* Oleksa Dovbush, Ukraine's very own Robin Hood, had met his death in 1745 at the hands of his girlfriend Dzvinka's enraged husband, Mr Stefan Vynchuk. Although this may seem rather arcane information to the visitor, for Kosmachans the very fact that Dovbush, the most popular and revered *houtsoul* folk hero who had outwitted soldiers, policemen and fellow outlaws for years, was killed in their village is a great honour.

> *Who was recently a prince and ruler of these mountains, an eagle of that air, a deer in those pine forests, a lord of those lords up to the very Dniester waters? Dovbush! Before whom did the brave and strong tremble, and the proud submit? Before Dovbush!* Ivan Franko.

Situated at the end of a grassy track, the museum is the brainchild of Mr Mykhailo Didushytkly, a sprightly septugenarian with a drooping moustache and a green felt hat apparently glued to his head. Eclectic and eccentric describe the contents which Mykhailo has lovingly assembled over the years—dozens of *houtsoul* axes, icons, wooden drinking cups, belts, flutes, bagpipes, *trembitas* and pieces of anthropomorphic wood, some deliberately chosen for its pornographic qualities, are stockplied and displayed in a space no more than six foot by twelve. It was a similar story in his workshop, reached by climbing up a perilously narrow staircase into the attic of his house. Almost as cramped, this time with tools and bits of wood, the pin-ups of busty ladies which adorned the walls helped to explain the inspiration behind his selection of 'natural sculptures', which either featured copious breasts or long erect penises. Since the recent death of his wife, Mykhailo has taken to writing poetry but sadly we did not have time to hear a recital; I was hoping his verses may have been a bit lewd as well.

The relentless rain had started again, so we retreated back to the house after cancelling the berry and mushroom picking expedition. I asked Nicola about the *houtsoul* attitude to sex, given the frank nature of some of Mykhailo's collection (I later read in the Ukrainian Observer that, '….Mykhailo also has a foot in paganism. For example, he carves wooden sculptures of the ancient "gods" and goddesses" of the pre-Christian Ukrainians').

"They are very earthy people. They like sex. It is said that when they go into the woods to pick berries and mushrooms, a *houtsoul* man will creep up behind a woman and lift her skirt up. If she is wearing knickers, he lets her go but if she is not wearing knickers, well, they just get on with it then and there." He mused for a moment, then continued: "You see, although Christianity is acknowledged as the official religion in Kosmach…."

I interjected: "You mean some people are not exactly Christian; more like half-Christian, half-pagan?"

Nicola looked nervously at me and continued: "There is the famous story of an old woman who entered a church and lit two candles — one for God, another for the devil. The shocked priest asked for an explanation. "Father, I am old," said the woman. "I think it is wise to have friends everywhere." And then of course there are the *znakharkas*."

"And who would they be?" I asked in all innocence.

"Old ladies who know the secrets of the plants in the meadows and the trees in the forests. Many people seek them out when they are ill. They apply potions, usually murmuring a spell in the process."

"Are they classed as witches?"

"Certainly not. These ladies are genuine healers and have nothing to do with devil-worship. Wizards or *koudesnik* are far more suspect but there are very few of them around these days. "

Just after noon, Maria and Ocsana arrived to make lunch; a mere three hours had elapsed since breakfast. I felt like a goose being fattened for foie gras as dinner, breakfast and now lunch seamlessly merged into a twenty-four hour food fest of *nalysnyky* (crepes), tomatoes, pork, borsch, *varenyky* (ravioli) creamcheese, *pidpenky* (mushroom sauce), mamaliga, dumplings, hard cheese, cottage cheese, eggs, bacon fat, *holubtsi* (stuffed cabbage rolls), all eased down with draughts of berry juice and the ubiquitous Carpathian *palinka* or *horilka* (including at breakfast). When Ludmila appeared at the door to collect us that evening, I saw her as an angel of nutritional mercy.

The following day, Nicola, Igor, Ludmila, Ilona and I set off to cross the Carpathians and discover Ruthenia, once a small country that had briefly appeared on the world map as an autonomous part of Czechoslovakia between 1919 and 1940. I had an old pamphlet with me, written in 1944, in which the author advised:

"If you want a luxury hotel, keep away from Ruthenia. She has never built up a tourist industry. Go to Ruthenia only if you are sound in limb and wind. Go to Ruthenia if your heart is young and if you like the simple things of life—mountain air, scenery, rocks and springey turf, the wind and the heather, loneliness and the companionship of youth. Go to Ruthenia if you travel light—if you want swimming shorts for the summer and skis for the winter. Go to Ruthenia if you are a man with a gun. Go to Ruthenia if you want snow-covered slopes and frozen mountain-lakes. Go to Ruthenia if you want wild sun-clad beauty. Go to Ruthenia if you want to see where the West meets the east; the mountain fastness of Central Europe."

Well, I had ticked most of these boxes and it was with an anticipatory air of adventure that we sped south, following the Prut, now in spate, through the town of Yaremche to the Yablunyts'kyi Pass, the 3,000 foot entrance to Eastern Ruthenia.

The snow-capped summit of Mount Hoverla was just visible to the South, enough to prompt Nicola to deliver another folksy anecdote.

"Long ago a young peasant fell in love with a beautiful girl from a noble family. Her father disapproved of any marriage, so he went off and became a soldier. When he returned, he went in search of his beloved only to find that she had been married to someone else of her own class. Such was his grief, that he turned to stone—Mount Hoverla—and his tears became The River Prut."

We had now arrived in mist-bound Rakhiv where the Ukrainian guide book 'A Trip Through Transcarpathia' accurately stated: ' In dull weather it seems that clouds catch on the alps, and the sky descends on the ground'. Just beyond the town lies The Centre of Europe, at least according to the Royal Academy of Sciences of Austro-Hungarian Empire, whose members erected this sign in 1887.

LOCUS PERENNIS
Dilicentissime cum libella lib-
rationis guae est in Austria
et Hungaria confecta cum men-
sura gradum meridionalium et
paralleloumierum Europeum.

MD CCC LXXXVII

Whatever the scientific justification for such a claim might be, I had the distinct feeling that I was standing on an extremity of Europe if not perhaps a few yards into Asia. Apparently there is a similar Centre of Europe in Lithuania. Across the road the Black Tisa river rushed past and a hundred yards on, its brown waters swollen with mud and branches, gurgled and gushed into the Tisa itself. This was the border with the EU's newest member, Romania, ironically symbolised by a high wire fence blocking the railway line, which had been built long before the current boundaries were put in place.

In the Ukraine, it is impossible to pass by a river without hearing a story and the Tisa was no exception. Nicola, that inexhaustible fund of folk lore, slipped once more into story-telling mode:

"A long time ago a poor widow called Hoverla had a very handsome only son named Prut. Many young girls were keen on him but Hoverla wanted him to marry the ugly and much older daughter of their wealthy neighbour Petros. Many times Hoverla reminded her son about the hundreds of acres of forest and meadows, together with the huge number of cattle, which would come his way if he were to marry her. But Prut was not in a hurry to tie the knot and spent most of his time trying to avoid his neighbour's daughter.

One day, Prut arrived in Rakhiv where he met a beautiful young lady called Tisa and immediately fell in love with her. From then on, Prut would take every opportunity to go and see her and before long, his mother discovered the illicit romance. Her hopes of riches severely dashed, she ordered the servants not to let Prut leave her mansion.

Not surprisingly, Tisa became very upset without her beloved. Then suddenly she got a message from Prut that he planned to run away from home on the first moonlit night, meet her at an appointed place and afterwards they would be married. When everyone had gone to sleep, Prut jumped out of his window, through the roof below and ran off towards his love. Woken by the sound of the crash, Hoverla soon realised what had happened and standing to her full height, hide the moon and the stars behind her. The sudden onset of darkness caused Prut to lose his way and he started running in the opposite direction. Meanwhile, Tisa had reached their rendezvous.

When daylight came, she found herself standing in front of her uncle, The Danube, to whom she told her tragic story. Then her uncle said: 'Don't be sad, Tisa. I will find Prut and you will be together again'. He kept his promise and the two hearts of Tisa and Prut flow together into the waters of the Danube."

It all sounded rather familiar.

My final lesson on *houtsoul* life was given by a delightful woman who was the guide at the Carpathian Biospherical Reserve Museum. Through a series of brilliantly designed tableaux, I was educated in the niceties of *houtsoul* Stone Age life, *houtsoul* rafting, *houtsoul* shepherding and *houtsoul* homemaking. A farewell supper at a *koluba* (inn) in Yaremche brought the expedition to an end. It had been a wonderful team—the ever efficient and flexible Ludmila, the skilful and stalwart driver Igor, Nicola, the walking *houtsoul* encyclopaedia, and the lovely, ever patient Ilona, my linguistic right-hand. I quoted the final sentence of my 1944 Ruthenian pamphlet—"If you have seen Ruthenia, you are at least a well-travelled man."—and transposed the lines of Roman Babowal's poem into the second person plural to thank them:

You brought me the moon, stolen,
hidden in your sleeve, with a pair of golden stars.

Now it's time for me to return to Moldavia the previous autumn.

En route back to my lodgings near Gura Humorului, I stopped off at the little church of Humor, founded in 1530 by a boyar, Toader Bubuiog, who archly included Petru Rares, Helena and Stefan behind his wife, Anastasia, in the votive wall painting of 1535. He paid the bill but gave the credit to his lord and master.

The Church of the Dormition of the Virgin at Humor, which is my personal favourite of all Romania's painted churches, is the smallest of the jewel boxes and the most exquisite. It exudes such tranquillity, friendliness and charm; once you are through the gates, the carefully tended flowerbeds of roses, the predominant pinks of the external paintings and the essential femininity of its chapter of nuns all coalesce into something akin to a spiritual greenhouse. The world of the devil is shut out and the world of Humor nurtures and sustains ones soul—in Romanian *duh*, the same word for ghost.

Like its peers, Humor boasts a splendid Last Judgment, Jesse's Tree, Akathistos Hymn and Procession of Saints, but it also glories in some wonderful frescoes of the military saints. Given Stefan's predicament with the Ottomans, it is fitting that this sanctified genre was advertised above the entrance to the church.

The idea of the Saint as a horseman has fascinated scholars over the ages. After its introduction to Aryan societies, the horse became so indispensable to everyday life, both military and civil, that it was inseparable from the idea of God. Christianity merely continued this tradition and one scholar found an early Christian church in Egypt where the paintings showed everyone on horseback, including Christ and all his Apostles. The mounted warrior as a symbol of Good versus Evil most probably stems from the Persian[45] cult of Mazdaism where the six great good spirits, the Amesha Spenta, are represented as mounted figures. One text describes how they are 'clad in warlike dress and coat of mail…brandishing their lances before the King.'

St George slaying the Dragon is one of the most popular images of Christian art, which has endured right up to the present day; indeed he became the Patron Saint of England and is still emblazoned on every gold sovereign. No historical details of St George's life have survived but it is probable that he was a soldier in Palestine who was martyred at the end of the third century. The immensely popular medieval book of saints, *The Golden Legend*, states that George was a Knight from Cappadocia who slew a dragon in Libya in order to rescue a fair maiden. Her father, the King, was so thankful that he allowed the baptism of 15,000 local people to take place. George fell foul of the Emperor Diocletian's anti-Christian purges and, after horrendous torture—the rack, two doses of poison and a dip in a bathtub filled with molten lead—he was dragged the length and breadth of the city of Nicodemia before he was finally beheaded. It was not only George who came to such a gruesome end; Alexandria, the wife of his torturer, had been persuaded to convert to Christianity as a result of George's stoic resistance. She was promptly hung up by her hair and beaten to death by her husband's henchmen.

Both the dragon and St George were popular with Kings and their Captains. Constantine the Great was said to have had his own figure painted over the entrances to his imperial palace, with a cross over his head and a dragon under his feet, thus portraying himself as

---

[45]   The statue of 7th C Sasanian King Khosrow II at Taq-e Bostan is of a mounted knight in visor and chain mail with a lance beneath his arm.

the champion of Good over Evil. After his victory over the dragon, George had asked for nothing from the King of Libya other than the King should fund monasteries and look after the poor. Thus, any gesture of charitable largesse by a medieval monarch enabled him to identify with this great folk hero and to gain instant political popularity.

For the Orthodox Church, St George is a profoundly mysterious image that affords a glimpse into what is normally unseen—the spiritual combat or secret warfare of the mystics. It is not a simple story of Good and Evil, of St George in his armour killing the dragon. Close inspection of any painting of George and the Dragon will reveal that despite being skewered by a large lance, the dragon remains with its eyes wide open, very much alive. It was only later in the story, after George had led the dragon into the city by the maiden's girdle, that he killed it with his sword. This is symbolic of the true battle fought by the Warrior Saints; it is man's own battle against his inner temptations. The horse is a symbol of strength and power. The dragon is merely pinned to the ground. The message is that man cannot destroy Evil— he can only control his own temptation by harnessing his strength and power. There is no violence in this action—hence the faces of the protagonists are not full of hate and anger. The warrior is the man who, having established attention and silence within himself, tames his earthly nature in order to become the recipient of divine influences.

The artistic interpretation of St George and the Dragon is another key to the separation of Byzantine and Renaissance art. Marzul de Sax, a German artist living in Spain at the beginning of the fifteenth century, paints the Saint in the thick of battle, probably depicting the Aragonians fighting against the Moors in 1096. Here, St George is more warrior than Saint and this was in keeping with his growing Crusader reputation as a winner of battles. Fifty years on, Uccello focuses on the dragon, which takes centre stage in the picture, with his magnificent finery, looking rather like an early airplane. Here is a picture full of medieval symbolism, essentially Byzantine in 'code' if not in composition e.g. the cave is the underworld. Then the link with Byzantium is broken. Tintoretto's St George of 1555-58 has been relegated to the background whilst the princess runs out of the picture towards the viewer, a staggeringly inventive composition but overtly sexual. Fifty years on, in 1607, Rubens puts St George back in the foreground with all the extra drama of a broken lance and swordplay. The showmanship of these flamboyant paintings has, wittingly or not, changed the meaning of the story, leaving the Byzantine tradition as the guardian of the true version.

The odd man out of the late Renaissance artists is Durer, whose 1505 portrait of St George shows a middle-aged and rather weary German soldier, carrying a flaccid dragon by its neck. It is difficult to make out whether the dragon is dead for its eyes are still open, yet the collapsed jaw and limp front legs suggest it is. Durer has absolutely understood the true meaning of the image of the warrior Saint and it is in the exhaustion, which this picture expresses, that we can all relate to the struggle between our better and worse selves. Although deviant from the strict pictorial limits of Byzantine art, Durer alone continues the spiritual and inner meaning of the painted image.

Under the panel of St George, in second place, comes St Demetrius, the bearded patron saint of Thessalonica and latterly of all Slavs. A contemporary of George with equally obscure origins, he was most likely martyred at Mitrovica in Serbia in the reign of Emperor Maximian. His crime? To preach Christianity. His fate? Death without trial. Like St George, he became a Warrior Saint and is usually shown, with a lance, killing Lysios, a gladiator in the service of the pagan Emperor. Demetrius often rides a red horse, possibly to differentiate him from St George, who rides a white horse. Like the dragon, the gladiator, whose attire varies from Avar to Turkish, is also very much alive despite the lance through his neck, again symbolic of man's inner battles with himself.

St George and St Demetrius enjoyed great popularity amongst the Crusaders on account of a vision, in which they both appeared, that preceded the fall of Antioch and the rout of the Saracens. With these divine credentials of military prowess, it was hardly surprising that the Moldavians embraced them with such fervour in those dark days of Ottoman invasions.

In third place comes St Mercury, a popular soldier Saint astride a black horse, who may have been of Scythian origin. He found promotion in the reign of Emperor Decius on account of his valiant deeds in battle. Asked to take part in a sacrifice to Artemis, he refused on grounds of his Christian faith and was duly tortured and executed.

Another favourite military Saint, although not depicted at Humor, was St Procopius who had more than one history attached to him; in fact, some medieval compilers of saintly lives identified no less than three separate versions. The one that appears on the walls of the painted churches concerns a duke whom the Emperor Diocletian ordered to attack the Christians. On his way to do battle, he experienced a vision[46] and promptly converted to Christianity. Torture and imprisonment followed at the hands of successive governors of Caesarea until he was finally executed around 303 AD.

The early life of St Theodore, one of the most popular of all the soldier Saints, goes unrecorded except for his martyrdom in the fourth century. He is said to have set fire to a pagan temple and after excruciating torture, died in agony. Over the centuries, he gained followers in Rome, Venice and Chartres, which all led to confusion about his rank. Was he a general or a mere recruit[47]? The answer was to recognise two St Theodores just like the three Procopius's.

Last but not least, there comes St. Eustace who started life as a Roman general under Trajan. On seeing a stag with a crucifix between its antlers, he converted to Christianity, changed his name and promptly lost his family and fortune. He was recalled to his command but after refusing to attend a pagan sacrifice, was put with his family into a large brass pot shaped like a bull and they were all roasted to death.

The popularity of these warrior Saints in sixteenth century Moldavia reflected the need to bolster morale in an age of almost constant conflict with the Turk. For ordinary men and woman, it was the victory of these Saints over impossible odds that set the example they needed to continue fighting. Modern man has long forgotten these early stalwarts of Christianity.

---

[46] On his way to exterminate the Christians in Alexandria, a brilliant cross of crystals appeared in the sky accompanied by a voice saying: "I am Jesus, the crucified son of God. By this sign you have seen, overcome your enemies and my peace will be with you."

[47] The confusion probably stems from Theodore Tyro ("of Tyre")—*tyro* can also mean recruit.

CHAPTER FIVE

MUSICIANS, MONKS AND MAPMAKERS

The hardy ploughmen were out in force, scattered across an otherwise empty landscape in little packets of two men and a horse; their ploughshares sliced silently through the ground hardened by drought, exposing seams of dark rich soil. I was wending my way to the village of Văleni, the family home of the Styrcea family. Was there a Moldavian equivalent, I wondered, of the eighteenth century Scottish song, The Ploughman?

The ploughman he's a bonny lad
And does his work at leisure
And aye when he comes home at e'en
He kisses me with pleasure.

Chorus:
Then up wi't now my ploughman lad
Up wi't all my ploughman
Of all the lads that I do ken
Commend me to the ploughman.

This particular part of my journey had started in London some months back, when a friend had introduced me to Michael Styrcea, an Anglo-Romanian destined to return home. Originally a Moldavian family 'of hoary antiquity' — their coat of arms is the Moldavian auroch and an arrow (the one that hit Matthias Corvinus at the battle of Baia where Stefan the Great trounced the Hungarians) — Michael's grandfather, Ion, was the Minister Plenipotentiary in Constantinople at the turn of the nineteenth century, a key diplomatic posting for the unified Romanian state was but a mere thirty-five years old and the Ottoman Empire its former suzerain.

His father, Victor, was born in the Minister's summer residence on the shores of the sea of Marmara, then brought up in Văleni, a small village near Piatra Neamţ, with occasional visits to the family's town houses in Chernivtsi[48] and Bucharest. Like many families of that time, half their property was in Romania and the other half in Bucovina, the South-eastern part of the former Austrian province of Galicia[49]. The village bearing the family name is now in the Ukraine, albeit only a few kilometres North of the Romanian town of Siret. The family also had an estate at *Krasna Il'ski,* not far from Chernivtsi.

Ion became a senator and courtier, finishing his distinguished career as Master of Ceremonies of the Royal Court when he played a prominent part in the 1938 state visit of King Carol II and Prince Michael to London. This could not have been easy since Carol had created a poor impression on his previous visit to England for the funeral of King George V. *Time* magazine wrote:

'The "Horrible Hohenzollern", buck-toothed King Carol II of Rumania, put his Jewish Mistress Magda Lupescu aboard his Royal Train at Bucharest and rattled off to Paris where Magda alighted and remained. His Majesty was brought to Dover on the British destroyer Montrose, received a 21-gun salute from Dover Castle, was met in

---

[48] Romanian Cernăuţi; German Czernowitz. Part of the Austrian Empire until 1918, then Romanian until 1944 when absorbed into the Ukraine.

[49] The name "Galicia" comes from the Latinized form of Halicz, a Ukrainian town, formerly the 11th century capital of the Duchy of Halicz and a major military center in the 14th -17th centuries.

London by the heir to the Throne, the Duke of York, and took up residence in the house of a sister of one time U. S. Secretary of the Treasury Ogden Mills. Her husband, the Irish Earl of Granard, was Master of the Horse to King George and in the earl's house Carol II was styled officially a "guest of King Edward VIII", the explanation being offered that other foreign kings and queens were occupying all available suites in Buckingham Palace.'

Victor, Michael's father, joined the Romanian legation in London as second secretary in 1937. When recalled by Marshall Antonescu in 1941, like many of his contemporaries he declined and stayed on, first to work with a group of Romanians who gave 'assistance' to the British Government and then the BBC. He died in 1990 'with a smile on his face' after hearing of the fall of the Communist regime.

Michael shared with me an inscription, which his father had written in the flyleaf of a book about the Moldavian Painted Churches and Monasteries:

'A birthday present for my beloved son Michael that he and his descendants may never forget their origins and especially Moldavia, the homeland of our forbearers, a number of which lie buried in some of these glorious churches. I quote but one example: Lord Constantin Stircea, commander of the castle of Hotin and his sister Ana, whose seventeenth century tombs lie in the church at Moldoviţa.

The house of Styrcea (Stircea), of remote Transylvanian origin (circa 1100) but established in Moldavia about 1359, the year of the Principality's independence from Hungary, was a family of Grand Boyars who owned vast landed estates.

Some of our Arbore ancestors whose blood flows in our veins through intermarriage, lie in the church of Arbore, built by the famous Grand Boyar Luca Arbor (decapitated in 1523) on his estate.

In many of these unique painted churches of the Bucovina i.e. the North-western part of Moldavia, as well as in a number of very old ones, there are tombstones of other of our ancestors and ancestors through intermarriage belonging, for instance, to the Musar dynasty, the Princely house of Movila which gave rulers to Moldavia and to the families of Ciogolia, Costin, Cozmescu-Sardrue, Flonder-Albeta, Grigorcea, Hasdiu, Hirta Rosea and Tautul (to quote but some of them) which just as the house of Styrcea were great in the first three centuries of the history of Moldavia i.e. roughly 1350-1650.'

No wonder the thought of returning to Romania filled Michael with pride. He had given me a map with the turning to Văleni marked next to Hanul Ancuţei, an old inn on the side of the Roman-Siret road. There are actually two inns there, the other by the name of Răzeşilor which was where I stopped for coffee. For some reason the waitresses all wore miniskirts, fishnet stockings and décolleté blouses as if they had come straight from the local 'disco'. Maybe they had since they were all very cross and bad-tempered.

After crossing the Moldova river, at this point wide and shallow with sloping banks of pale grey shingle, I reached the village of Tupilaţi, then followed a rustic avenue of tall graceful poplars which meandered through beech woods skirted with oaks, hugging a secret channel cut through the sandy soil by mysterious hands. Michael told me how, when on holiday as a child at Alfriston in Sussex, his father had pronounced on the similarities between the South Downs and the Cuckmere valley and this gentle landscape of woods and hills dissected by lush valleys with small rivers.

Then the road rose up, and just over the crest I spied the village, stretched out on either side of a small valley. The focal point of Văleni is a grassy square in front of the church; from here everything is less than a minutes walk—the school, the mayor's parlour, the police station, the vet and the priest's house. I tried the gate set in the church wall but found it locked. Then I heard a horse and cart clattering and squeaking its way up the knoll behind me and as if by magic the verger stepped down from his dicky and introduced himself, all the time waving a large bunch of ancient keys to signify my problems were over. Inside the walls, in the centre of the precinct, stood a little whitewashed sixteenth century church with a gothic portal and great door with a huge double lock stamped 1519. The inside of the church had been restored by Michael's great-grandmother, Ecaterina Stircea, in 1874 which explained why the iconostasis was in such fine condition and also provided a provenance to the curious pulpit with looked like an exquisitely decorated hunter's seat reached by an elegant ladder.

On the walls of the entrance porch hung two oil paintings each about a meter square; joined together they depicted the Last Judgment. One showed the Blessed and the other the Damned. It was the latter that engaged my attention for The River of Fire had been replaced by a dragon's mouth out of which emerged a very large snake with twenty labels wrapped around its skin, each chaperoned by a devil. Was this *Revelations 20:2?* "...the dragon, that old serpent, which is the Devil and Satan..." I imagined that twenty deadly sins must be inscribed on the labels. If so, it struck me as unfair on the villagers that the standard Seven Deadly Sins had been tripled. In the centre of the painting stood an ugly red-haired man with a rat's tail protruding from his coccyx and sharp black horns popping out of his knee caps. Wearing a fetching orange T-shirt with scalloped sleeves and collar and a mini-skirt not unlike the waitresses at the Hanul, 'Ginger' is blowing a horn pipe with his right hand and holding a scroll in the other. Below him on the canvas, three very pretty village girls with cat-walk legs are dancing with three devils who look like a cross between a kangaroo and a donkey. At the very top of the painting are the scales, weighing a gold plate with a small crucifix on it against another gold plate, this time with ten devils clutching its sides. The symbolism was lost on me although I wondered whether there could be a connection with the church's most prized possession, a relic of St Cosmas, the physician and brother of St Damian.

The belfry, which is separate from the main church, boasts a set of bells cast in Bohemia and brought to Moldavia by Lady Ecaterina. Unknown to me, the verger had gone off to find the priest and the two appeared as I was staring up at the bell tower, wondering what the bells sounded like and how amazing it was that the two clock faces both told the correct time unlike in an English village. I soon found out when I was invited to stand on a narrow wooden beam a few feet beneath them and listen to their boom and clang while Father Gheorge demonstrated them one by one with gusto. With the shockwaves of the impromptu bell-ringing reverberating round my head, I was then taken on a tour of the village and the first stop was the schoolhouse, formerly the Styrcea family home. The little neo-Palladian house was not grand, a modest single storey building like most Moldavian *conac* or manor houses[50] of its time (the recently restored Russet manor house at Pribesti to the South of Iaşi is a typical example). To its front stood an arboretum, now ragged and unkempt but it was just possible to make out a circular vista of the hills beyond. Further up the hill from the schoolhouse was an old barn, constructed of wattle and timber, vibrating quietly to the sound of a maize threshing machine that was being voraciously fed with cobs by dust-covered farm lads.

We all retired to the priest's house for coffee, hitching a ride with the verger on his cart. Father Gheorge proudly showed me his vineyard and beehives and then presented me with a litre of wine and a litre of honey, a gesture impossible to refuse. He was very keen to show me some photographs on his PC, for the church had been re-consecrated the day before, an event that had been attended by 'sons of the village' from all over Romania. As to why, I could not make it out other than a document dated 1864 had recently been discovered, thus triggering off a chain of events which seemed to culminate in yesterday's service attended by droves of bishops richly robed in gold and silver vestments and their extended flock of Faithful.

Assiduous as ever, Father Gheorge insisted on introducing me to the mayor, Mr Ion Stoleru, and we walked over to his office in the town square. Seated behind a table tactfully draped with the EU flag, Mayor Stoleru apologised for not getting up but explained he had hurt his foot at some stage during the celebrations the day before. Palinka was served, gifts exchanged—I managed to find a large Havana cigar in the bottom of my rucksack and presented it to the mayor with the caveat that it would be unwise to inhale it. This produced loud laughter from Vasilica Aungurenci, the village policeman, who had also joined the party but a frown of disapproval was registered by his wife, Catalin-Valentin Aungurenci, who is the village schoolteacher or to give her proper title, Director of Education. Their small daughter, who

---

50   However, these houses usually had an extensive network of large, barrel-vaulted cellars.

had furtively followed them in, had surreptitiously sat down at the table and nodded sagely as she swivelled her head from one speaker to the other like a Wimbledon umpire.

The consensus was that life in the village was improving, in that it had emerged from a local government reorganisation a few years ago with the status of its own 'locality' and mayor. But in terms of living standards there remained much to do, especially the need for mains water and sewage; none of the houses had bathrooms or indoor WCs. On this note, I proposed a toast to 'Mr Thomas Crapper' and down went the palinka.

"Meester Tamas Crappa!"

Weighed down with presents, I left Văleni behind, hidden in a timeless valley gilded by the soft afternoon sun of late autumn, and reflected on the friendliness and hospitality of this out-of-the-way village. These little Moldavian villages are full of surprises. A little further North from here, on the banks of the Prut river, lies the small village of Liveni; today it is known as George Enescu in honour of its most famous son and Romania's most illustrious composer. His is indeed an extraordinary story. Born in 1881, the twelfth and only surviving child of musical parents, the young George showed such astonishing aptitude for the violin, piano and even composition that the Vienna Conservatory offered him a place at the age of nine. Four years later he enrolled at the Paris Conservatoire where he soon became a favourite in the salon of the Romanian princess Helene Bibescu and, through her, met the composer Camille Saint-Saens to whom he showed his first work, *The Romanian Poem*. Encouraged by the great man's favourable response, Enescu conducted it at the Bucharest Athenaeum in 1898, a brilliant debut for the seventeen-year-old conductor and composer.

Other works soon followed and before long, Queen Elizabeth, the Sapphic and artistic wife of King Carol I of Romania, invited him to join her circle of musicians, painters and poets at Peles Castle. It was here in 1907 that he met Princess Maruca Cantacuzino (née Rosetti[51]), who possessed 'a combination of great beauty and an unusual (and at times bizarre) vivacity of spirit'[52]. A fellow Moldavian, her family home, a pretty, late nineteenth century *conac*, was in the village of Tescani, tucked into the deep folds of the Carpathian Mountains North-east of Moineşti. It was a case of two people falling 'head over heels'[53] in love. Three years older and married to Prince Mihail Cantacuzino, the eldest son of the twice Prime Minister and fabulously rich Prince George 'Nabob' Cantacuzino, and mother of his two children (her son Bâzu Cantacuzino became a dare devil pilot), she became inseparable from the young musician and finally married him twenty years later in 1939[54].

His two *Romanian Rhapsodies* had made him world famous; the first one in A major is one of the most played and recorded Romanian musical works of all time. Enescu modestly considered them 'sins of my youth' and always hoped to be judged on other, more complex compositions, much the same as Bedrich Smetana, the Czech composer felt about his hugely popular symphonic poem, *Ma Vlast*. These Rhapsodies are resonant of George's Moldavian antecedents, for as he himself wrote[55]: 'I feel connected to Moldavia with all my strings. My connection with the land, the skies and the waters of Moldavia cannot be unbound…in Liveni I return among people and things which rejuvenate my memories. We keep the native land, with all of it, all our life in our hearts and it is present in our songs, in poems, in paintings, in what we do. Without it we would be empty.'

The first performance in 1906 in Paris of his *Symphony No 1 in E flat major*, called by some critics the Heroic Symphony, was such a success that two years later George's agents organised a concert at the Theatre des Arts consisting entirely of the young composer's works. Such was his versatility as a musician that Enescu established

---

[51]   A prominent political family who fielded two Prime Ministers in the nineteenth century.
[52]   Noel Malcolm's *George Enescu: his life and music* 1990
[53]   Sherban Cantacuzino to author, December 2006
[54]   They did in fact marry in Lausanne in 1919 after Maruca's divorce but failed to complete the correct paperwork for the marriage to be recognised in Romania.
[55]   A. Rauta, 'Lupta', 1936

136

himself as one of the great solo violinists of his generation — together with Jacques Thibaud and Fritz Kreisler — and appearances in Berlin, Budapest, Amsterdam and Rome followed.

During the First World War, Enescu abandoned his international career and worked tirelessly to raise money for the Romanian Red Cross by giving recitals in cities and towns across the country. These were followed by visits to military hospitals where he would play his violin at the bedside of wounded soldiers. One told him how 'you returned to me in those moments the will and the wish to live, which I had lost.'

With peace restored in 1918, Enescu resumed his international career, touring the US and Canada. On his return, he bought some land in Sinaia on which to build the villa Luminis. This was to be his only permanent home for despite his fame, Enescu retained the modest lifestyle of his youth: 'I try to remain a student forever. People meet me often in tram cars, I live at the Hotel Bratu....I eat there also, surrounded by all sorts of workers, of modest persons. All only ..... because my work demands a simple atmosphere. Where I work there must be no luxury....my simplicity is liberation of material needs. To create for yourself as few necessities as possible, that's the philosophy of life....'

In 1927, the child prodigy Yehudi Menuhin came to study with him and from thereon the two remained exceptionally close. Many years later, Menuhin wrote: 'Starting that day, Enescu exerted a supreme influence on me and I am not the only one to say so. Go all over the place, ask musicians that knew him, that played with him and you will find the same reaction: Enescu was the supreme influence that determined their existence, not only in music...' That same year came the first performance of his *Third Sonata for Piano and Violin in A minor* 'in Romanian folk character', another testament to Enescu's Moldavian roots with its *lautari* or gypsy fiddlers. His one and only opera, *Oedipe*, based on Sophocles's tragedy, had its first night in Paris in 1936. George wrote 'this is the work of my life...I've put in this work all the substance of my being, my whole soul'. Fortunately, it was well received.

The Second World War years were spent in Romania and although he went on a tour to Moscow in 1946, he decided to leave that September for the United States. The story goes that as he embarked for New York on SS "Ardealul" at Constanţa, he was overheard to incant:

> *Oh, my dear Moldavia,*
> *Those who leave you*
> *Are terribly aggrieved.*

Despite the onset of a severe illness which caused his wrists and fingers to contract, he stoically gave master classes, all the time missing Romania which remained agonisingly far away, both physically and politically for Maruca had had to 'donate' her house at Tescani to the new Romanian communist state[56]. But the nostalgic pull of Romania was too strong, so they moved to Paris from where he continued to tour, give master classes and make recordings. He died in May 1955 in genteel penury and was buried at Le Père Lachaise cemetery alongside such musical greats as Bizet, Chopin, Fauré and Poulenc. His wife, Maruca, survived him and died in 1968 aged ninety. Speaking to the distinguished Le Figaro music critic and author Bernard Gavoty before he died, George summed up his life: 'It's over. This story starts far away on the plains of Moldavia, and ends here, in the heart of Paris. Reaching out from the village (where) I was born to the great city (where) I end my days, I walked a difficult path, guarded by trees that are lost in sight. It was, of course, a long way. It seems short to me!'

So ended the story of a young Moldavian boy who dazzled the world's musical scene with the brilliance of a multi-faceted diamond — violinist, pianist, and composer and conductor of symphonies, chamber music and opera[57]. To all of these varied musical activities that he supremely mastered, he brought boundless

---

[56] It is now an Enescu Cultural Centre.
[57] And he could sing as well! In 1937, when rehearsing Act III from Siegfried with the Romanian Radio Orchestra , a bass singer failed to turn up and Enescu sang Wotan's part from the conductor's desk with his "full, expressive and accurate voice", surprising the audience who burst into applause and cheered loudly.

creativity, untrammelled originality and inexhaustible energy, single-handedly taking Romania into the forefront of contemporary Western musical culture.

A footnote to this Moldavian romance is the story of Maruca's son, Constantine 'Bâzu'[58] Cantacuzino. A wonderful athlete—he captained the Romanian ice hockey team in the 1933 World Championship—and an audacious and talented racing driver, setting a new record of forty-four hours from Bucharest to Paris—Bâzu took to the skies and by the time war broke out, had logged over 2,000 hours as well as winning the national aerobatics contest.

In 1941 he was named chief-pilot of LARES, the Romanian national air transport company, but soon managed to get to the front line as a fighter pilot, where he claimed four victories and two 'probables' before being demobilized that October. He returned to active duty in July 1943 and flew day and night missions against the Allied air forces, shooting down both Russian and American aircraft.

After 23 August 1944, when Romania quit the Axis and joined the Allies, the Germans started bombing Bucharest from airfields close to the capital. Bâzu's Fighter Group was brought in to protect the city and he shot down several German bombers. He went on to see action in Transylvania and by the end of the War, he was the highest ranking Romanian ace with fifty-seven confirmed 'kills' and thirteen 'probables'. He is one of the few pilots, if not the only one, who shot down Soviet, US and German aircraft and in the process flew British Hurricanes, German Messerschmitts and American Mustangs!

At the end of the war, when the communists confiscated his private property and threatened him with imprisonment, Bâzu now known as 'The Prince of Aces' managed to escape to Italy and then on to France and finally Spain. There the Romanian community helped him to buy an aeroplane so that he could earn a living at air shows.

---

58   Pronounced 'bee-zoo'

He died in May 1958, leaving two versions of his death: the first was that he died after an unsuccessful surgical operation, the second that he was killed when he crashed his aircraft.

His friend Ioan Dobran denied the latter: 'He did not die in a plane crash. He died because of his illness. He ate well, drank well and had lots of women. From countess to cook! He was a man to admire in some respect.'

Why Bâzu? It is the sound of an aeroplane.

From Văleni I headed West into the foothills of the Carpathians in search of Râşca monastery where I had arranged to meet the Abbot and Simona Tatulescu-Cighur, a friend from London who was putting together a fund-raising plan for the monastery. Râşca comes from the Slavic word *recica* for water and the monastery sits on the banks of the aptly named Ruska river.

Etymology is a feature of the Romanian Orthodox monastic scene, never simple but always intriguing. Starting with the Abbot, one has to go back to the Aramaic *abba* or father; although the Greeks used exactly the same word αββας it didn't equate to abbot! Father Mihail was styled Archimandrite—Greek αρχι plus μανδρα—the chief shepherd in charge of the sheepfold or the shepherd of souls. The image of the shepherd and the lamb—the Good Shepherd—was widely used in early Christian iconography; how sad it was when it slowly lost popularity and disappeared from Christian art.

From the third century onwards, the fundamental terms of Christianity came to be created, usually from Latin and Greek and of course the new faith required new expressions to communicate its thinking. In the Romance languages about thirty religious terms were borrowed from Greek, for instance (in the order of Greek, Romanian and English): αναφορα / anafur / wafer, καλογερος / clugr / monk, ηγουμενος / igumen / abbot. Others were borrowed from Latin and adopted by the English as well, like (in the order of Latin, Romanian and English): altarium / altare / altar, angelus / înger / angel, crux / cruce / cross, and sanctus / sânt / saint. Some Latin words were only used by the Romanians—basilica / biseric / church, draco / drac / devil, and peccatum / pecat / sin.

Later, after the Bulgarians became Christians and colonised Romania in the tenth century, a number of words of Slavic origin entered the Romanian church language such as *duh* 'soul, spirit, ghost'; *rai* 'paradise'; *vladic* 'bishop'; *pop* 'priest'. Several words describing Slavic heathen beliefs were also borrowed by Romanians: *vraj* 'charm, spell, magic, witchcraft'; *basm* 'fairy-tale' (cf. Slavic *bajati* 'to conjure'); *moroi* 'ghost, phantom'; *vârcolac* 'werewolf, vampire, ghost' and *zmeu* 'dragon'.

In 1888, an adventurous English lady, Mrs Mary Walker, arrived at Râşca with two companions and she recorded her experiences in *Untrodden Paths in Romania*. Her splendid account deserves to be quoted at length:

> 'The track winds among bushes and tall grass; suddenly, at a turning, the glittering crosses and cupolas of the monastery come into sight— a joyful promise of rest! But we are not yet there; many a turning and winding and more streamlets have to be endured, before our carriage rolls with the accustomed rumbling sound over the planked flooring of the Cloportnitza; these gateways have always sonorous wooden floors.

> Two *caloyers*[59] are sitting outside in the shadow of the wall. They wave a welcome and we pass in ... to a scene of such soft, sweet promise of repose that, as with one voice, the exclamation "No! nothing shall induce me to start again today; we will stay and enjoy this peaceful haven of rest," discarded the original intention of simply taking luncheon here and hurrying on. Worn out by the fatigues and tremors of our long and venturesome drive, wetted, and travel-stained, and very hungry, we looked at the Guest-house with its broad shady balcony, its plot of garden beneath, clusters of bright flowers adorning

---

[59]   Jolly old monks

the steps and the terrace before the apartment of the *Archimandrite*, where the projecting roof is shaded by a lofty lime tree that sends its flickering shadows across the fresh dewy grass; verily, such a sweet spot could not be rashly abandoned! Around the quadrangle, here and there a vine-trellised pathway leads into the modest monastic cottages, and in the centre stands the strangest, most picturesque old church that we have seen, not as yet ruined by whitewash, left in all its native quaintness of grotesque pictorial effort. But we do not at once note all these details.

We have stopped at the door of the *Fundarik*. The place seems deserted; a moment later a servant comes forward, a sort of wild-man-of-the-woods, bare-footed, with a mass of shaggy, black curling locks over his forehead and shoulders; he is dressed in coarse linen, confined at the waist by a leather belt. This wild apparition proved, however, very gentle in his ways; helping down our luggage, he conducts us to a room on the upper floor and departs to announce the arrival of guests. The restorative '*dulces*'[60] and water, followed by coffee are quickly brought, and before long the temporal director of the affairs of the monastery comes to bid us a cordial welcome. This gentleman—M. Pisoschy—is not a monk; he is the nephew of the Archimandrite—an old man in very failing health. He lives with his uncle, to whom he is much attached, and is the general administrator of the affairs of this small community, which is cited as being the best regulated and most orderly of the monasteries in this country.

Our kind entertainer gives us the best rooms in his delightful guest-house. They are exquisitely clean, and furnished with every comfort of carpeted floor and soft divan; a large bouquet is on the table; the scent of flowers and of new-made hay comes through the open windows, and the gentle waving of the lime tree shadows on the many-tinted church walls spreads, as the evening sun touches the bright cupolas with golden sparkles.

A very hospitable dinner is served in the large dining-room, in which a well-made mămăligă plays a subordinate part amongst fowl, eggs, fruit, vegetables, cream, and that exquisite Moldavian bread. We are waited

---

[60]   Spoonfuls of rose-flavoured jam.

on by the 'wild-man' (we have named him 'The Druid'), assisted by a youth, both in spotlessly clean linen blouses, with a deep band of coloured embroidery round the throat, and richly ornamented belts. These wild-haired beings, looking like ancient Dacians fresh from their mountain home, performed their duties (to our great astonishment) with the quiet, gentle watchfulness of the highly trained waiter. Coffee was served in a delightful room overlooking the large garden at the back of the monastery, into which we presently descended with M. Pisoschy. Here, as in the guest-house, all is in the most perfect order. It is a blaze of colour—all our familiar garden flowers growing luxuriantly in the rich loamy soil, in which flourish also fruit trees heavy with promise; some trained, some tall standards; raspberry-bushes and clean strawberry-beds are bordered by roses and tufts of lavender. A second vegetable garden of a sterner nature, showing great plots of artichoke and homely cabbage, leads into the farm enclosure. The animals are all in the fields, but the vast receptacles for the maize—the principal growth of the country—are worth examination. It is stored in immense wattled basket-work, thatched over. This basket, standing some fifteen feet high, narrows towards the bottom, where it is raised from the ground on stones or sections of logs; a small door in the basket-work near the base lets out the grain when wanted. This being quite a model farm, possessed two or three granaries in the finest condition. Near poor cottages these maize-baskets, dilapidated and out of balance, with rebellious sticks shooting up in picturesque confusion, form a most effective foreground object against the soft bloom of distant plain and tree-clad mountain slopes.

On returning to the guest-house it proved that the 'savages' had made up our beds most scientifically. They met us with a tray of dulces and coffee—always a different variety of the delicate preserve—a little later a large bowl of milk, with strips of the snow-white bread, closes our repasts for the day, but even the night is provided for—a tray being left in the room with more sweetmeats and glasses of fresh water. The careful attendance of our Druid and his assistant were beyond all praise.

We were quite sorry on the following day to leave this charming retreat, and wandered once more around the old gateway, the tower—

the bit of fortified wall still remaining—and across the sweet green
meadow of the enclosure, where gliding figures are returning to their
several cottages after the morning service.

After a very elaborate and hospitable breakfast, we proceeded to
pay a visit to the Archimandrite, a venerable old gentleman, looking
exceedingly ill. He receives very kindly, however, our thanks for the
great hospitality of our reception, and assures us that we are the first
English ladies who have visited that monastery. They remember
only one English gentleman several years before—the late **Mr.**
Alison, of eccentric memory; his sojourn left a vivid impression,
now softened, we must hope, by the more subdued manners of our
little party, each member of which receives on leaving the blessing
of the venerable man.

At the moment of starting the rain comes down in torrents. I seize
the opportunity of delay to make a sketch of the' Druid,' who
submits calmly to the infliction, and afterwards proceeding to one
of the balconies for a sketch of the church, I am watched by a very
dirty old monk, emerged from a neighbouring room. He presently
asks, "Are you come to disturb and upset the arrangements of
the monastery?" taking us, doubtless, for Government agents
in disguise. He has placed his frugal breakfast—mămăligă and
black beans—on a stone near the door of his cell, while he
comes anxiously forward. He proves to be a Russian, capable of
speaking a few words of French. I seek at once for information;
but he instantly shuffles off in a great fright, "*Non! Je suis vieux!
Je suis vieux!*" in such dread of entanglement that he even forgets
the little tin dishes in his precipitation; presently he stealthily
emerges like a rat from his hole and carries back his food.'

With Mrs Walker's account fresh in my mind, I crossed the pock-
marked bridge over the Râşca river and found the little monastery
lying in the fading light below the darkening mass of Mount Pleşu. It
was on the wooded slopes of this mountain that the monks had always
sought shelter and God's love when confronted by the recurring threats

of raiding Tartars, invading Ottomans or marauding Hungarians for as Stefan the Great never tired of saying, Moldavia was surrounded by enemies. In these thickly forested hills, sixteenth century Moldavia sustained a large population of hirsute hermits and thus it comes as no surprise to see their scantily clad, emaciated, long-bearded images painted on the church wall in the Procession of Saints, usually on the lowest register.

Râşca 's very origins stem from this tradition: 'Somewhere, in a silent meadow of the forest, St John of Râşca, the holy Bishop, sank in the depth of Godly love and knowledge, bringing back for us glimpses of holiness from the life to come. There, among the trees, the Mother of God appeared to him three times, leading him towards where her miracle-working icon was hidden. This icon is today the monastery's most precious treasure.'[61]

The life of a hermit continued well into twentieth century Romania, when one of its most famous adherents was the Archimandrite Cleopa of Sihastria. Born as Constantine Ilie in 1912, the ninth of ten children, his religious upbringing was so devout that five of his ten siblings, along with their mother in her later years, took up the monastic life. In the spring of 1929 Constantine and two of his brothers entered the monastery at Sihastria and after seven years of probation the young novice was tonsured a monk with the name Cleopa. For the next ten years, Cleopa and his brothers tended the monastery's sheep on the high pastures of the Carpathian Mountains, where 'the breeze of silence gently blew across the hillside whispering to the aspiring hearts of the young brothers.'

Cleopa would later remember these early years with profound affection:

'In the years that I was shepherd of the skete's sheep together with my brothers, I had great spiritual joy. The sheepfold, the sheep—

---

[61]   A guide to Râşca

I lived in quietness and solitude on the mountain, in the midst of nature; it was my monastic and theological school.

It was then that I read *Dogmatics* by St. John Damascene and his *Precise Exposition of the Orthodox Faith.* How precious this time was to me! When the weather would warm up, we would put the yearling lambs and the rams in Cherry Meadow, which was covered with green grass and surrounded by bushes. They would not stray from there. "Stay put!" I'd say to them, and then I would read *Dogmatics.*

When I would read something about the Most Holy Trinity, the distinctions between angels, man and God, about the qualities of the Most Holy Trinity, or when I read about Paradise and Hell—the dogmas about which St. John Damascene wrote—I would forget to eat that day.

There was an old hut in which I'd take shelter, and there someone from the skete would bring me food. And when I would return to the hut in the evening, I would ask myself, "Have I eaten anything today?" All day long I was occupied with reading... When I was with the sheep and cattle I would read and the day would pass in what seemed like an hour...

I would borrow books from the libraries of Neamţ[62] and Secu Monasteries and carry them with me in my knapsack on the mountain. After I had finished my prayer rule, I would take out these books of the Holy Fathers and read them next to the sheep until evening. And it seemed as if I would see Saints Anthony, Macarius the Great, St. John Chrysostom and the others; how they would speak to me. I would see St. Anthony the Great with a big white beard and in luminous appearance he would speak to me so that all he would say to me would remain imprinted on my mind, like when one writes on wax with one's finger. Everything that I read then I will never forget...'

In 1942 Father Cleopa temporarily took charge of Sihastria monastery in place of the ageing Abbot who was confined to his sick

---

62   He would have had a choice of 18,000 books collected over 600 years!

bed. In January 1945 he was ordained Deacon and named Abbot at the relatively young age of thirty six. Two years later, following the Soviet occupation and the ensuing communist takeover, many monasteries were closed and countless hierarchs, priests, monks, nuns and other faithful Orthodox were imprisoned, many tortured, some murdered. Although Sihastria had managed to remain untouched due its remoteness in the Carpathian Mountains, Abbot Cleopa was already famous as a national spiritual leader and thus a threat to the communist government. In May 1948, on the feast of Ss. Constantine and Helena, he delivered a homily that included these words: 'May God grant that our own rulers might become as the Holy King and Queen were, that the Church might be able to also commemorate them unto the ages'. The next day the state police arrested him and flung him into prison without bread or water for five days. On release, he wisely fled to woods in the mountains above the monastery, where he lived in a hut constructed mostly underground.

During this time of trials and tribulations, Abbot Cleopa told his followers that he was visited by the Grace of God in the following way. When he was building his hut, birds would often come and sit on his head. However, the first time he served Liturgy on a stump in front of his hut, as he was communing the Holy Mysteries, the birds came and gathered around him in numbers such as he had never seen before. As he gazed upon them in astonishment, he noticed that each one had the sign of the Cross marked on its forehead.

Another time, having read all the prayers, he set the *antimension* on the tree stump and began the Liturgy with the exclamation, 'Blessed is the Kingdom of the Father and the Son and the Holy Spirit, now and ever and unto the ages of ages!' Once again the birds appeared, and as they perched in the branches of the trees, they began to sing in beautiful and harmonic voices. Abbot Cleopa asked himself, 'What could this be?' And an unseen voice whispered to him, 'These are your chanters on the *cliros*[63].'

---

[63] The cliros or choirs for readers and chanters is found at the end of the solea near the side walls of a church.

These signs and others encouraged him immensely during his time of exile and on his return to monastic life in 1949, after moving to the monastery of Slatina with thirty monks, Cleopa was asked by the Metropolitan of Moldavia to assume the spiritual guidance of most of the monasteries in the region, including Putna, Moldoviţa, Râşca and Sihastria. Arrested for a second time in 1952, he once again retreated into the mountains until the situation normalized. From 1959 to 1964, the Church of Romania suffered acute and persistent harassment under the Communist regime, with the monasteries undergoing their most difficult days of the twentieth century.

In 1959 the government decreed that all monks under the age of fifty-five and all nuns under the age of fifty must leave their livings and by the spring of 1960 the state police had forcibly removed more than four thousand monastics from Romania's monasteries. Yet again, Father Cleopa was forced to flee to the mountains where he regularly spent more than twelve hours a day in prayer. It was during this time of persecution that he wrote several of his well-known guides to the spiritual life.

In the summer of 1964, to the great joy of all the monks at Sihastria, Father Cleopa returned from the forest, broke his silence and within days consoled the dozens of pilgrims who had filled the monastery seeking his counsel and direction. The following year, he began to write homilies, teachings, and epistles for laymen as well as monastics; the most important of these works include *Discourse on Visions and Dreams*, *On the Orthodox Faith*, *Homilies for the Feasts* (1976), *Homilies for Monks*, *Homilies for the Sundays and Feasts of the Year* and *Homilies for Laymen*.

On the evening of his death, Father Cleopa had just started to read his morning rule, when his colleagues said to him: '*Geronda*, its evening now. These prayers should be read tomorrow morning.' Cleopa replied 'I am reading them now because tomorrow morning I am going to my brothers.' At 2 a.m. the next morning, this last great hermit of Moldavia died and departed for eternity and His Christ.

Simona, my fund-raising friend from London and a successful entrepreneur in her own right, was waiting for me at the monastery with her two young children and her mother in tow. We had first met two months earlier to discuss her ideas about publicizing Râşca in England and had agreed to try to link up when she was next over in Romania

"Have you seen the Abbot?" I asked. "I can't find him anywhere."

"He is in the the forest."

Heavens above, had he been threatened with arrest? I wondered.

"It is the logging season", Simona added by way of explanation to soothe my patent consternation.

A few hours later, Abbot Mihail arrived in his long black robes, full of apologies for his lateness. He ushered me and Simona into the small guest refectory and poured out three glasses of home-made palinka. The traditional toast of "Naroc!" completed, still wearing his black woolly hat and designer dark-glasses, the Abbot launched into a breathless exposition.

"They (the forest authorities[64]) only give us fifteen days to take timber out of our thirty hectares of forest, so the whole of the monastery—all twenty-five of us— has moved up to the mountains to work. From the minute it gets light in the morning to the second it gets too dark to work."

He reflected for a moment and corrected himself: "Well, I left the six oldest fathers behind. They commute between the church and their rooms. No use on the farm or in the forest."

"Farm?"

"Oh yes. We have sixty hectares here, mainly cattle and pigs. We're also building a pond for carp…and, yes, of course there are also our vegetable and fruit gardens. The monastery is self-sufficient and self-financing". He paused. "It has to be."

Simona had told me that when Mihail arrived at Râşca from Putna in 1991, the monastery had been closed since 1960. There were literally no means of support and for the first year, the tiny contingent of five monks lived hugger-mugger in a single small room. Since

---

[64]   Romsilva, the national forest administration.

then, under Mihail's leadership, the monastery has been transformed into a viable religious 'house' with the farm modernized, the church restored, visitor accommodation added, a shop opened, a summer school built for orphans and a forest saw-mill commissioned.

A nun quietly entered the refectory and laid the table for dinner. She was one of two 'on loan' to the monastery to look after guests and serve behind the counter in the shop. Curious to know how the monastery recruited its monastics, I volunteered the information that 'I live next door to a Benedictine monastery in England. They find it hard to attract novices but it must be easier here.'

It was hard to predict the reaction of the Abbot behind the beard and dark glasses. His answer surprised me.

"Up to 1995, we had an influx of young people; there was a large backlog from the bad days of communism. The problem was that motivation in those days was in some respects more to do with financial security rather than with Faith. This is no longer the case for there are plenty of jobs in Spain and Italy and we have also had to tighten up on recruitment to weed out what we term 'asylum' seekers. I can now decide who enters the monastery. After 2000, we had ten joiners; four have since left. This year, not a single new entrant."

He ruminated for a bit. "Maybe our vows are becoming unfashionable—poverty, chastity, obedience."

Mihail is the son of a doctor and entered religious orders at Putna when he was fourteen. Abbot since 1996, the youngest Archimandrite in all of Romania at the time, his presence is palpably impressive, exuding that curious and mysterious concoction of physical, intellectual and spiritual energy, which defines so many charismatic leaders.

He joked: "This is nothing new. At the end of the eighteenth century, Râşca was a prison—for runaway monks! Usually the sons of nobles who had changed their minds about the monastic life but unfortunately they had taken their vows. When they were caught, they were locked up here, behind these great walls, and could only get out if their families paid very large sums of money. It made such a good prison that the Habsburgs even used it for political prisoners—Mihail

Râşca Monastery

IN MRS WALKER'S FOOTSTEPS

Simona and the Abbot

New heads on old bodies ...

THE RÂŞCA OVERPAINTED PANELS

... don't get along

Kogalniceanu, the future prime minister of Romania, was exiled here for six months in 1844. He lived in our bell tower."

Given that the Abbot was trying to raise Euro 90,000 to put thirty orphans through summer camp from June to September in the coming year, I said I would look out for runaway monks on my way down to Bucharest. Abbot Mihail rewarded my questionable wit with a huge laugh followed by a slap on the back which resembled being hit by one of his felled trees.

"By the way," he concluded, "our main project is to restore the paintings in the church. They were, how to say, over-painted in the nineteenth century? Underneath are the originals from 1540. For this, we need one million Euros."

By now it was late, the palinka decanter empty and we agreed to meet early the next morning before the Abbot had to return to the forest to supervise his team of holy lumberjacks. Outside, the old monks who had been spared the travails of the forest were making their way to prayer, black shadows flitting slowly across the moonlit quadrangle.

Who were the Moldavian artists who had painted the outside of these sixteenth century churches? We know some of their names and where they came from but unfortunately little is known about them as individuals. The list of churches and artists reads:

Arbore—Dragos from Iasi
Moldoviţa—Toma of Suceava, a courtier and master artist
Voroneţs—unknown
Humor—Toma Zugravul[65] and three other masters
Suceviţa—Ioan and Sofronie Zugravul from Crimca
Râşca —Stamatelos Zakynthos from Greece.

---

[65] Zugravul (Slavic Зографски) was a common surname for artists, deriving from the Greek word Ζωγράφ for painter.

Bălineşti—Gavril Ieromonah

Most likely, they would have come from painting families and been apprenticed as small boys to their fathers or uncles and in the course of their training, they would have acquired an encyclopaedic knowledge of the Bible and the lives of the saints. Although the centre of the arts in Moldavia was at Suceava, most artists led an itinerant life, moving from job to job, although once on site, it could mean staying put for anything up to two years.

Much as their Moldavian princely patrons would have liked to commission works in mosaic, that favourite medium of Byzantine art, it was expensive and scarce; the Emperors of Rome and Constantinople had deliberately used it for its ostentation and luxury to flaunt their wealth. So paint was substituted and this is turn governed the artist's 'timetable' for churches could only be painted five years after their construction to give time for the foundations to settle and the mortar to set.

In the modern era of ready-made enamels, oils and acrylics, paint is mass-produced and available in unlimited quantities. The supply and availability of paint in the fifteenth and sixteenth centuries was a very different story. Individual artists had first to source the ingredients and then make up their own concoctions, some of which would have been highly toxic. Of the most important colours and pigments, ochre was obtained from soils and deposits and used as the basis for all flesh colours. White, used to highlight faces and hands, was obtained through the oxidization of lead using vinegar, a process that took about four weeks before it could be ground into powder. Black was produced by burning wood or bones, hence 'bone' black.

Red came from quicksilver, a process known for over three thousand years in Georgia. Carmine[66] red or St John's Blood was discovered in 1517 through processing the Polish cochineal louse (*Porphyrophora polonica*), then imported from the Mexican variety in the seventeenth century when it was widely used in icon painting.

---

[66] The word 'carmine' is itself derived from the 'kermes' dye which comes from another inset, *Kermococcus vermilio*, (kerm being Persian for worm).

Red also came from an indigenous Romanian plant, '*rioba*'. Indigo[67] blue could be made from woad or 'dyer's knot' but usually came from a dye plant *indigofera tinctora*, widespread in the forests of India. Green or *verdigris* was extracted from glauconite and volconsconite soils found in Bohemia and Verona as well as in Novgorod in Russia. It could also be made from Dyer's Buckthorn.

Like Carmine red, the colour purple was obtained from a marine snail known as the *Murex brandaris* or the *spiny dye-murex*, a messy business that nearly resulted in the unfortunate mollusc's extinction. There were several yellows—yellow orchre came from clay, orangey or gold-coloured orpiment usually from realgar, a highly toxic arsenic-based deposit, and traditional yellow from the berries of the buckthorn tree *Rhamnus Infectorius*, cooked with other plant juices and combined with chalk or alum. And, of course, gold itself came from the precious metal and was not, in itself, regarded as a colour but as 'a shining', a radiance to which all other colours were subordinated. Modern analysis shows that the colours were mixed with lime, egg, gall, vinegar, honey, some turpentine and water.

Before applying the paint to the church wall, the artists and their assistants had to prepare the surface. First, a layer of mortar, two parts sand to one part lime, was applied with a trowel to a thickness of about one and a half centimetres. Once dry, a second coat of around eight millimetres was applied, and finally a third coat about five millimetres thick, this time of a very fine lime mixture. At this stage, the Master artist would have probably sketched out his overall design and given his 'students' the job of sketching in the detailed panels. But this is supposition—no sketches remain—and so it is quite possible that once the last coat was dry, experience and knowledge took over and the walls were duly painted, with instructions given verbally. Such a method of working would have left little lassitude for mistakes.

Working outside meant that the artists had to take into account both the daily and seasonal changes of light and the concomitant reflection of the sun's rays. This may seem a statement of the obvious but the light in this part of North East Romania is extraordinary. In the

---

[67] From the Greek word *indikon* for dye.

summer, it can be a brilliant, glaring white, so strong that it obliterates all others colours. In the winters, snow lies thick on the roofs of the churches and on the ground around them, another opportunity for light to play yet more reflective tricks. The 'al fresco' solution adopted by the artists was to select a primary colour—blue, red or green—adapt it to the surroundings and then use it as the background throughout the exterior paintings, hence the legacy of Voroneţ 'blue', Humor 'pink' and Suceviţa 'green'.

Râşca provided an opportunity to admire two more themes of Moldavia's painted churches, one external and the other internal. Mrs Walker had noticed on the exterior of the apse 'a ladder....winding upwards, showing the efforts, mostly vain, of the despairing souls. Some are hurled, shrieking, into the fiery jaws; others cling wildly; one aged man, half-way up, is suspended by one hand, whilst a demon in mid air hangs on to the other, and to make the strain and pull of this imp more effectual, a friend has clutched his tail and hangs his added weight; the old man is almost gone! There are many others of these grim conceits, mingled with heavenly visions, but these last are pale and insipid beside the roguish malice of the little demons.'

What she missed was that this is the Ladder of St John Climacus. Famous as a Holy man throughout the Middle East, John entered the Monastery of Sinai when he was about sixteen years old. Here was the dramatic country of the Old Testament with Mount Sinai, the mountain of Moses, rising 7,000 feet high above the monastery. Inside the fortress walls erected by the Emperor Justinian in the sixth century, John would go on to experience the three forms of monastic life—the communal, the solitary existence of a hermit and 'the life of stillness shared with one or two others', the semi-eremitic life. After forty years as a hermit, including a year of silence, John was elected Abbot.

Klimax is the Greek word for ladder and it refers to John's book, the Ladder to Paradise, where moral perfection is reached through a series of spiritual exercises, expressed as the scaling of thirty rungs of a ladder reaching from Earth to Heaven. The number thirty refers to the thirty 'hidden' years of Christ. In ascending order, the rungs of the Heavenly ladder represent: Renunciation of Life, Dispassionateness, Pilgrimage and Dreams; Obedience, Penitence, Remembrance of Death, Sorrow; Placidity and Meekness, Malice, Slander, Talkiveness and Silence, Falsehood, Sloth, Gluttony, Chastity and Temperance, Avarice, Poverty, Insensibility, Sleep and Prayer and Psalm singing, Wakefulness, Timidity, Vainglory, Pride and Blasphemy, Meekness and Simplicity and Guilelessness and Wickedness; Humility, Discretion, Solitude, Prayer, Tranquillity, Faith and Hope and Charity.

The imagery of a ladder was not in itself new, for the ladder as a mystical symbol was known in Ancient Greece and Egypt nor was it exclusive to John Climacus for St John Chrysostom talks of a ladder from Earth to Heaven and so does St Theodoret. However, although his book was addressed to his fellow monks, the Ladder came to have a great popular appeal. John writes: 'God is the life of all free beings. He is the salvation of believers or unbelievers, of the just and unjust, of monks or those living in the world, of the educated or the illiterate, of the healthy or the sick, of the young or the very old. He is like the outpouring of light, the glimpse of the sun, or the changes of the weather, which are the same for everyone without exception.'

Only found at Sucevița and Râșca , the visual 'text' of the ladder deals with the fight between Good and Evil, with the rungs both sins and virtues. At Sucevița, fifteen monks ascend the thirty steps, each numbered and identified by either a sin or virtue. As they climb the ladder, assisted by no less than fifty-two angels willing them on and by St Gabriel fighting furiously with a group of devils, some of them fall off and hurtle down towards a dark, purplish Hell. At Râșca , their descent is more precipitous as they plummet, head first, into a Satanic abyss.

John ended his great work with an exhortation, which has been pictorially captured so well by the artists: 'Ascend, my brothers, ascend eagerly. Let your hearts' resolve be to climb. Listen to the voice of the one who says: "Come, let us go up to the mountain of the Lord, to the house of our God" (*Isaiah 2:3*)'

Even today, St John's book is read aloud in Orthodox monasteries throughout each Lent.

The interior over-painting at Râşca to which the Abbot referred was purely a technique applied in the eighteenth and nineteenth centuries to cover up the unsightly damage to the frescoes caused by incessant burning of candles, seeping rain-water and general wear and tear over the centuries. In several cases, such was the extent of the deterioration and dilapidation that the church had to be completely rebuilt. Just to the South of Râşca , a competition was held in 1858 to choose an artist to paint the frescoes in the newly built church of the monastery of Agapia. The winner was a young man called Nicolae Grigorescu, who went on to become one of Romania's greatest artists, loved and revered by successive generations.

Born in 1838 in Pitatu, a village outside Bucharest, Nicolae's father died when he was five and he moved to Bucharest with his mother where he started to train as an artist. His three-year apprenticeship at the age of ten to Anton Chladek, a Czech painter living in Bucharest, was followed by work as an iconographer for the Orthodox churches at Băicoi and Căldăruşani, and as muralist for the Zamfira monastery. In 1858, when he won the competition to paint the murals at Agapia, he made the acquaintance of the Prime Minister of Moldavia, Mihail Kogalniceanu, who was a keen art collector. Kogalniceanu was instrumental in obtaining a grant for the prodigiously talented Nicolae to study in Paris.

Arriving in the great city, arguably the cultural capital of the world in 1861, Grigorescu was admitted as a student to the School of Fine Arts of Charles Gleyre and Sebastien Cornu. Pierre-Auguste Renoir joined at the same time. The young Romanian traipsed up and down the museums and galleries, perfecting his artistic techniques through copying works by Rembrandt, Rubens, Salvator Rosa,

Prud'hon and Gericault. Summer sojourns in Barbizan enabled him to meet Millet, Troyon, Rousseau and Daubigny and to join in their reaction against the stylised excesses of Ingres and Delacroix.

In 1867 he returned to Romania, to Botoşani in Moldavia, but soon went back to France, where he got his lucky break—in 1868 Napoleon III bought his *Vase with Flower'*. Five years later, he held his first major exhibitions in Bucharest and Vienna where he introduced his hallmark portraits of peasant girls in their traditional costumes, their faces wrapped in an aura of mysterious sensuality. The influence of the Barbizan School was clearly demonstrated by his love of the outdoors, of contrasting light and shade and of the spontaneity and simplicity of everyday rural life.

Although nearly forty, Grigorescu volunteered as a war artist to cover the Russian-Romanian-Turkish war of 1877-78, when the Romanian and Russian armies helped to win Bulgaria's independence from the Ottoman Empire. In portraying the principal events of the war, Grigorescu followed his true-to-life artistic principles and made countless pencil sketches of the battlefield and also some in oils which later on provided the groundwork for his large compositions like *The Attack at Smyrdan* and *The Battle of Rahova*. Like a modern war photographer, he tersely and promptly recorded scenes in the rear echelons and moments of fierce action in the front line, accurately capturing the campaign atmosphere and the men's mood. An interesting facet of Grigorescu's wartime work was his visual empathy with the columns of demoralized enemy prisoners as they trudged past him in the snow, resigned to captivity in unknown places. In his portrait of *Turkish Prisoners*, he depicted the despondent and dejected faces of men who had been sent to fight for a cause that was neither of their doing nor of their concern; for Nicolae understood that this was the universal lot of the conscript soldier.

After The War of Independence, he returned to France, where he discovered Brittany first as a tourist and then as a painter, glorying in the medieval town of Vitre with its narrow streets and paint-peeled walls, its peasants and fishing folk and Atlantic coastline. All these he painted with verve, playing on his favourite relationship between light and shade, with the technique of applying colour patches to suggest movement. His beach scenes and seascapes are some of his finest paintings, marking his elevation to the front ranks of contemporary Romanian artists.

After his return to Romania in 1887, he bought a house at Câmpina in the Prahova valley to the north of Bucharest where he embarked on what has come to be known as his 'white period', so called because of the milky grey veil he spreads over the greens of vegetation and blues of summer skies. A succession of personal exhibitions were organized at the Romanian Athenaeum in the 1890s and in 1899 he became the first Romanian artist to be admitted as a full member of the Romanian Academy.

Almost blind in his old age, Grigorescu died in July 1907, leaving unfinished on his easel the picture *Return of the Fair* (*Reîntoarcerea bâlciului*). According to his last wish, his body was laid on the top of a farm wagon and pulled by four oxen to his grave. His legacy to Romanian art was over 3,000 pictures and a record of peasant life that has been cherished ever since by the Romanian people. Whether working or feasting, whether gathered together or alone in the solitude of an empty landscape, Grigorescu's peasants, confident yet fatalistic, are on an equal footing with everything around them—the simple huts, the clump of trees, the oxen-hauled carts, the sheepdog and his flock, the shepherd boy and the shepherdess. His painting was homage to the common man in celebration of those essential human qualities of vitality, robustness and spirituality.

If Enescu and Grigorescu came from humble backgrounds, the same cannot be said of Dimitrie Cantemir. This extraordinary gifted prince and scholar was born in 1673, second son of a successful soldier, Constatin Cantemir, Prince of Moldavia from 1685 to 1693. According to family legend, the founder of the family was a Tartar, Khan Temir[68], who had settled in Moldavia in the sixteenth century.

---

[68] Better known in English as Tamerlane the Great or Christopher Marlow's Tamburlaine.

The name had become elided to Cantemir. Educated first at Iaşi in the Classics and Slavonic languages, Dimitrie demonstrated an astonishing memory and when he was sent to Istanbul in 1688 in bond for his father's good behaviour as Prince, he enrolled at the Academy of the Orthodox Patriarchy and soon gained access to its great treasury of Islamic learning, becoming fluent in Turkish, Arabic, Persian and Tartar.

The young Prince also became an accomplished *tanbur*[69] player and a popular figure at the Imperial court at Topkapi Sarayi where he presented the Sultan with *The Book of the Science of Music through Letters*, a study dealing with the melodic and rhythmic structure and practice of Ottoman music including 350 scores. His residence in Ortaky, which he had bought in 1693 from the Sultan's brother-in-law, became a centre of intellectual and political debate, attracting philosophers, polyhistors, rhetoricians, annotators of the Koran, musicians, painters and miniaturists, mathematicians and translators. What a brilliant galaxy of talent and learning he surrounded himself with.

In March 1693 Dimitrie was elected Prince of Moldavia by the boyars on the death of his father but by April he had failed to come up with the money demanded by the Ottomans and had to stand down in favour of another candidate, Constantine Duca, who had been bankrolled by the Prince of Wallachia, Constantin Brancoveanu. Dimitrie returned to Istanbul as the representative of his older bother, Antioh, who was subsequently appointed ruler in 1695.

In 1699, the year of his marriage to Cassandra Cantacuzino (from the *Kantakouzenos* line of Byzantine Emperors), the daughter of Serban Cantacuzino the former ruler of Wallachia, the Peace of Karlowitz between Vienna and the Porte changed the Moldavian political landscape forever. The Habsburgs recovered all of Hungary except the Banat, all of Croatia-Slavonia and the whole of Transylvania. Poland consented to withdraw from Moldavia, which it had been

---

[69] An Iranian guitar-like instrument. Its derivatives include the Greek buzuki and the Indian sitar.

occupying on and off for the last decade, and the Porte abandoned its claims to the Ukraine (Russia took a further two years to reach agreement with the Sultan: Azov was ceded to Moscow in 1702). These dramatic changes all meant that Turkey was now perceived as a power in decline.

For Moldavia therefore, the new reality equated to living next door to two new superpowers, the Habsburg Empire and the up-and-coming Russian one. When he finally succeeded to the Moldavian throne in 1710, Prince Dimitrie had long ago come to the conclusion that a war between these regional superpowers was inevitable; furthermore, Moldavia would be right in the middle of it. In November that year, the Ottomans predictably declared war on Russia, so Dimitrie did a deal with Peter the Great; in return for Moldavian support, Cantemir secured the hereditary title of Prince and , as an insurance policy, a pension and estates in Russia if it all went wrong. And that indeed was just what happened.

Peter who had recklessly advanced way ahead of the main body of his army, found himself and his advance guard of 38,000 facing a well-equipped 135,000 strong Turkish army at Stanilesti on the River Prut in July 1711. A 50,000 force of bloodthirsty Crimea Tartars swam across the river to engage the Russians whilst the main Ottoman body of troops secured the bridges and outflanked Peter. Surrounded and short of supplies, Peter proposed terms which were readily agreed to—Azov was handed back, a large bribe was paid to the Grand Vizier and Russian interference in the affairs of Poland renounced. Dimitrie, now horribly exposed to the Porte for his duplicity, had no choice other than to flee. He managed to escape the clutches of the Turks by swathing himself in the rugs of the Empress Catherine's barouche and thus began life as an exile in Russia.

Cantemir was lucky. His opposite number in Wallachia, Prince Constantin Brancoveanu who had done a similar deal but with the Habsburgs rather than the Tsar, was summoned with his family to Istanbul in 1714 and summarily beheaded with his two sons and son-in-law.

Dimitrie's wife Casandra died in 1713, leaving him with six children[70] under the age of fourteen. Now aged forty-four, he married Princess Anastasia Trubecka, a seventeen-year-old Russian princess the same age as his eldest daughter Maria[71]. He lived the rest of his life at Harcov near Moscow and died on his estate at Dimitrievska in 1723. What an extraordinary life Dimitrie had lived; born of noble birth in Moldavia, educated at Iasi for the first fifteen years of his life; the next twenty-two years in Istanbul spent as a hostage, student and courtier; one year as prince of Moldavia and then twelve years in exile in Russia, famed throughout Europe for his erudition.

Cantemir's legacy was his three great histories, all written while in exile in Russia. *Descriptio Moldaviae*, written between 1714 and 1716 and printed in Latin, German and Russian, was an extensive survey on the history and culture of Moldavia with a fine map attached, drawn by the Prince himself, who sits in the bottom left corner in Emperor's robes with a dashing legionnaire stationed behind him. His second Romanian history was entitled *A Chronicle of the Entire Romanian Land* and was written in Romanian between 1719 and 1722. Here for the first time was advanced the spurious claim that all the inhabitants of Romania—Moldavians, Transylvanians and Wallachians—were the descendants of Trajan's colonists and had pure undiluted Roman blood. Nothing was left of the Dacian gene.

But his greatest history was *Incrementa et decrementa Aulae Othmannicae* or *Growth and Decay of the Ottoman Empire*, a history of the Ottoman empire published in Latin, English, French and German. His knowledge of this subject was so encyclopaedic that 485 pages of notes supported the 579 pages of text! A second sister volume, '*System of the Mohammedan Religion*' offered a commentary about the faiths, cultures and education of the Arab, Turkish and Persian peoples, taking a sympathetic view of the moral and artistic facets of the Islamic world.

---

[70]   His son became the Russian ambassador to France and a talented playwrite.
[71]   She later became the mistress of Peter the Great.

I went to the church in search of Abbot Mihail the following morning for he wanted to show me the interior frescoes. The entrance hall or pronaos is always painted with scenes from the *Menologion*, the daily calendar of the Church year that pictorially records the lives or rather deaths of the early Saints. Most Saints met their end by decapitation — at Humor, one can identify Saints Callistrate, Anastasia, Maxence, Basilissa, St John the Baptist, Platon and Ardenie departing this world without their heads. Invariably the executioner looks suspiciously Ottoman and his scimitar of Asiatic design, although all of these deaths preceded the conversion of Constantine to Christianity in the fourth century.

Other scenes show the godly kneeling with their hands tied behind their backs, then propelled to the bottom of a pit of water with the aid of a baton e.g. St Clement; crucified e.g. St Peter; stretched out naked, then beaten to death with a hammer; burnt on a stake; grilled alive, stretched out over a brazier; suffocated by stones piled on top or by a slab winched down from above; split in two — a complicated death, requiring the victim to place his head between his knees, hitch his feet to two bent trees entwined with rope, which, when released, effectively and agonisingly divide him into two over a period of time; defenestrated e.g. St Jacob; spit roasted over a fire; flayed alive — skin removed by instruments resembling garden rakes; sawn in half from head to toe; and dragged behind a horse until dead.

These 'killing' methods were not figments of the artist's or chronicler's imagination. Man's inhumanity to man knew no bounds in the persecution of the Christians by Nero and Diocletian. In medieval times, little had changed and indeed some of the excesses of Vlad the Impaler in neighbouring Wallachia surpassed even those of the Persian (inventors of the impaling and crucifixion methods) and Roman Emperors.

There is an opinion which suggests that such scenes of death are particular to the Orthodox Church; this view studiously ignores the 'Roman Church' paintings of Hans Memling, Hieronymous Bosch and many others who earned their living by depicting, in the most lurid anatomical detail, the agonies of death by flaying alive, boiling in a pot and splitting down the middle. It is the very lack of detail in the Byzantine version which reminds us, yet again, that art belongs to heaven, not to man.

I found the Abbot, somewhat agitated, waiting for me and after a quick look round at the over-painting, I persuaded him to get back to his sawmill and we would confer at a later date. On this occasion, the Abbot belonged to the forest, not the church!

"Domnul fie cu voi!" boomed the Abbot as he wished me God's speed.

Driving South on the road to Bucharest, I once again followed the course of the Siret river, past Petru Rares's walled monastery of Probota and through the busy town of Pascani, the site of the charming seventeenth century Iordache Cantacuzino house, one of the best preserved of its type in Moldavia. In the Second World War, the land between here and Iaşi was the scene of a titanic struggle between Russian and German armies. From April to June 1944, the Russian Second Ukrainian Front, nearly 550,000 men in all, tried to force their way through to Ploieşti in a bold move to deprive the Germans of oil and knock Romania out of the war at the same time. Opposing them were around 300,000 German and Romanian soldiers. After their first offensive had been stopped at the end of April, the Russians re-organised and launched a new one on 2 May; so intense was the bombardment that one German soldier wrote, 'at 04.20 hours the world seemed to disintegrate. The front was ablaze. The flash of bursting shells was all that was visible as far as the eye could see', and another noted, 'there began a firestorm the likes of which had seldom been seen before.'

Remarkably the line held with over 220 Russian tanks destroyed in the first day. By 8 May, the offensive had run out of steam and come 26 May, the *Stavka* ordered a halt to offensive operations in Romania. However, the German high command, the OKW, was not privy to this information and launched a major counter offensive on 30 May. By the end of the first week of June, the front had once more stabilized and no further significant action took place until August. It was an extraordinary feat of arms by the German and Romanian army and a humiliating experience for the Russians. Not surprisingly the victorious Red Army of 1945 has written little about it.

Looking at the rolling hills with flocks of sheep grazing contentedly, the position of tiny villages revealed by wisps of smoke rising in thin grey plumes above them, it is hard to comprehend that, just sixty years ago, nearly 19,000 young Russian soldiers were killed in action here and over 74,000 wounded; and on the German and Romanian sides, over 45,000 young men were killed and wounded.

Moldavia has indeed buried and mourned more than her fair share of the dead.

Chapter Six

QUEEN OF HEARTS

The drive to Bucharest from Râşca was diabolical; rain, sleet, traffic, potholes, road works and diversions all conspired to reduce my progress to a crawl. By the time I reached the outskirts of Ploieşti, it was dark and so I stopped to ring ahead and book a hotel room in Bucharest city. To my chagrin, there was not a single hotel bed to be had, something to do with a trade fair and conference. I then tried the hotels in Ploieşti and found it was the same story. Never usually one to despair on such occasions, I felt my spirits distinctly sinking as I surveyed the rain swept concrete landscape of the former oil capital of Romania. Fortunately a call to Hélène Cantacuzino, from now on known as The World's Greatest Travel Agent, produced an alarmingly simple solution. Go to Sinaia for the night: it was, after all, only a one-hour drive.

Sinaia, a sleepy mountain town high up on the pine-clad slopes of the Carpathians at the head of the Prahova valley, was once the summer playground of the Romanian royal family. The two palaces of Peles and Pelisor, both beautifully maintained, remain the focal point of the town, attracting thousands of visitors throughout the year.

The history of the Romanian royal family is comparatively

short. In 1866, a young German Prince, Carol von Hohenzollern—
Sigmaringen, was elected Prince of newly independent Romania.
Married to a brilliant if eccentric fellow German, Princess Elizabeth
of Wied, Carol was crowned King in 1881 after Romania selected a
monarch as head of state. Heirless, he adopted his nephew, Prince
Ferdinand ('Nando') von Hohenzollern—Sigmaringen as his son
and heir. Nando married Princess Marie Edinburgh, Queen Victoria's
granddaughter, and they had six children, including the philandering
and deeply insecure Carol II, who became King in 1930. His son,
Michael, took over from his father in 1940 and had the unenviable
task of extricating his country from the Axis camp. In 1948, he left
Romania and today lives in Switzerland. If it only lasted for sixty-
seven years, the story of this exotic royal family is nonetheless
exciting, sometimes erotic and always riveting.

History approves of Carol I as an upright decent man, a
courageous soldier and a stolid politician. The one black mark against
him was the ruthless suppression of the peasants' revolt in 1907.
His 'Bohemian' wife Elizabeth is best remembered as the poet and
author, Carmen Sylva. Brilliant, batty, and eccentric, Queen Victoria
hugely approved of her, so history gives her a tick as well. Posterity
awards Nando, always overshadowed by his magistral uncle, with
the tag of a nonentity—'he never entered a room except sideways'
according to Marte Bibescu—but his consort, Queen Marie, was the
Haley's comet of twentieth century royalty and left behind her a
trail of light so bright that it is her memory that still lives on in
Romanian hearts. Her son, Carol II, rarely put a foot right—leaving
his wartime post, running off with commoners, abdicating not once
but twice, being horrid to his widowed mother (she called him 'a
rotter') and so on. However, he was far from stupid and did much
to put Romania on the world map in the inter-war years. Ex-King
Michael is still alive and like his grandmother enjoys the widespread
affection of the Romanian people.

Queen Marie was half-English, her father was Queen Victoria's
second son, and half-Russian, her mother being the daughter of Tsar
Alexander II. It was a potent mixture that propelled her through an

Peles Castle, home to ...

CARPATHIAN CAPERS

... the Royal Ruritanian Theatre Company

QUEEN MARIE "TO BE ROYAL WAS TO BE… THEATRICAL."

extraordinary life, during which she incurred the love of millions and the disapproval of hundreds. Her admirers greatly outweighed her detractors and rightly so for she loved life and lived it to the full.

In his biography of *Queen Mary* (of Teck), James Pope-Henessey opined that the Princess Marie 'developed into a very theatrical person…neurotic and self-satisfied as her cousin Kaiser Wilhelm II'. Presumably he found theatre and royalty incompatible, which King William IV and the lovely Mrs Jordan certainly did not. However, as Lesley Blanche writes of Queen Marie in *Under a Lilac-bleeding Star*[72]:

'to be royal was to be, in a sense, theatrical: whether she believed, like her ancestors, in the divine right of kings or whether she moved with the times and sensed the growing artificiality of the metier, she dressed the part. Besides, she frankly liked dressing-up. With each change of costume she revealed another aspect or mood. The Princess in her Carpathian castle, shadowy pillared halls, divans piled with bearskins, walls hung with rare ikons, and the Queen, splendid in her trailing robes and jewels, enthroned among her courtiers and admirers. The fairy-tale Roumanian Princess visiting her remote provinces on a shaggy pony, wearing top-boots and embroidered aprons, who will wave her wand, put on her golden crown and right all the wrongs. The lovely and fecund mother, joy of the dynasty, in a tea-gown, all softness, surrounded by her beautiful brood; the mature woman, the Mother Queen, Mama Regina to her soldiers, in a nurse's uniform, at the front in the hospitals—and here she was playing no part, but was flung into the tragic ordeals of her country, sharing, retreating, upholding with selfless devotion.'

So what better way can there be to tell the story of Queen Marie than as scenes from a quintessentially regal if somewhat Thespian life?

---

[72] The enchanting story of Lesley Blanche's travels in Bulgaria and the Balkans, originally published in 1963, is available in Quartet paperback ISBN-10:0704302128.

ACT ONE
Scene One

September 1892. Rosenau castle, a vast fortress overlooking the medieval town of Coburg in Germany.

From a window, the Duke and Duchess of Edinburgh watch their children at play in the gardens—Alfred 18, Marie 16, Ducky 15, Sandra 14 and Baby Bee 9.

Their gaze is directed at Missy as the family calls Marie and they discuss the options for her marriage. The choice is George, Edward VII's second son and by that time, after his elder brother's untimely death in January 1892, the heir to the throne of England; Grand Duke George Michaelovitch of Russia; or Prince Ferdinand (Nando) Hohenzollern–Sigmaringen, the nephew of King Carol I of Romania and heir to that throne.

Prince George and Marie were childhood sweethearts but he is under pressure to marry his late brother's fiancée, Princess Mary of Teck.

Grand Duke Michael is Missy's first cousin and thus forbidden to marry her under the rules of the Orthodox church..

Nando is keeping the company of a commoner albeit an aristocrat, the clever and beautiful Elena Vacaresco[73]. His uncle, the King of Romania, is not amused although his wife, Queen Elizabeth, has been encouraging the affair.

Their choice is Nando.

It is ironic that at one time Elizabeth, the current Queen of Romania, was put forward as a prospective wife for the Duke of Edinburgh.

---

[73] See *Blue Blood and Ink: Romanian Aristocratic Women before and after World War 1* by Doina Pasca Harsanyi (Women's History review Vol 5 No 4 1996)

Scene Two

Jan 1893. The wedding[74] at the town church of Sigmaringen. The sartorial politics are attended to. The German Emperor wears the uniform of Admiral of the British Fleet as does the Duke of Edinburgh, though his sports the Romanian Order of the Star. The King of Romania has donned a Romanian General's uniform as has Prince Ferdinand, who wears the broad orange band of the Order of the Black Eagle, with which he had been personally decorated by the Kaiser the day before. Princess Marie is dressed in white corded silk, embroidered with pearls, her skirt trimmed with bouquets of myrtle and orange blossoms.

Scene Three

Feb 1893. A steam train crosses snowbound Europe. Marie and Nando sit awkwardly facing each other in the stuffy splendour of King Carol's private carriage.

Scene Four

Bucharest. It is snowing. On the platform King Carol, a tall, gaunt, bearded figure and Queen Elizabeth, diminutive, plump and nervous, await them in thick winter furs; courtiers in flamboyant uniforms hover around. A band strikes up as they alight. Marie is presented to the Romanian cabinet on the platform—she is wearing a violet and gold cape over a long green velvet gown, her head buried in a huge fur collar.

Scene Five

June 1893. The Royal family drive to their summer residence, Peles Castle, in the foothills of the Carpathians. As it comes into view, Marie has her nose pressed against the carriage window; she is pensive and despondent. 'Just like your granny's place in Scotland[75]' quips the Queen.

---

[74] Eyewitness account from *The Graphic*, London, 21January 1893.
[75] It was Sacheverell Sitwell who dubbed it 'a sort of tropical Balmoral'!

Scene Six

Summer 1896. Marie is in Moscow for the coronation of her cousin, Tsar Nicholas II. She meets her first cousin, the dashing Grand Duke Boris Vladimirovitch. Tongues wag throughout the courts of Europe.

Scene Seven

1897. Cotroceni Palace, Bucharest. Now twenty-four and mother of Carol, four, and Elizabeth, three, Marie is bored with the stuffiness of the Romanian court. Her adored sister Ducky, married to the dicky Grand Duke Ernst of Hesse, has come to stay. Marie has bought a black Bechstein piano—they paint it white and decorate it with roses.

Scene Eight

The Palace dining room. King Carol tells her he is impressed with her riding and has decided to make her Colonel of the Fourth Hussars.

ACT TWO
Scene One

June 1897. Marie takes her first review of the Fourth Hussars as their Colonel. That evening there is a regimental ball; a gypsy band plays after the waltzes—she dances with a dashing young cavalry officer, Lieutenant Zizi Cantacuzino..

Scene Two

August 1898. Zizi is installed in the Palace as a gym instructor to Prince Carol. Marie goes on holiday with him to Constanţa on the Black Sea where they stay on board a yacht anchored offshore. Their cover is his thirteen-year-old niece whom Queen Elizabeth asked Marie to take with her. Foolishly, they ride around Constanţa in an open carriage.

Scene Three

Autumn. King Carol tells Marie in no uncertain terms that she is to cease seeing Zizi—anyway, it is too late. He, the King, has already posted him to another regiment and out of the country. He orders her to go with Nando to France and get their marriage back together.

ACT THREE
Scene One

Summer 1902. Prior to Edward VII's coronation, 27-year-old Marie stays at Cliveden in Buckinghamshire, where she meets the young 23-year-old American millionaire, Waldorf Astor, and promptly falls for him. For the next five summers, Waldorf and his sister Pauline come to stay at Sinaia. But in 1906, Waldorf marries Nancy Shaw and Marie is forced to give up her attentions.

During the same period, an 18-year-old naval cadet, Ioan Andrie, sings, plays the guitar and writes poetry for Marie in exchange for her affections.

Scene Two

1907. Marie is now installed in her own home, Pelisor Castle, next to Peles. She has four children; the youngest Nicky is four.

Princess Marte Bibesco, vivacious, scheming and very clever, introduces Marie to Prince Barbu Ştirbey, a brilliant lawyer, substantial landowner and astute businessman. He talks knowledgeably about politics and the international scene, hitherto subjects out-of-bounds to Marie. This is the beginning of the love affair of her life—she has discovered the man who will shape her destiny.

Scene Three

June 1914. The Tsar of Russia and his family arrive on their yacht off Constanţa. The hidden agenda is to introduce Marie's eldest son, Prince Carol, to Grand Duchess Olga.

That night there is a gala dinner; Queen Elizabeth excels herself—
she forgets to wear any jewellery—the Tsarina out of good manners
removes hers. Marie does not. Elizabeth has arranged some
entertainment—fireworks, readings and allegorical tableaux. Little
girls with angel wings skip across the stage—it collapses into a tangle
of broken scenery and limbs.

It has not been a success; for Carol and Olga, it is a case of hate at
first sight.

Scene Four

October 1914. King Carol dies. Marie is staying at Mogoşoaia with
Princess Bibescu. She is telephoned in the early hours of the morning.
It is Ştirbey: 'You are Queen.'

Scene Five

Romania has managed to keep out of the war until 25 August 1916
when she enters on the side of the Allies. By October, the war has
gone disastrously wrong—in the South the Romanians are being
attacked by Germans, Turks and Bulgarians; to the North by Germans
and Hungarians.

23 October 1916. Buftea, Prince Ştirbey's house outside Bucharest.
Marie's youngest child, Prince Mircea, four, has typhoid fever. His
eyes are bandaged and he is screaming—he grinds his teeth and
clacks his jaw. At 9.30pm on 29 October, he dies.

Marie's book *My Country* is published by Hodder and Stoughton:
'This is a small country, a new country, but it is a country I love.
I want others to love it also; therefore listen to a few words about
it. Let me paint a few pictures, draw a few sketches as I have seen
them, first with my eyes, then with my heart.'

Scene Six

November 1916. Bucharest. A German army is advancing on the city. Marie is evacuated and arrives at Iaşi (Moldavia) on the royal train. Nando and Ştirbey remain behind. The situation in Iaşi is even worse than in Bucharest. A city of 100,000 has become a city of a million displaced persons.

Despite the protests of her courtiers, Marie goes straight to the scene of a terrible accident—an ammunition train has blown up. She tends to dying soldiers and civilians in the vicinity of the explosion.

Scene Seven

Winter 1917, the coldest for fifty years. Marie is still in Iaşi. There is starvation on the streets. Wolves roam the city at night. Disease is rife—more than 300,000 have died. Black typhus, brought in by Mongolian trench-diggers, decimates the ranks of the army. For Marie, there is no such thing as personal risk: she refuses to wear gloves in typhus wards as she visits the sick—'they can't kiss rubber gloves.'

Scene Eight

May Day 1917. The Tsar has abdicated. Mobs of ill-disciplined Russian soldiers free prisoners from Iaşi's jail and march on Government House, demanding the overthrow of the King and Queen. Five days later Russian extremists try to storm the Palace and massacre the royal family. Allied officers intervene.

Scene Nine

A retrained Romanian Army goes on the offensive in July but it can go no further without Russian support. In November, news reaches Iaşi of Lenin's coup. Russian soldiers respond to this by killing their officers and going on an orgy of looting and raping as they head back to their homes. It is all over—despite Marie's protestation, 'I am ashamed of being Queen of cowards', Romania has to sue for peace with Germany and in December hostilities cease.

Scene Ten
March 1918. The French military mission is leaving Iaşi; everyone sings the Marseillaise and cries. A tall man remains behind and approaches Marie. It is Colonel Joe Boyle, a fifty-one-year-old Canadian Klondike adventurer. It was Boyle who arrived from St Petersburg[76] in December 1917 after a death-defying journey with the remnants of the Romanian crown jewels and Treasury gold, which had been sent the previous year for safekeeping in St Petersburg. Marie writes: 'He is a man that captivates you with his strange charm, who fears nothing and due to his unusual willpower and courage overcomes every situation; a true Jack London character'.

Within forty-eight hours, Boyle is off again, this time to rescue a group of 78 Romanian aristocrats, politicians and businessmen who are facing execution by the Bolsheviks in Odesa. He brings them to safety by boat and receives a hero's welcome.

Scene Eleven
April 1918. Marie withdraws from public life to Cotofanesti, her little wooden house outside of Iaşi. Boyle joins her and helps to make it habitable for her and the children. Boyle then has a stroke flying back from Bessarabia and Marie moves him to the royal estates at Bicaz to nurse him back to health. 'He was always a solitary and he finds incredible that his only woman, only companion, only comrade is a queen. The faith seems to be very weird. Who would possibly understand how the events in our lives come to pass?...'

Scene Twelve
August 1918. Prince Carol falls 'violently in love'[77] with Ioana Zizi Lambrino and deserting his army post, runs off with her to Odesa where they get married. Marie sends Boyle to remonstrate with him.

---

[76]   Boyle had originally been asked to sort out 'the Moscow knot' — 10,000 freight cars that were paralysing the Russian rail network. He resolved it in 48 hours.

[77]   A.L.Easterman: *King Carol, Hitler and Lupescu*.

ACT FOUR
Scene One

March, 1919. The Treaty of 1916, signed between Romania and the Allies, has been deemed invalid by the Supreme Council of the Allies in Paris. Ştirbey and PM Bratianu send Marie to Paris to negotiate—hoping for *le success de jolie femme.*

Marie is staying at the Ritz with her daughters; she has turned her suite of twenty rooms into a floral extravaganza, a tribute to Byzantium.

She meets with Clemenceau at Quai d'Orsay—he bounds down the steps to meet her. He attacks her for signing the armistice with the Germans. She counters. It is *un success.*

She meets with Lloyd George—Marie wears a dress of mousseline de soie with hand-painted roses. She flirts over lunch and indulges his vanity. Another *success.*

She meets Woodrow Wilson. It is 8.30 a.m. at the Ritz. Her room is a 'whole world of flowers'. Wilson is not interested in hearing her plea. *Un échec.*

She counter-attacks by arranging lunch with Mrs. Wilson two days later. American chalk sits down with Romanian cheese. Another *échec.*

Finally, in December, the Americans sign and Romania carries off the prizes of Transylvania, Bessarabia, the Banat and Dobrugea that were justly hers by treaty.

Scene Two

August 1919. Prince Carol has been allowed back to Bucharest with his wife Zisi Lambrino. To sabotage the marriage, the court comes up with the ploy of reintroducing him to Maria Martini, with whom he had an affair in 1916—and a baby girl. The result? A baby boy. Then Zisi has a baby boy, Mircea. Carol renounces his succession.

Boyle comes to the rescue once more and by January 1920, Carol has rescinded his decision.

Scene Three

April 1920. Marie tells Joe Boyle that he must leave –'the politicians are jealous of your place at court.'

Scene Four

February 1921. Carol marries Princess Helen of Greece. An heir, Michael, is born in October. He is Marie's first official grandchild.

Scene Five

1922. The long delayed coronation of Nando and Marie finally takes place in Alba Julia, in the middle of Transylvania. It is a magnificent neo-Byzantine ceremony, designed by Marie down to the last detail. Under a canopy on a large field—inside a church was considered too politically tricky—surrounded by the hills and open grasslands of the countryside, Nando crowned himself King and then placed a gold crown on Marie.

Scene Six

1923. Colonel Joe Boyle, CBE, DSO, has died a pauper in London after gallantly rescuing an old friend from a communist jail in the Crimea. Marie arranges a Romanian headstone for his grave, 'a man with the heart of a Viking, and the simple faith of a child.'

Scene Seven

1925. After attending the funeral of Queen Alexandra in England, Prince Carol absconds to Paris with his mistress, Elena (Magda) Lupescu, whom he will eventually marry in a hotel bedroom in Rio de Janeiro in 1947.

Have you heard about Magda Lupescu
Who came to Romania's rescue?
It's a wonderful thing

To be under a King –
Is democracy better, I ask you?

Marie's *The Country that I Love* is published by Duckworth: it is a compilation of the articles she wrote in the war. ' Myself a refugee, a Queen with empty hands, a mother who had just buried her youngest child…the intense suffering around me tore me away from my own sorrow, gave me the ardent and intense desire to be of use to my people, and through them to my country, at a moment when all hope seemed to be abandoning us.'

Scene Eight

January 1926. The citizens of Brasov give the fairy-tale castle of Bran to Marie. She restores it, builds a rose garden and a teahouse, entertains there and writes books. Flowers, especially lilies, are everywhere. She takes to wearing Romanian peasant costumes.

Scene Nine

July 1927. Nando dies of cancer after a long illness. A Regency is put in place for the heir to the throne, six-year-old Michael.

Scene Ten

June 1930. Carol has returned in a coup and taken the Regency from his son.

Scene Eleven

February 1931. Ştirbey needs a hernia operation and must travel to Paris; an attempt is made to kill him on the Orient Express. He does not return home for ten years.

Scene Twelve

Marie goes to see Ştirbey in Paris from where they continue their journey to Briac in Brittany to stay with Ducky who has married her childhood sweetheart now the Tsar-in-waiting, Grand Duke Kiril.

At his sister Ileana's wedding in July 1931, Carol takes her to one side and informs her that her real father is Ştirbey, reducing the newlyweds to tears.

Scene Thirteen

1938. The children's nursery in Pelisor. Marie is seriously ill with liver cancer. Ştirbey is in exile in Switzerland. She lies dying in great pain; she broadcasts to the Romanian people:

> I was barely seventeen when I came to you. I was young and ignorant, but very proud of my native country, and even now, I am proud to have been born an English woman.....but I bless you, dear Romania, country of my joy and grief; the beautiful country which has lived in my heart.

She asks the Lord 's Prayer to be recited in English and then expires at 5.38 pm on 18 July.

Scene Fourteen

Her wayward son gives her a magnificent state funeral. On her instructions, her coffin is draped in mauve, not black. Her body is taken by train to Curtea des Arges where she is placed in the vault next to her husband.

Scene Fifteen

Her heart is placed in a gold casket and sent by train to Constanţa where it is taken by her aides to the yacht 'Mircea', which sets sail for Balcic, her final resting place.

POSTSCRIPT

1940. The Bulgarians seized Balcic. The casket containing Marie's heart is moved to Bran by the late Queen's aide-de-camp, General Zwiedineck.

In the same year, Carol abdicates for the last time and flees to Mexico with Magda Lupescu. It is rumoured that he takes thirty million pounds with him.

In June 1941, Romania's military leader, General Antonescu, takes his country into war on the side of Nazi Germany.

In August 1944, King Michael stages a coup against the General and declares Romania on the side of the allies.

Barbu Ştirbey is sent by Michael to Moscow to sign the peace treaty. The following year he is proposed as Prime Minister but is rejected by the Communists. He dies at Buftea in 1946.

Beverley Nichols[78] eloquently sums up the life of Queen Marie:

'Be beautiful and dumb by all means. Or even better, be brilliant and hideous. But just you try to be beautiful and brilliant, and a queen, and see what happens! Marie was a woman who has lived fully and loved deeply; who has braved the crowd and commanded it. And though life has brought her many days in which her crown lay heavily upon her, she has always worn it with grace.'

I suspect he was referring to the gossips who would have it that Ferdinand was the father of Carol and Elisabetha, Grand Duke Boris of Mignon, Waldorf Astor of Nicholas and Barbu Ştirbey of Ileana and Mircea; and that Marie's rumoured pregnancy during her time with Zizi Cantacuzino resulted in an adoption[79].

---

[78]   Beverley Nichols: *No Place Like Home*
[79]   Paul Quinlan The Playboy King: p. 15, p. 17, p. 23-24.

For those who would like to read more about Queen Marie, in addition to her autobiography *The Story of My Life*, there are two biographies: *Maria of Romania: the intimate life of a twentieth century queen* by Terence Elsberry and the much admired *The Last Romantic: a biography of Queen Marie of Roumania* by Hannah Pakula. My friend Diana Mandache recently unearthed some later papers of Marie and these have recently been published as *Later Chapters of My Life: the Lost Memoir of Queen Marie of Romania*. Paul Quinlan in *The Playboy King* extensively covers King Carol II's relationship with his mother.

A complex, restless, passionate character, Marie possessed an intense creative energy, which she applied to the design and decoration of her homes and gardens[80]. As she herself put it[81]:

'All through my life I have had a real passion for building wee houses or huts. ...It is only in these last years that I have been able to indulge more completely in this passion; my huts have grown larger, have even become goodly sized habitations.

With the years, I had learned to understand and appreciate the art and architecture of the country, and had become the chief promoter of a movement tending towards resuscitating a national style, instead of imitating all that came from the West. It sometimes needs a foreigner's eye really to appreciate the beauties of a country, especially when that country is struggling towards development. Those in the ferment of evolution are apt to overlook their own treasures whilst straining towards that which other countries offer.'

---

[80] *Art and Design in Romania 1866-1927* by Shona Kallestrup (ISBN 0-88033-582-3) is easily the best book about the Royal houses.

[81] Most of these quotes come from *My Dream Houses* by H. M. Queen Marie of Roumania from *Roumania Anniversary Number* (edited by Horia I. Babes), The Society of Friends of Roumania, Inc., New York, 1935.

However, when she first arrived in Romania, she had no choice other than to stay with her in-laws here in Sinaia, where they had their summer residence in the mountains, a veritable Balmoral of the Balkans. The building had been started in 1873 by King Carol I when he instructed Wilhelm Doderer, a German architect, to draw up plans. Doderer proved somewhat dogmatic in adhering to his original design, so he was replaced by Johannes Schultz in 1876, a man more amenable to change or what his predecessor called 'interference'. Although completed in 1883, many more alterations were carried out between then and 1914 by the Czech architect Karel Liman and today's castle is an ungainly hybrid of Royal whims and Germanic fashion or as Queen Marie put it bluntly 'German mauvais goût at its worst'.

On the outside, Peles Castle is attributable to the German neo-Renaissance style: vertical profiles, asymmetrical, irregular shapes and an abundance of towers, timber frames and decorative elements. The steep gabled roofs are reminiscent of medieval Nürnburg. The Castle terraces, overlooking the fir-covered mountains, were designed in the Italian Renaissance style, crowded with statues, urns, vases and columns, somewhat incongruous with the main house yet equally eccentric.

The interior is predominantly defined by the cumbersome and ponderous taste of King Carol, occasionally enlivened by the fanciful character of Marie's mother-in-law, Queen Elizabeth, alias the authoress Carmen Sylva, the most sensitive and artistic of souls. The daughter of two highly educated and cultured parents—Prince Hermann of Wied, a philosopher and author of *The Unconscious Life of the Soul and the Manifestation of God*, and Princess Marie of Orange Nassau[82], a poet and faith healer, writing and spiritualism ran in her genes. All over the Castle are poignant reminders of her tenure: above the fireplace in the Concert Hall, which was added in 1906, is her portrait by Jean du Nouy, depicting her, pen in hand, at work as a poetess. Music was yet another artistic arrow in Carmen's cultural

---

[82] Was considered as a bride for Edward VII but disgarded because of her deafness. Nearly became Queen of the Netherlands.

quiver. The American writer William Curtis glowingly reported in 1911: 'She is a brilliant pianist and was a favourite pupil of Rubinstein and Clara Schumann. She is equally accomplished as an organist... she has composed symphonies and other pieces. She plays the harp gracefully.....'

One of the few rooms with any enduring charm in the entire palace is the Theatre Hall, an enchanting space seating sixty people with a wonderful frieze by Gustav Klimt and Franz Macht. It was here that Carmen the Tragic Muse gathered around her a coterie of neophytic, adoring handmaidens dressed in Oriental robes, whom she referred to as her children and led them fearlessly in the pursuit of beauty. Princess Anne Marie Callimacki[83] recalled ' as a mere baby, I remember attending Queen Carmen Sylva's musical séances, where, dressed in long flowing robes, her white hair bearing a sort of halo covered with long lace draperies hanging down her back and shoulders...'

According to Queen Marie, the irony of Carmen's luxurious and indulgent life at Peles was that she hated it. 'The Queen had been allowed little part in the plans of the castle; her conception of life being ardently fantastic, she was seldom consulted about things that had to be built of brick and stone. Indeed, I had always the impression that Carmen Sylva never really loved the castle; its sumptuous magnificence seemed to oppress her.'

Marie found life at Peles with her parents-in-law both overpowering and dull. Make what you will of her poem, *The Bad King*:

> *In the hall down there,*
> *In a black carved chair,*
> *Sits a king who owns*
> *Eleven white thrones,*
> *But dark as night is his heart.*

---

[83] Callimacki: *Yesterday was Mine.*

The bride he has won
Sits out in the sun
And weaves a white sheet
Which lies at her feet,
Like snow that is turning to ice.

The dark man on the throne
Sits alone, quite alone,
And he knows full well
The voice of the bell
That will tell the tale of his death.

His bride knows it too
And what she will do
With the shroud she's spun
When the sinking sun
At last will have set her free.

So she sings a wild song
To the fear-filled throng
Which is winding its way
To the castle grey
Where the king lies dead in his blood!

So her solution was to build a small home for her family, Pelisor, next to the main Palace. Using the Czech architect, Karel Liman, to design it, Marie imposed her own ideas on Pelisor with great success. It was an intimate as opposed to a grand house; it was personal as opposed to official; and above all, she stamped her romantic personality on every room. Marie hated the sterility of the neo-classical movement and the sombreness of German neo-Medievalism, so together with the Viennese furniture designer Bernhard Ludwig she devised[84] an Art Nouveau style liberally embellished with Byzantine and Celtic motifs. The riotous result can be seen in the Golden Room where the walls are embossed with thistle leaves, a symbol dear to her both as the emblem of the town of Nancy in France, the home of Art Nouveau,

---

[84] Marie exhibited her own paintings and designs at the annual 'Artisitc Youth' exhibition in Bucharest.

and of her father's Scottish title. The ceiling has a skylight in the shape of a Celtic cross, another device beloved by Marie, always conscious of her English roots. Much of the décor and ornament was made specifically to Marie's instructions and includes work from the best designers of the day—Emile Galle[85] and the glassmaking Daum brothers of Nancy, Josef Hoffmann of the Wiener Werkstätte and Louis Tiffany of New York.

The Crown Princess had another trick up her sleeve at Sinaia. In 1897, she had been to stay with her sister and brother-in-law at the Hesse Palace at Darmstadt, where the Duke showed off his new drawing and dining rooms designed by the British Arts and Crafts architect, Mackay Hugh Baillie Scott. So taken was Marie that she commissioned him to design a tree house for her along the lines of Dante Gabriel Rosetti's poem: 'The blessed damosel leaned out / From the golden bar of heaven'. She herself records:

> ' This was built for me in the forest of Sinaia, where for many years Cuibul Principesei (the Princess' nest) was the amusement of every-one; a queer little log hut suspended across several giant firs. It could be reached only by climbing the steep stairs of a wooden belfry, from which a drawbridge was let down; once on the other side, the draw-bridge could be pulled up and my house became impregnable. It hung on the very edge of a steep incline, and over the tree tops I could look into the valley below. This tree-dwelling had two rooms, a diminutive kitchen and balconies on both sides. I arranged it with loving care, and many a happy hour we spent in it between earth and sky. The "nest" lasted until after the war, when one night it suddenly collapsed during a violent storm; but I must own (up) that I had forsaken my cuib before that fatal day . . .'

Although Marie was conscious that neither Pelisor nor the Cotroceni Palace in Bucharest were actually hers, this did not stop her from carrying out major modifications and 'improvements' to the latter. Originally a seventeenth century monastery and home of

---

[85]   The leading artist of the École de Nancy, famous for his glass, wood and ceramic designs.

the Cantacuzino family, Cotroceni was converted by Prince Cuza in the 1860s as a summer residence for himself, then given to Nando and Marie as their townhouse in 1893. The French architect, Paul Gottereau, was commissioned to restyle it and Marie created what Carmen Sylva described as 'something between an Indian temple and a fairy tale'. Another visitor[86] found it a 'cross between a Church and a Turkish bath'. A heady mélange of Pre-Raphaelite romanticism, Arts and Crafts, Art Nouveau, Baillie Scott, Neo-Byzantium, Celtic symbolism, Norse mythology and Brâncoveanu neo-Romanian architecture, Cotroceni was indelibly and gloriously branded by the maverick and whimsical taste of its chatelaine.

Never one to sit still and admire her handiwork, Marie 'romanianized' the exterior of Cotroceni between 1913 and 1915 with a Brâncoveanu wing designed by Grigor Cerchez and later, in 1925, he and Karl Limann, Marie's pet architect, redesigned the old dining room into today's white barrel-vaulted chamber. She was proud of her achievements at Cotroceni: 'Everything Roumanian in style at Cotroceni is my work, as are the roses that in early summer turn our terraces into a sea of colour. To one coming upon Cotroceni when they are in bloom, the house looks like the Sleeping Beauty's enchanted palace, reached only through a maze of flowering thorns.' And of course there were her 'wee huts': a gypsy *bordei* with a roof of floppy maize (1896) and a Maori tea-house, a picturesque blend of a Maori *whare* and an English summer house.

Then to her surprise and delight, in 1913 George Filipescu, a former Conservative Deputy, left his comfortable country house at Copaceni to Marie in his will.

> 'With joy and enthusiasm I set about becoming my own rival, which was easy, as there the budget at my disposal was less meagre. We enlarged and beautified the big house. I planned the garden, making

---

[86] Princess Anne-Marie Callimachi

two long grass borders running in straight lines from the house to the woods, and turned the lake's banks into fields of irises of every possible tint. In the evening, when the sun is sinking, those irises become a thousand small lanterns of light.'

At her husband's hunting lodge at Scroviste, she continued to erect more 'wee huts'.

'Pursuing my passion for miniature houses, I persuaded the King to let me have a tiny fisherman's cottage that stood at the very edge of the water. He laughingly gave it to me and I turned it into the dearest little habitation—everybody falls in love with it, wondering why they never thought of building one like it. The objects within its whitewashed walls are all quite simple, but the color-scheme is pleasing and each thing is exactly in the right place and of exactly the right kind to suit the house. Later, just before he died, the King allowed me to build another wee cottage near mine, for Ileana. Having become with the years an expert in small houses, this last little cottage is perhaps the most charming of all. Its floor and curtains are blue, all the vases are blue, and even the bath is blue; and blue flowers grow all around it I delighted in making this little dwelling perfect; and once we hoped that Ileana would realize her first dream of love beneath its broad red thatched roof.'

Life in Iaşi under German occupation was miserable for Marie but she managed to buy a wooden house in Cotofanesti from where she could continue to visit the wounded soldiers in the city. A constant visitor was Joe Boyle, who bought an abandoned house nearby and converted it into a home for three refugee families.

Then 'the incredible came to pass'; no more wee cottages but a real castle of her own. Marie takes up the story:

'It was before I built the blue cottage that Bran came into my life— Bran, that forsaken little fortress beyond the mountains. Many years before, on an excursion across our frontier, I had seen it standing in stolid solitude upon its projecting rock, and had imagined what an enchantment it would be to possess that stronghold and turn it into a home. What romance it would represent—a little feudal castle, verily a fairy-tale come to life!....About two years after the war the authorities of the town of Braşov came in solemn procession and offered me the castle of Bran, in free gift, for my very own! This was indeed a marvelous event.'

The Castle of Bran, had originally been granted by Ludovic I d'Anjou to the good burghers of Bran to defend the South-west approaches to the city of Brasov for, before the pass at Predeal was completed in the late nineteenth century, Bran was the front door to Transylvania from Bucharest. With her customary energy, Marie set about converting an uninhabited jumble of towers and battlements into a country house fit for a Queen, yet at the same time very much a private house. As far as Marie was concerned, 'there is no court, not even a lady-in-waiting. And I ask here only the people I like.'

In her distinctive style of writing, Marie records that

'Bran was a new field of activity, a new dream of beauty to shape into life. Seconded by a faithful old architect as enthusiastic as myself, I set about giving life to the dead walls, lending a soul to the old fortress which had never really lived. I woke it out of its long torpor, I made out of a blind thing a home with many eyes looking out upon the world beneath. Somnolent, aloof, impregnable as it had seemed, it nevertheless allowed itself to be turned into a snug and cozy abode. I did nothing to mar its feudal aspect, modify the steepness of its stairs, heighten the ceilings of its galleries, or straighten its crooked rooms. The doors have remained so low that on entering you have to stoop; the walls are several feet thick; heavy beams span the unvaulted ceilings, and there are so many levels to the castle that it is difficult to know on which floor one is.

Bran today is a small museum full of quaint treasures brought from many lands; its courtyard is a mass of flowers, and from every window hang geraniums and nasturtiums. All around it gardens full of flowers have sprung into being, flowers in such profusion that I am able to fill the castle with them; they stand everywhere in huge earthenware or metal jars and bowls, splashing the white walls with their ardent colors. No house loves flowers more than the little castle of Bran. At night, when the lights are lit, it stands against the sky, a fantastic shadow pierced by a hundred lights[87].'

When she died, Marie left Bran to her youngest daughter, Ileana, Grand Duchess of Austria. After the war, the castle and gardens were seized by the Communist regime in 1948 and left neglected until 1958 when it reopened as a museum. Today the castle has been given to Ileana's son who has reportedly put it on the market for forty million pounds. Maybe Madame Tussauds will buy it.

Despite her town and country palaces, manor houses, tree houses, cottages, gypsy huts, medieval castles, there was something missing in Marie's architectural portfolio. With childhood holidays spent in the Isle of Wight and then a lengthy stay in Malta when her father commanded the Mediterranean fleet, Marie missed the sea. The royal couple had built a large 'official' house, *Cara Dalga* (Black Wave), on Mamaia beach, a fashionable resort to the North of Constanța and Marie had managed to erect one of her 'wee huts' at the end of the terrace. But one day, with Bran now a reality, another dream came true.

'…. as I rambled with my son Nicky through Dobrodgea, I suddenly came upon a spot near the sea which awoke in me a quite particular sensation: I had the feeling that this place had always been waiting for me—or was it I who had always been waiting for this place? It was not as if I had come here for the first time.

That old tree hanging above the turquoise-blue sea from the top of a high crumbling wall, beneath which flowed a spring of clear moun-

---

[87] 'And, here, at a sudden point, what appears to be a whole rock, or hillside, lit with lights, towers above the road…this is Queen Marie's Castle of Bran, with a light burning in every window…' Sacherverell Sitwell.

tain water ... Somehow this spot was familiar to me, it had something to do with the very foundation of my being; here was peace, beauty, sea and fresh water, and that huge whispering tree bending right over the shore as if listening to the song of the waves.

I sat down in the shade of the great tree and gazed out upon the light-spangled sea, watching the play of waves against the shore. A feeling of complete, almost overwhelming, well-being took possession of me—I belonged to this and this belonged to me. Now and again along the long road of life this sensation has come; it is simply the feeling of coming home, of being entirely and absolutely accepted by one's surroundings.

....There was also this about Balcic—it was my return to the sea, my first love. Born on an island, I have in my soul an eternal deep craving for the sea. Ileana has inherited this love for the sea. She belongs to Balcic and Balcic belongs to her. I cannot think of Balcic without Ileana, and it was together with her that I developed my dream.'

And so there came to be built the *Tenya Yuvah*, the Solitary Nest, executed by the architect Emil Gunes to the designs of the Queen and the Balcic artists Alexandru Satmari and Cecilia Cutzescu-Storck and built by the Romanian army. The result was a spectacular multicultural muddle, Romanian *cerdace* (wooden balconies), an octagonal domed bathroom, a Turkish minaret, a small Orthodox church and five terraces of gardens toppling into the sea. It has been suggested that this diversity of styles was influenced by her interest in the Bahá'í faith at the time[88].

Lesley Blanche met the caretaker when she visited The Solitary Nest.

---

[88] Queen Marie wrote: 'Saddened by the continual strife amongst believers of many confessions and wearied of their intolerance towards each other, I discovered in the Bahá'í teaching the real spirit of Christ so often denied and misunderstood: "Unity instead of strife, hope instead of condemnation, love instead of hate, and a great reassurance for all men".'

'Did the Queen often come here?' I asked the caretaker, who was still hanging around eyeing me speculatively.

'As often as she could. She loved it here,' he replied, 'when she fell ill the doctors said it was no good for her by the sea. They said she must go to the mountains. It broke her heart to leave. She never came back. She wanted to die *here*... but she told them to bury her heart here, beside the chapel. It's been taken away now, though.... Change... change... nothing's the same, except the flowers....'

He snipped the heads off some dead marigolds, and stared at me again, his dark eyes bold and questioning.

'You are interested in the Queen? You are English, as she was? You never knew her? But you like this place... the others who come here...', he shrugged, 'they only want to see the bedroom....'

'Her Majesty used to watch the sunsets from the minaret,' he volunteered, 'there's a little staircase leading up beside her bedroom... the moon will be up before the sun is down... you should go up to the minaret,' and offering me a handful of dried sunflower seeds, he lounged off, chanting some sad-sounding song89.

In her poem, *Dark Vision*, Queen Marie has a foreboding:

> *Down by the sea where the wild waves weep,*
> *Where the ten tossing tides rise out of the deep,*
> *I met a lone man with the face of a ghost*
> *And asked him the way to the sad sea-coast,*
> *There where my love was lost.*
> *But never a word did the pale man say,*
> *But stood silent, letting the salt sea spray*
> *Splash like the silver sun over his head;*
> *And looking at him I saw he was dead,*
> *Dead as my love was dead.*

---

89   *Under a lilac-bleeding star.*

And dead were his lips and dead were his hands,
And beyond him I saw a wide vision of lands
Where the snow-swans swarm upon silent strands,
Where their last song's sung and the last star stands
Watching the lonely night.

And the man—with his hand he showed me the shore
Where the dead lie dumb amid seas that roar,
And laid himself down where the dark star fell,
And though he was dead, oh! I knew quite well
That a day would dawn for us both.

Queen Marie was a great romantic in every sense of the word. In an interview with Cosmopolitan Magazine in 1925, she was quoted thus:

"Love lies in all things: in the silence of night, in the fires of dawn, in the great waves of music, in colour, sound and harmony. Love lies at the core of every faith, every hope, every ecstasy. Love banishes fear and makes a hero out of the coward; love understands and forgives, hopes, believes; love has tender hands and gentle lips; a word of love can turn the wicked back from his sin, can open out a vision of light to the man who was hopeless."

She lived her life accordingly.

I wrote to Canon Ian Sherwood, to ask him if, during his Anglican chaplaincy in Bucharest, the memory of Marie had lived on. He replied:

'Queen Marie was spectacular—politically, religiously, physically and in so many ways—as you know. When I was chaplain in Bucharest, I used to treat the chair where she sat regularly at the Anglican liturgy with reverence. Once a month I used to polish her chalice.

Her late daughter, Princess Ileana (Mother Alexandra) corresponded with me regularly. I used to receive small donations from her through the diplomatic bag, and buy Nescafe, Scotch, and other items of "currency" for one remaining member of the royal household.

That survivor was Constantine Lazarescu. He accompanied the royal family to the border when they departed by train in the late forties[90]. He was charged with handing them their passports at the border and then returning to Bucharest. The whole railway line was peopled by those waving sad farewells before that dreadful Communism ate up humanity.

Constantine was a lawyer, and married to an English woman. He was arrested as soon as he got back to Bucharest, and imprisoned from 1948 till 1968. All the inmates with whom he shared his cells during those gruesome years died in prison. Under the new Ceausescu regime, things began to look up — what a fantasy!

The prison gate guards, giving him his civilian clothes when he was departing the prison, asked him where he lived. He said that twenty years was a long time and he did not know if his wife would still be in Romania. He gave them the address; they found a phone number. His wife answered the phone. She had stayed all those years in hope, when she might easily have lived safely in England.

They were reunited — now elderly. Mary Lazarescu soon died, and Constantine always blessed her. Constantine became my friend and my contact with the *real* world that had prevailed even under the terrible falsehood and evil that posed as reality. Queen Maria was very much part of the pleasure of our discussions.

Constantine is with God now, and I cannot, even now, write or talk about him without weeping for sorrow and joy — so I just write now and don't talk!'

---

[90]   3 January 1948.

CHAPTER SEVEN

BANAT BATHS AND BOARS

On the two occasions I have visited Timişoara, the omens were inauspicious. The first time, in 1990, it proved impossible for myself and other passengers on the Malev flight from Budapest to disembark from the aircraft due to a pack of snarling, ravenous wild dogs who had materialized from the long grass to take up position at the bottom of the steps. The intervention of some burly security guards finally dispersed them. This time as I drove into the city, an elderly man in a wheelchair pushed by a concerned middle-aged lady manoeuvred heroically between the rows of traffic, begging for alms. To state his case, the incumbent of the chair had rolled up his trouser legs to the knees to show off the toeless stubs of his feet and the weeping ulcerous sores on his shins.

Best known as the flash point of the 1989 revolution—one should never forget that over 1,000 civilians were killed here between 16 and 21 December—Timişoara was put on the map by the Romans, who grasping its strategic importance as 'a turtle in the middle of a marsh', built a camp there and called it Zambara. That fort was to dictate the town's history. Possibly a Cuman settlement in the eleventh century, Andreas II of Hungary recognised it as *Castrum Temesiensis* in 1212 and soon it became the capital of the Banat, an area that encompasses the South-west corner of modern Romania. Almost a perfect square, its boundaries follow the River Mures East from Szeged to Zama; South from Zama to Orsova; West along the Danube to Belgrade and then back North to Szeged.

A particularly gory episode was enacted in the city in the early sixteenth century. A Hungarian peasants' revolt over 70,000 strong led by György Doja arrived beneath the city walls in the summer of 1514 and laid it to siege. The timely arrival of the Prince of Transylvania's forces saved the day and over forty of the rebel leaders captured. After fifteen days of unrelenting torture, only ten were left alive including Doja. He was seated on a red-hot iron throne and, in a word, barbequed. The nine other survivors were forced to eat his flesh before his body was quartered and sent to various cities for public display. A statue of the Virgin Mary has thoughtfully been erected on the spot where this happened.

It was the first area to be occupied by the Ottomans after the defeat and death of the young Hungarian King Louis II at the Battle of Mohacs in 1526. After a hard-fought siege, Timişoara surrendered in 1552 and the head of its Spanish mercenary captain, Alfonso Perez, was scalped, stuffed and sent to the Sultan. Ottoman rule was harsh, especially the fiscal burden, so many peasants voted with their feet and before long the rural areas of the Banat were almost deserted. The city itself continued to prosper as a trading centre, as evidenced by the Turkish traveller Evliya Çelebi who found over 400 shops there in 1660. He also observed a tin cock on top of one of the gates. When the wind blew, 'the cock would hiss, spin round and indicate the direction of the wind.'

Fifty years later, in September and October 1716, the Habsburg Imperial Army commanded by the great Prince Eugene of Savoy, *der edle Ritter*, finally succeeded in driving the Turks out and the province was ceded to the Habsburg Emperor Charles VI at the Treaty of Passarovitz in July 1718. The Banat was now considered a crown territory of the Holy Roman Empire and from 1718 to 1778 was duly administered from Vienna; from 1778 to 1848 it was incorporated into the political administration of Hungary.

The expulsion of the Turks in 1718 resulted in a resettlement program sponsored by the Habsburgs to bolster the meagre number of the inhabitants left in the area, mainly Serbs. The Habsburgs had three aims: to fortify the region against any future Ottoman invasion, to develop the farm land to feed the ever-expanding empire and, most precious to the heart of all Emperors, to further the Roman Catholic religion in Eastern Europe. Thus they offered Catholics of the South-western German states inducements such as free agricultural land, building plots, construction materials, livestock and exemption from taxes for several years.

The colonization of the Banat was entrusted to one of Prince Eugene's best generals, Claudius Florimund, Count of Mercy. He sent his agents to Baden, Wurtemberg, Alsace, Lorraine, the Rhinelands, Westphalia, Bavaria and Swabia as well as other areas. Confronted by this *pot pourri* of new arrivals from various regions and speaking various dialects, the Hungarians decided to call them Swabians, and thus the name came to be applied to all the Germans who settled in the Danube valley

The colonization came to be known as *der Grosse Schwabenzuge* or The Great Swabian Trek. The majority of the migration took place in three phases which were named after their Habsburg sponsors: the 15,000-strong 'Karolinische Ansiedlung' from 1718-37; the 75,000 'Maria Theresianische Ansiedlung' from 1744-72; and the 60,000 'Josephinische Ansiedlung' from 1782-1787.

A Swabian ditty succinctly classifies them as:

> *Die Erste hat den Tod,*
> *Der Zweite hat die Not*
> *Der Dritte erst hat Brot.*
>
> *The first encounters death*[91]*,*
> *The second need,*
> *Only the third has bread.*

---

[91] From 1749 to 1771, over 9,651 were buried in the parish of the citadel in Timişoara alone. Considering that the population of the city in 1771 was about 10,000, an entire generation was wiped out by the plague, war and earthquakes.

During these migrations, other nationalities also settled in the plains of the Banat, among them Serbs, Croatians, Bulgarians and Romanians, and to a lesser extent, Slovaks, Ruthenians, Czechs and a few French and Italians. By the end of eighteenth century, more than 1,000 German villages had been established in the Banat and by the end of the next century, there were more than two million Germans living in the Hungarian territories.

1848 brought demands for independence by both the Romanians and the Serbs of the Banat. Worried by the increasing stridency of the Serbian minority, the Hungarians at first showed some sympathy for this aspiration but soon the shutters came down and in 1849 direct rule was re-imposed by Vienna until the *augsleich* when the Banat formally became part of Hungary. From here on, the Romanians adopted a non-aggression policy towards Vienna and Budapest, hoping to bring about change through dialogue and using existing political institutions rather than rebellion.

World War I was a turning point for the Banat. Even before the war was over, nationalities within Austria-Hungary were eager for independence. In October 1918, the Czechoslovak Republic was declared and the Yugoslav National Council proclaimed independence from the Dual Monarchy. The Hungarian Republic was formed in November and in December, when the German army had left, the Romanian National Assembly declared unity with the Banat and Transylvania. When the war ended, the Habsburgs were no longer in power; Austria-Hungary had been dissolved. Revised final boundaries for Hungary were agreed at the Treaty of Trianon in June, 1920, and this resulted in the loss of two-thirds of her former territory. Land in Transylvania and most of the Banat was awarded to Romania. Yugoslavia gained land in Southern Hungary, including a strip of the Western Banat. The Swabian villagers whose families had lived in Hungary for almost 200 years now found themselves in three different countries.

The result of all of this turmoil radically altered the ethnic mix of Timişoara. In the space of a hundred years[92], the Romanian population dramatically increased from 6,312 to 270,487, the Hungarians marginally from 19,162 to 25,131 while the Germans declined from 30,892 to 7,142, down from 40 per cent in 1900 to 2 per cent in 2002. Like their Saxon counterparts in Transylvania, most of them left after 1977 in search of a better life in West Germany. Has this changed the character of the city? Not really since from its inception, Timişoara has seen its dominant populace change from Roman to Cuman to Hungarian to Turk to Serb to German and finally Romanian; its inhabitants have always been happy to go along with the description of a twelfth century Arab geographer, 'a nice city offering lots of riches'. Its progress since 1989 has amply endorsed this epithet. Yet there are some strange cultural legacies.

In Victoria Square, the great Orthodox Cathedral rising to 270 feet with its nine towers, each with a gilded cross, emphatically announced the change of national ownership after Trianon. Built between 1936 and 1940, its naos is dominated by a great gilded iconostasis carved out of lime wood, undeniably one of the most impressive in the whole of the Orthodox world. At the far end of the square, the late nineteenth century Helner and Fellner[93] Baroque-style opera house received a face-lift after a catastrophic fire in 1920; it went horribly wrong, resulting in an undecorated triumphal blind arch plonked incongruously in the centre of its façade. The interior fared better, a riot of neo-Byzantine design.

Fortunately this nationalistic architectural exuberance was not visited on the exquisite early eighteenth century square of the Piata Unirii. As I arrived, the pale yellow exterior of St George's Roman Catholic Cathedral had been transmuted into soft orange by the late afternoon sun and fusing with the other pastel colours of the square, created one of those familiar scenes left behind by the Habsburgs over far-flung corners of their empire. This could have been the

---

[92] Census figures from 1900 and 2002.
[93] These gentlemen had the contract to build opera houses all over the Empire, which is why most of them look identical.

centre of Cluj or Kosice. The Cathedral's altar designed by Emanuel Fischer of Vienna is classic Baroque, drenched in gold to assuage the parched consciences of the parsimonious burghers. In the centre is a Rafaelesque canvas by the Viennese artist, Michael Unterberger, of St George impaling a dragon on the end of his lance. Wearing eighteenth century armour, a red cloak billowing out behind him, I wondered whether this St George was really Prince Eugene and the dragon the Turk. Services are still conducted on Sundays in Romanian, German and Hungarian, reflecting an older tradition of race and creed as indeed are the performances at the theatre and the opera.

On the opposite side of the square stands the curious Palace of the Serbian bishop and next to it, the Rascian[94] Cathedral built in the 1740s by the Serbs on the site of their original wooden church. Presumably in the spirit of friendly competition after watching the RC Cathedral going up to their front, they erected a classic Austrian Baroque church, adding twin towers in 1791. In the forecourt are two blackened iron stands for burning candles, one marked in Cyrillic 'за живе' (za shee-vee) or 'for the living'. Between the two churches, in the centre of the square, stands the Monument of the Holy Trinity, erected in 1740 by a Frenchman, Jean de Hansen, to mark the end of the terrible plague of 1738-39 when so many died that their bodies had to be burnt. Carved in Vienna out of sandstone, it was transported down the Danube, then up the Tisa and finally along the Bega canal. The bas-relief panels on the pedestal show scenes of the plague: a mother raising her arms to heaven implores God to spare her children; a man carries a dead body slung across his shoulder. An almost identical statue of St John Neopuk stands in the nearby Liberty Square, another eighteenth century implant from Vienna, this time by Herr Blim and Herr Wasserburger[95].

Making my way back to my hotel in Romulus Street (yes, you go along Remus Street to get there!), I passed the Orthodox Cathedral and went inside to observe the evening service. The heady

---

94 A name given by the Austrians to Serbian and Romanian Orthodox believers.
95 Like Helner and Fellner, they had a lucrative contract to produce lookalike Catholic statues for erection all over the Empire.

Cotroceni

Pelisor

SOME OF QUEEN MARIE'S HOUSES

Copaceni

Serbian

TIMIŞOARA COMPETING CHURCHES

Orthodox

Roman Catholic

smell of incense mixed with the chants of the priests enraptured the congregation. Many were queuing to pray at the shrine of St Joseph the New of Partos. Born in 1568 in Dalmatia, Joseph had become bishop of Timişoara in 1650. Renowned for his miraculous powers of healing, his relics had been brought to the city in 1956, an act difficult to reconcile with the professed atheism of the Communism regime. An old lady had pressed herself against the glass that covered his full-length portrait, motionless as if glued to the icon. I felt her prayers must have been important.

I had dinner in a small restaurant in Romulus Street. Escalope of pork Cordon Bleu had been lovingly translated as 'Porc Gordon Blue'. Never mind the spelling, the ping of the microwave oven was all that mattered and no pun of Gordon Ramsay intended.

The road to Baile Herculane from Timişoara is notoriously slow, so I decided to take the train instead. First Class travel on Romanian state railways is a misnomer but it is at least relative to the deprivations of comfort experienced in other classes and a fraction of the cost in most other European countries; my three-and-a half hour journey by *Rapide* cost ten pounds. A couple were changing their baby's nappy in the waiting room, squabbling while the child squealed. Everyone else was asleep. The train was spot on time, that time being determined only on the day of travel. The First Class WC, although 'free', was mysteriously occupied by a large tractor tyre that effectively prevented any act of mitrication or defecation.

After an hour's journey South, the land began to rise and soon the snow-covered ridges of the Munti Tarcu appeared in the East, the three peaks of Baicu, Gugu and Godeanu looming up on the far horizon. Traditional villages passed by with their low houses, gaggles of geese, pear-shaped haystacks and rank mizzens. The fields were organized into either neat strips of maize or fallow, often fenced or hedged with orchards separating them, suggesting a Swabian influence. The first lambs had appeared, identified by their pristine white wool jackets against the grubby coats of their parents. At Armenis, where the Timis valley narrows, the Rapide began to struggle as it dragged itself uphill between the steep beech-clad slopes. I spied a family of gypsies who had set out a stall of bottled honey by the roadside; the women and children sat round a camp-fire whilst their men folk nonchalantly solicited passing motorists.

At the point where the River Cerna takes over from the River Timis, the Rapide got its wind back and charged downhill towards the Danube, slowing down at the town of Mehadia, claustrophobically positioned under a towering limestone bluff, until it came to a stop at Baile Herculane station. Here, I alighted and, after being politely accosted by an elderly dwarf for alms, hired a rickety taxi to take me to the valley of the 'Baths of Hercules'.

It was down this valley that the left flank of Trajan's legions marched in 101 AD, bent on the final destruction of the Dacians, a troublesome tribe, with a charismatic teenage leader called Decebalus, that ruled the lands north of the Danube, and also a very rich one since it owned the fabulous gold mines of the Apuseni. The Emperor's hidden agenda was to rectify his cash crisis and pay off the arrears owed to the army. Prior to the attack, Trajan realised that without a bridge, he would be unable to ferry enough troops and supplies across the Danube river to secure a bridgehead; so he built one. Modern surveyors have traced the remains of its foundations and have calculated that its bank-to-bank span reached about 3,900 feet[96].

The chronicler Ziphilini who was familiar with the history written by Dion Cassius, the governor of Pannonia under Hadrian, tells us that the bridge was built by Apollodorus, the architect both of the Forum Trajanum and of Trajan's column in Rome, the Norman Foster of his day. He states that each of the twenty piers was 150

---

[96] Julius Caesar's famous bridges over the Rhine in 55 BC and 53 BC only covered an estimated 400-1400 feet.

Roman feet high, sixty feet thick and 175 feet equidistant from each other. At each end, there were robust defensive towers. Cleverly sited on the widest part of the river to disperse the force of sudden floods and also to enable the ice to break on the widest possible surface, the bridge was defended by a tower at either end. Once across, the Roman engineers constructed the Via Trajana, partly cut into the rock and partly supported on wooden beams, which combined the functions of a tow path and a covered passage for troops.

After the final conquest of Dacia in 106 AD, the new Roman province was populated by soldiers and settlers from across the whole Roman world (*ex toto orbe Romano*). Divided into two parts, *Dacia Superior* and *Dacia Inferior* (corresponding roughly to what is today Transylvania and Oltenia, respectively), the Northern part was later divided into *Dacia Porolissensis* in the north and *Dacia Apulensis* in the South. The new province was a Roman outpost in *barbaricum,* and as such, intermittently subjected to attack by Germanic tribes and the odd-sounding Iazyges. How many actual Dacians survived Rome's 'pacification program'? The chronicler Lydus estimated the number of prisoners taken to Rome by Trajan to be about 50,000 but it is impossible to confirm the charge of genocide though undisputedly their numbers had been savagely culled.

During the reign of Gallienus (253-268 AD), Eastern Transylvania was abandoned and Eutropius recorded that the Romans subsequently created two other provinces South of the Danube, *Dacia Ripensis* and *Dacia Mediterranea*. After the final withdrawal in 275 AD, the lower Danube became again the Roman *limes,* the frontier of the Empire against *barbaricum*, and the last Roman hung up his towel in the Baths of Hercules.

The approach to the Baths was uninspiring, past a number of modern functional but environmentally unsympathetic hotels, until the sides of the valley of the River Cerna began to contract and soar up like the spires and towers of Gothic cathedrals, becoming sheer limestone cliffs that mysteriously captured the sun's fading rays and converted them into a heavenly white light. After about three miles, the old town appeared and the haunt of Emperors, both Roman and Habsburg, Kings and Queens, Princes and boyars, magnates and burghers, and English vagabonds was revealed. I had read two previous accounts by English travellers. John Paget in his 1860 journey to Transylvania warned of *ennui* following the *de rigeur* parboil and the 'deficiency of accommodation ....a crying evil...new arrivals not infrequently are obliged to sleep on tables and chairs in the public dining room'. Seventy years later, the young Paddy Leigh Fermor passed through this 'ornate and incongruous watering-place' which he imagined had been a haunt of 'ailing burghers of Eastern Europe, in crinolines and stove pipe hats, sabretaches and czapkas, or mutton-chop sleeves and boaters' for over a century.

It may have been low season and mid-winter but nothing could have prepared me for the shocking condition I found the town to be in. Having fortuitously chosen to book a room in the Hotel Ferdinand, as it happened the only hotel open in the old town, I set off to explore this 'echo of the Austrian-Hungarian Empire at its farthest edge'[97] and discovered rampant ruination on a truly tragic and massive scale. The Cerna river (from the Slavic Черной or *chernoi* for black) was ruined by tangled piles of filth and plastic detritus; the woodland paths were ruined by litter and lack of upkeep; the houses, be they pavilions, sanatoriums or the great sulphur baths themselves, were ruined by neglect and vandalism. The Decebalus Hotel looked like an unpaid Roman legion had just stayed there. Nowhere have I ever seen such dereliction brazenly presented as normality. Not a single construction worker was to be seen anywhere.

To be fair the Baths do not over-promote themselves on their web site; they sensibly stick to historical facts, not hyperbole. Unlike Leigh Fermor whose evening at the Casino 'spun itself into a golden haze', mine was a more sombre occasion and I certainly did not find myself dancing with a girl studying English in Bucharest to the tunes of *Couchés dans le foin* and *Vous qui passez sans me voir*. In fact, the

---

[97]   Leigh Fermor: *Between the Woods and the Water.*

Hotel Ferdinand was full of footballers and handballers, at least forty, wearing bright blue tracksuits and shod in trainers, all sponsored by commerce and industry and accredited to the University of Craiova. I assumed they were here to train and 'parboil'—and eat prodigious amount of meat and fruit. The hotel itself was devoid of charm save for Erno Tauber, the Maitre d'Hotel, who apologised to me about the demise of the soup.

"Soups finished. There will be some tomorrow."

"I'm not here tomorrow."

"So sorry."

He sported a moustache and moved purposefully around the dining room like a combination of Groucho Marx and Basil Fawlty on nefarious errands. I volunteered my opinion that the town looked a bit shabby.

"Postcards? You like to see old cards?" I momentarily demurred, wondering exactly what sort of cards he had in mind, before assenting and he returned to the table with an envelope.

The contents were certainly evocative of the past: the Hotel Carol circa 1924 would not be out of place in Cap Ferat today; the same could be said of the Salanul de Cura, for the casino was shown in all its splendour with a magnificent coffered ceiling; and the Hotel Severin circa 1927 featured the latest open–top tourer in the foreground. All of these buildings are now abandoned and derelict.

Maybe the explanation was as simple as the failure of The Baths post–1989 to wake up to the fact that they had to compete with all the other spas in Europe—in Hungary, Slovakia, Slovenia and Czech Republic let alone France, Germany, Italy and Switzerland—and the resultant implosion of its prosperity was similar to that of the factories and collective farms that now lie all over Romania like the rusting carcasses of industrial dinosaurs. However, I was convinced that some unregistered economic tidal wave, definitely man-made, had hit the valley, destroying all enterprise before it.

There was music throughout dinner played over the loudspeaker system—'*Greatest hits from English football songs*'. Never had Vienna seemed so far away. It had been disappointing not to hear the Craiova 'ballers' join in; after all, Leigh Fermor had been treated to members of the Bucharest Opera gaily launch themselves into an impromptu and fine rendering of *The Barber of Seville*.

On my way back to the station the next morning, after a final walkabout had verified my gloomy first impressions, I asked my taxi driver for enlightenment.

"Why is this town totally decrepit?"

"Under communist, everything OK." This is a fairly standard and understandable answer in Eastern Europe, providing you were not sacked/tortured/had your children expelled from school/hospital appointments cancelled/banned from travel etcetera. It is also a fair comment about the artificial prosperity that Communism delivered on-and-off for forty years before its command economy broke down.

"Now economics very bad. Corruption very bad."

"In what sense?" I asked.

"Personal pocket."

"Whose?"

"Designed by politicians."

I hope that some of the twenty billion Euros earmarked by the EU for Romania stays clear of this pocket and finds its way to buy real building materials and pays real workmen to restore this ancient curative town.

What happened in Baile Herculane after the Romans left? I had always paid scant attention to the list of wandering tribes that swept into Romania from the East and this was a good moment to review it.

In the third century, the *Carps* inhabited the territory of what today is Moldavia. Living in tribal unions, their main trade was agriculture and animal breeding. They made several incursions into Transylvania and Oltenia but by 297 AD, had been soundly defeated and subsequently settled within the frontiers of the Roman Empire. The derivation of the word 'carp' comes from the Latin *carpa (Cassiodorus)* for a Danubian fish. Was it then applied to this tribe pejoratively?

The *Sarmatians*, originally from Western Iran, were nomadic shepherds and horse soldiers and were mentioned by Ovid, when he was living in exile in Constanţa during 9-17 AD, as crossing the Danube in a Southerly direction. Tacitus reported them living in the first century AD between the Danube and the Tisa and after the Roman retreat, the Sarmatian *Iazyges* occupied the central part of the Banat. In 332, they were attacked by the Goths, but with help from Constantine the Great, managed to stave them off. However, in the course of the war, the ruling faction called *Sarmati Argaragantes* scored an unfortunate own goal; they had armed their slaves, the *Sarmati Limigantes*, who promptly revolted and sent their former masters packing.

The *Roxolani,* another group of Sarmatians, also lived in considerable numbers in Moldavia and Muntenia towards the end of the second century and during the first half of the third. Then they disappeared, probably migrating to the great Hungarian plain.

The *Alani,* the last wave of Sarmatian peoples in South-eastern Europe, started to migrate West of the Don in the first half of the third century and reached Moldavia and Muntenia during the second half of that century. I am proud to record that one group of these peoples, the *Alanians*, still live in the Caucasus in present day *Ossetria*. The idea that the name 'Alan' means either 'little rock' or 'handsome' in Breton or 'harmony' in some Celtic languages is flawed; we 'Alans' are Sarmatians, descendants no less of Scythian warriors and Amazon women..

The *Goths* belonged to the Eastern branch of the Old Germanic populations and migrated from the area around the estuary of the Vistula in a South-eastern direction; by the second half of the second century AD, they were living on the frontiers of *Dacia Traiana*. The first battle between the Goths and the Roman army took place during the reign of Emperor Caracalla, probably in 214 AD, and was followed by constant attacks throughout the third century. From the end of that century, the Goths divided into two branches: *Ostrogoths* and *Visigoths* (Eastern and Western Goths, respectively). The Visigoths migrated in large numbers into the areas West of the

Prut river, namely Moldavia, Muntenia, Oltenia and Transylvania. That country was accordingly called *Gothia*.

In the third century BC, the *Huns* lived in parts of Northern China, in the present day provinces of Sansi, Sensi and Hopei. After having been attacked by the indigenous Chinese, they migrated Westwards and lived for a long period of time in the region of the Volga. In 375 AD, they attacked the Goths in Moldavia and Muntenia and soon occupied all the territory formerly dominated by the Goths. The power of the Huns was at its height in the mid-fifth century. In 451, the West Roman Empire defeated them at the Battle of Chalons or Catalaunum (near Troyes in France) and the forty-seven-year-old Attila[98], conqueror of Gaul, died in 453, most likely from drink on the eve of marrying a new and beautiful young wife. In the following year, a coalition led by the Gepidae defeated the Huns at the Nedao river in Pannonia[99], which marked the end of Hunnish power in Europe. As the Romans would have put it, '*Sic transit gloria mundi*'.

The *Gepidae*, another branch of the Old Germanic peoples, this time living along the shores of the Baltic Sea, started to migrate Southward in the mid-third century. They settled in the region of the upper Tisa, now North-east Hungary, South-west Ukraine and the Maramures. Most of them managed to stay put during Hunnish rule and they regained their independence in 453 AD after Attila died. In 471, they occupied the town of Sirmium[100] and made it the residence of their kings from where they ruled over a large territory from the Sava to the eastern Carpathian Mountains. In 567, the Avars, in coalition with the Longobards, defeated the Gepidae and summarily abolished their kingdom.

Probably coming from Mongolia, the *Avars* occupied the steppes of Southern Russia some time before the sixth century. In 558, they sent an envoy to Byzantium, offering their services in exchange for land and money. Nine years later, they attacked the Gepidae, defeated

---

[98] Attila has a mixed reputation but it's not all bad—he was so beastly to the inhabitants of North Italy that they fled to the lagoons around Venice and hence we have that glorious city to enjoy today!

[99] Nobody knows where this river was in Hungary—it has been 'lost'.

[100] Sremska Mitrovica in Serbia.

them and occupied their territory. During the second half of the sixth century and the first three decades of the seventh, Byzantium suffered many Avar invasions including a joint attack with the Persians on Constantinople. At the height of their power, the Avars reigned over a vast territory between the Alps, the Adriatic Sea and the Black Sea. The power of the Avars was finally broken in 795-96, when the Franks destroyed the vast tented residence of the *kaganat* known as the *hring*. The chronicle of Nestor affirms that all the Avars died, but some are known to have made it back to Transylvania, East of the Tisa.

The *Bulgars* were a semi-nomadic people, originally Huns from Central Asia, who since the second century had inhabited the steppe North of the Caucasus and the banks of the Volga. When Attila's empire fragmented on his death in 453, the Eastern-most wing of the Huns solemnly migrated back to the steppes of the Ukraine but by the middle of the seventh century they re-emerged as a force to be reckoned with under the ebullient Khan Kubrat. He united the Kutrigurs and Utrigurs, the two main Bulgar hordes, and founded an empire centered on the Azov region that stretched as far East as the Volga and as far West as the Carpathians. The Westward migration of the Bulgars overlapped with that of the Slavs and soon they both had crossed the Danube and made their way into the Balkans. By 681, Khan Asparukh had forced Emperor Constantine V to recognize the first Bulgarian state, whose capital was at Pliska, near modern Shumen. By the middle of the ninth century, following the successes of Khan Krum against the Avars, the Bulgars occupied most of modern-day Romania and by 892, were shipping salt from Transylvania to the Moravians. But not for long for by the spring of 895, Arpad and his formidable Hungarians (they could accurately shoot off volleys of arrows while swimming across a river!) had flooded through the Eastern Carpathian passes and conquered all before them in their pusuit of treasure, slaves and plunder galore.

Did any of the above visit Baile Herculane? There is, to date, no evidence in the affirmative. What we do know is that the Roman habit of body washing took many centuries to return to civilisation!

The waiting room cum ticket office at Baile Herculane station is housed in a splendid rotunda pavilion that could have been transported here from an eighteenth century English garden. Mosaics of Roman gods and goddesses executed in the Art Nouveau style cover the panels in the dome; Hercules himself watched over me as I purchased no less than four separate tickets needed to travel on *The Inter-City* to Timişoara. Three scruffy dispirited teenagers lay draped over the benches, one even precariously slept on top of a radiator until prodded into life by a well-meaning cleaning lady whose concern was clearly for the hygiene of the radiator. An unkempt tramp watched with disinterest. The dwarf who had met me the day before had been replaced by a diminutive gypsy with a shock of black hair who, with a cigarette stuck to his lip, swaggered up and down the platform with all the assurance of Humphrey Bogart in *Casablanca*. As soon as the train arrived, the three teens upsticked and hurled themselves on board like dervishes, only to be energetically pursued by a squad of transport police. Great consternation ensued as the chase gathered momentum up and down the corridors. Eventually the police emerged triumphant at the end of the train with the three dejected runaways and we were on our way North. It had been a sad spectacle to witness the plight of three young people whose youth had been stolen from them by an unforgiving society in painful transition.

It was on this very railway that Captain David Russell of the Special Operations Executive (SOE) made his own getaway sixty-three years ago.

Aside the road to Ploieşti, fifteen miles North-east from Bucharest, lies a well-tended graveyard, its borders hemmed with woods and fields. With its familiar Lutyens cross inset with an inverted sword, it contains the graves of British and Commonwealth servicemen killed in Romania during the two World Wars. In the last row stands a headstone to the memory of Captain David Russell MC, Scots Guards.

Born on 28 August 1915, David Russell was educated at Eton and went up to Cambridge where he read Agriculture and Estate Management. He continued his studies at Cirencester before starting farming at Broke Hall near Ipswich. At some stage as a young man, Russell spent time in Germany for in his SOE file there is an entry 'Germany—lived there for 3 years' (where he became fluent in the language) as well as references to other travels on the Continent. These journeys may well have stemmed from his daredevil interests—flying, motorcycle racing, skiing and climbing.

After the outbreak of war, Russell was commissioned in May 1940 and joined the Scots Guards Training Battalion that October. After an uneventful two years in England, Russell was posted to the Middle East where in June 1942 he joined 'L' Detachment of the SAS. Described by Sir Carol Mather as 'a wild and independent character with a zest for life'[101], David Stirling tasked him to attack soft-skinned vehicles in the Axis build-up area behind Alamein. Russell excelled on this mission, personally destroying eight trucks. It was during this operation that Headquarters Middle East ordered Stirling back to Cairo to assist in planning Operation Agreement, a daring raid on the main Afrika Corps supply base at Tobruk.

The brainchild of an eccentric Arabist, Colonel Jock Haselden, the plan was ambitious. Force B, guided by the LRDG[102] to the Tobruk perimeter, was to assault the coastal guns protecting the port. A sea landing was then to be carried out by Force C and once a perimeter had been secured, Force A, consisting of two destroyers, HMS Sikh and HMS Zulu with marines on board, was to sail into the harbour and destroy it.

The method of inserting Force B was audacious. Haselden explained to his men: 'We are going to drive openly into Tobruk one evening just at dusk. We will enter as prisoners-of-war captured at the Alamein front, under the guard of German soldiers (and in German designated captured Allied trucks).' This guard was provided by the Special Interrogation Group (SIG), a sub-unit of D squadron SAS,

---

[101]   Sir Carol Mather: *When the Grass Stops Growing.*
[102]   Long Range Desert Group.

commanded by Captain Buck MC; his second-in-command was none other than David Russell.

On 6 September, Force B left Cairo and after reaching the outskirts of Tobruk a week later, joined the stream of German traffic. Apart from a tense moment when there was a minor accident with a German staff car, the commandoes reached their jumping-off point just as a diversionary RAF air raid began. Haselden with Russell and other members of SIG soon took their objective, allowing Lt Tubby Langton (formerly Irish Guards) of the SBS[103] to signal Force C to land. However, in the darkness and heavy gunfire, only two of the sixteen MTBs[104] were able to land their detachments and it proved impossible to secure a perimeter.

Then HMS Sikh was hit by shore batteries and all three raiding Forces now concentrated on extricating themselves. Haselden gave the order for Force B to withdraw in the remaining trucks. Russell joined in the desperate rearguard action, holding off the attacking Italians until Haselden was killed by a grenade. Then together with other members of SIG, he headed for Allied lines. After marching for over sixty days, Russell was spotted by a British armoured car on 18 November. Bearded, long-haired, starving and in rags, he seemed quite composed at meeting them. Tubby Langton had also managed to escape; in all, only six members of Force B made it back.

On 8 January 1943, Russell's MC was gazetted. The citation read that he 'exhibited great bravery and complete disregard for his personal safety throughout the operation…In circumstances of extreme danger and difficulty, this officer displayed the highest courage, endurance and devotion to duty.' After Operation Agreement, the SIG was disbanded and in April 1943, Russell was posted to the Romanian section of SOE Cairo.

---

103   Special Boat Section.
104   Motor Torpedo Boats.

The background to events in wartime Romania was complex. In 1933 Germany imported 100,000 tons of oil from Romania. Hitler knew that consumption would increase tenfold in the event of war and therefore the security of Romanian oil supplies was crucial to German strategic planning. Romania herself adopted a policy of non-alignment but following the fall of France, the Soviet Union exercised its secret agreement with Germany and annexed the two Romanian provinces of Bessarabia and Northern Bucovina by force.

King Carol II of Romania now decided to ingratiate himself to Hitler but it was too late. On 30 August 1940, the Vienna Diktat, issued by Germany and Italy, ceded Northern Transylvania to Hungary[105]. With Romania now stripped of most of her post-First World War gains, Carol decided to abdicate on 6 September and General Ion Antonescu, a professional soldier, took over. In November, Antonescu went to Berlin to sign the Tripartite Pact with the Axis and announced to the Romanian people 'Romania on her own initiative has entered the political sphere of Germany and Italy'.

The only credible opposition to Antonescu was Iuliu Maniu, the leader of the National Peasants Party and Prime Minister on three occasions between 1928 and 1933. SOE, concerned by the unrestricted access Germany now had to Romania's oil fields, needed to open up W/T[106] communications with him as soon as possible, for a carefully planned coup—with the Romanian army behind it—would cause the Reich serious problems.

Code-named Operation Ranji, on the night of 15 June 1943, Russell and his wireless operator, Nicolae Turcanu (Call Sign Reginald), parachuted into Yugoslavia, where Russell persuaded the Chetnik commander, General Mihailovic, to second Petre Mihai, a former sergeant major in the gendarmerie, to his mission as a guide.

---

[105]   43,000 sq.km and about 2.6 million people.
[106]   Wireless Transmissions.

The Ranji team crossed the heavily patrolled Danube river on 2 August and after moving fifty miles across enemy territory, arrived at Mehadia where the former mayor, Madgearu, was a well-known Manist[107]. After staying the night in his house, he suggested that they would be safer in one of his two vineyards and insisted that they left their weapons and uniforms with him so that he could hide them.

As an afterthought, Russell asked him to stash the propaganda leaflets they had brought with them. Leaving them alone for the following night, Madgearu disappeared and returned the next morning, completely drunk. On sobering up, he told them he had already distributed the leaflets throughout the town. By now Madgearu was such a liability that Turcanu persuaded him to go off and find a car to take them to Timişoara 'where they had important business'. As soon as he had gone, they promptly made their way to Mehadia station, caught a train to Turnu Severin and then backtracked to the village of Varciorova.

Here they made contact with the Pitulescu brothers, the eldest of whom had been the Postmaster General of Romania and was now the leader of the local National Peasants Party. The problem was that the team did not have a password and therefore Pitulescu had to go to see Maniu in Bucharest before he could engage with them.

For three weeks, the SOE mission remained in the woods close to the village. Towards the end of August, due to increased enemy patrolling, they moved to a valley called Fundul Vâdiţei, where they occupied an abandoned fishermen's hut dug into the ground and covered it with branches. Every day, Turcanu went down to the Pitulescu house to send messages (composed by Russell) while the others remained at the hide.

On 4 September, Russell was killed in mysterious circumstances, found shot in the back of the head. An investigation immediately started, both on the ground and back at SOE HQ in Cairo. Ivor Porter, a member of the next SOE mission into Romania, writes in his book, *Operation Autonomous*, that it was generally thought that the Serb Chetnik guide had murdered Russell for his gold sovereigns. However,

---

[107] Supporter of Iuliu Maniu.

an examination of the Ranji files leads to a different if inconclusive verdict.

According to Turcanu, after staying at the Pitulescu house until the early hours of the morning of 5 September due to poor radio conditions, he had returned to the hut and found Russell dead. Everything had been turned upside down. Both Russell's watches were missing and Petre Mihai was nowhere to be found. He then recovered the mission's money and sensitive paperwork cached in a tree about fifty meters away and made his way to Bucharest where, after making contact with the Manists, he was able to continue his transmissions.

To his surprise, Petre Mihai arrived shortly after and told Turcanu his story. 'We (Petre and Russell) bathed in the stream, drank a brandy and then went into the hut where we continued talking until we fell asleep. At about 9.30 or 10.30 pm, I awoke to the noise of crackling leaves …steps became louder and louder…I then burrowed my way out of the back of the hut. I see suddenly a flash of light, exactly like the light of a torch….and at the same time, I hear the shout "Hands up or I shoot" and I could hear a number of shots being fired as if from an automatic rifle.'

As far as the Pitulescu family in Varciorova was concerned, the finger pointed at Dumtru Burcu, a woodsman, who had known of the team's whereabouts. He was spending money 'freely on his young women' shortly after the incident. Mrs Pitulescu also had in her possession a long written statement by Petre Mihai, who had presented himself to the family the day after the murder, but she could not decipher it since it was in Serbian.

There was also considerable evidence of police and military patrols in the area and several bands of cut-throat thieves including Serbian guerrillas. In an OSS[108] report dated 3 November 1944, a source claimed that between 29 August and 19 September 1943, Romanian officials knew about a three-man British W/T party.

The investigation into the murder weapon was equally perplexing. Police reports stated that the bullet was a 12 mm or .455. When the mission had stayed with Madgearu, they had allowed him

---

[108] The American Office of Strategic Services, forerunner to the CIA.

to cache two out of their three .455 revolvers. This was made clear by Russell when he signalled Cairo on 24 August: 'only weapon is one pistol. Please send colt automatic and magazines'. So was Russell shot with his own weapon?

In its weekly Progress Report No. 61 dated 23 September 1943, SOE wrote 'in conclusion, it is pointed out that Russell probably undertook one of the most difficult of missions, bearing in mind that Romania is an enemy country and no reception arrangements could be made for him. The result of this mission is that we are now in W/T communication with Romania, which we have been trying to establish for the past two years.'

On 1 June 1944, Russell was posthumously mentioned in despatches, a somewhat low-key award given the importance of his mission. His grave had been left unmarked but when the area came under the control of the Allied Commission, a headstone was erected with the inscription 'Captain David Russell, a gallant gentleman who died in the battle for the liberty of Europe'. Later his remains were moved to the Commonwealth War Grave outside Bucharest.

About twenty miles to the West of Armenis, that point on the railroad where the train almost expires, lie the small towns of Lupac and Carasova where the locals speak *Torlakian*, the Slavic dialects of South-east Serbia and North-west Bulgaria. The Bulgarians who can never agree about anything call it *Shop*. To add to the confusion, the 5,000 locals who chat away in Torlakian are known as *Krashovans* or for reasons known only to the Romanians as *Cocoşi*—cockerels. In the 2002 census, most of the Krashovans declared themselves to be Croats on the Romanian census form in order to 'clarify' their position and presumably to heap even more confusion on an outsider like me.

Originally fourteenth century refugees from the Timok river area around Zaječar fleeing the Ottomans, they have miraculously stayed put over the centuries and now present a challenge to language

Baile Herculane in decline   *The gallant David Russell*

BANAT DIARY

Delia, Ion and last night's dinner

Bulci

MOCSONYI MANSIONS

Căpâlnaş

students. The good news is that the noun case system has all but been lost and the 'h' has also vanished; the bad news is that 'l' can serve as a vowel. So Question One: how to pronounce влк or vlk, meaning wolf? Question Two: how to pronounce жлт or shlt, meaning yellow? Answer is to transpose the 'l' for a 'u'!.

The train from Timişoara to Arad was classed *Personal* rather than *Rapide* or *Inter-City*. This meant that it stopped at every station. The earth is so flat in this part of Romania that one can seriously sympathize with the notion of a flat planet and the awful probability of falling off its edge. This thought was brought on by the nauseous motion of the train, not dissimilar I imagine to the experience of early seafarers crossing the Atlantic in small boats. Four unexpected visitors arrived in my compartment: a distressed middle-aged lady thrust a notice in my face declaring she had terminal cancer and needed money—I gave; a motherly lady spread a collection of cheap wallets and pens on the carriage floor and asked for offers—I passed; a soulful gypsy youth, proffering pictures of the Saints, implored me to buy one—I bought; a cocky gypsy wearing a white Stetson pulled packets of razor blades from the recesses of his overcoat like a conjuror—I declined.

I was making for Bulci, the Styrcea family home on the River Mureş, but knowing that I would not get there that evening, had decided to stay overnight at Pensiunea Geza in Minis, a village on the edge of the Zărand hills. My host, Géza Tüdös (pronounced *too-dush*), collected me from Radna Station in his Land Rover, and after pointing out the great eighteenth century pilgrimage church of St Mary with its twin towers and adjoining Franciscan monastery, whisked back to his old farmhouse where he combined his dual lives of winemaker and restauranteur. On arrival, he shook my hand and introduced himself as: 'Géza'. I realised then that all the preliminary chat in the car had been about testing me and somehow I had passed muster!

Immediately and easily persuaded by Géza to sample his 1999 Cabernet, grown on the slopes above his house, I congratulated him on his excellent command of English. He modestly accepted my compliment but qualified it with the admission that he also spoke

Hungarian, Romanian, German, French, Italian, Spanish and Russian. Eight languages is almost the basic skill set in this part of Europe. Dinner was served in a room that seemed to double up as an antique shop, the walls groaning with shelves ladened with a calamitous clutter of pewter, glass and porcelain, dressers on the point of collapse with candelabra, decorative plates and bric-a-brac. Pride of place went to a photograph of former Tsar Simeon II of Bulgaria who had visited 'Chez Géza' two years ago.

I have neither the credentials nor experience to write about food and wine but in deference to Géza's exceptionally good cuisine, here is my first and wholly inadequate attempt. The hors d'ouevres arrived on no less than nine different plates—*Ceapa roşić* (raw onion), *ardei gras* (red peppers), *brînza* (goats cheese), *cîrnati de casa* (cold homemade sausages), *salam* (traditional Hungarian salami), *ciuperci murate* (pickled ceps), *pateu de ficat* (chicken liver pate), *salată de vinete* (aubergine mousse) and that Romanian favourite, *maruntaie de porc* (sliced and salted pig's fat). Each one was delicious. Next on was *supă de piu* (green cabbage, carrots, potatoes and gnocchi in chicken broth). What more can one want on a cold winter's night? The main course then appeared—*papricas miel* (lamb-on-the-bone goulash) with *sparac pireu* (creamed spinach) and *spaghete* (thin spaghetti cooked with olive oil and herbs). A terrific combination with all the components complimenting each other. I had to leave half the pudding—*strudel cu Visine* (a delicious strudel of sour cherries with a frost of icing sugar)—due to gluttony.

Large as he is, Géza managed throughout dinner to be supremely attentive but in a mysteriously unobtrusive way as he padded round the dining room with the shambling gait of a performing Balkan bear. When he passed by, it was as if the moon had gone behind a cloud and then reappeared, illuminating an invisibly replenished glass of wine. The restaurant had begun to fill with other diners and I noticed Géza surreptitiously change the mood-music on his boom box from Chopin's Nocturnes to Irish rebel songs. Dinner finished with a seven-year-old brandy, 'the best in Western Romania'. Smooth and powerful, it was the perfect nightcap to shut out the yelps and barks of the village dogs and the plaintive angry tunes of Irish patriots.

After breakfast the next day, this time to the sounds of Mozart's Piano Concerto in C Major, we walked up onto the hill behind the house to inspect his vineyards. Géza had moved here in 1989 from Brasov where he had spent the first forty years of his life as a Hungarian in a Saxon town. Although he had read import-export business studies at University, he had worked all his adult life in hotel management in the Brasov-Predeal area.

"I had many foreign friends—German, French, Italian. Securitate sometimes made it very difficult."

"Surely this must have been *Catch 22* if you worked in the tourist sector. How could you have avoided meeting foreigners?"

"Of course. It was stupid."

He mused for a moment and then pronounced: "For bad people, it was easy in those days. But if you liked freedom, it was very hard."

He had certainly embraced his new freedom with gusto, becoming the first recipient in Romania of the Agro-Tourism Certificate for his Pensione.

"We had twenty litres of petrol for one month; sometimes, we could only use car every second Sunday. And no electricity from 5 pm to 11 pm." He visibly winced. I suddenly saw his Land Rover in a new light: it was his symbol of freedom to go anywhere at anytime.

Our talk now turned to his wine business. The upkeep of his two hectares of vineyards and the vendage were contracted out, allowing Géza to concentrate on his wine making. His yields varied from 3,000 to 7,000 kilos of grapes, which equated to between 1,950 to 4,550 litres of wine. As he had to close a wine sale in Arad, he bid me goodbye and hurried off down the hill back to the house.

Suddenly he stopped and turning round to face me, shouted: "By the way, I forgot to tell you, I am mushroom enthusiast for fifty years. Please come back in the autumn for the pickings!"

The sandy track followed the line of the ridge, through neat rows of vines busy with larks and wayfarers until it emerged on the crest of the hill. Finches darted for cover as I tramped past their homes in thickets of sloe and rose hip; a small flock of brightly coloured waxwings flashed past, trilling nervously. On the top of the hill were signs of a ditch and a rampart, maybe Roman originally, most certainly early Hungarian. And for good reason for, from this vantage point, I could see the Mureş river flex its muscles as it powered its way across the plain to join the Tisa; even in the gloom of an overcast winter's day, I could make out the city of Arad twenty miles away. Behind me to the East, like scenery on a deep stage, layer after layer of beech and oak forests stretched to the distant summits of the Apuseni Mountains.

From here in the thirteenth century, the Mongol scouts would have reported to their Khans that they had found an endless great plain. The Ottoman armies would have rejoiced that from here onwards they could unleash their cavalry and replenish their supplies for between Minis and Budapest there are no more natural barriers save the rivers. And in reverse, the seventeenth century Hungarian *kurucs*[109], during the uprisings against their Habsburg masters, would have retreated Eastwards into the safety of the vast Transylvania forests in the knowledge that the Imperial forces would be reluctant to pursue them.

The Mureş here acted as the border between the Austrians and the Ottomans for twenty-eight years after the treaty of Karlowitz in 1699. The Hungarians' history of allying themselves with the Porte meant that they were thoroughly distrusted and disliked by Vienna, so border guards were recruited exclusively from the 200,000 Serbs, led by Patriarch Arsenije Cernojevic of Pécs, who had migrated into Southern Hungary to escape the Ottoman army. Their descendants remain to this day.

---

[109]   Rebels.

Before he left, Geza had ordered up a taxi to take me to Bata, a small town in the Mureş valley about twenty miles West of Minis. After a hour's drive, past the great fifteenth century Hunyadi fortress at Lipova—the Castle of Şoimoş—that guards this entrance to Transylvania, through forests dotted with woodcutters' clearings, we had a merry time tracking down the house of my putative hosts, Ion and Delia Micurescu. Our first attempt was a farmhouse with several pieces of antique agricultural machinery outside its barn; two villagers had independently directed us there after we had given them the house number. There was of course no number on the door but I still knocked on it. No answer. Vasile, my driver, hollered. No answer. After about ten minutes, an old lady sauntered down the track towards us and gave us one of those lighthouse smiles that illuminate the darkest of moods. She came up to the car window, still smiling, and after a few words with Vasile, sweetly pronounced that she was Ion's eighty-four-year-old mother, her house was Number Sixty Four, his house was Number Sixty Nine and pointing to the centre of the village, gave clear instructions as to how to get there. She then temporarily purloined my mobile, dialled a number, barked a few concise instructions down it and handed it back to me with that same winning smile. Later I found out that widow Micurescu's acumen and energy are legendary throughout the village. Maybe there is something in the water in these parts because Vasile, who was a well-built fifty-something, had told me on the drive down that his eighty-five-year-old father consistently beat him at arm wrestling—"Skandabeg!"[110]

The Micurescus had bought the former hunting lodge of the Mocsonyi family—it had passed through several owners since 1948—from the receiver in 2001 and it was here that Delia, alerted by her mother-in-law, was waiting for me by the front gate. She had thoughtfully recruited the village English teacher, Teodora Anca, to join her since when we had previously corresponded, we had worked out that our common language was French and for me that meant a fair amount of words would 'go missing'.

---

[110] Skandabeg was the Albanian national hero who kept the Ottomans at bay for over twenty years in the fifteenth century. His connection with arm wrestling is unclear!

A welcome *ţuica* and then to work: How was my programme? Was this or that idea OK? Was I sure? Delia volunteered that she was the author of four books about Bata—a regional history, a novel dedicated to her husband, a bicentennial history of the school and, work in progress, an 'exclusive' study of Bata folklore. I particularly felt drawn to the title of her book, *Bata Ioane*, which she had written as a historical novel to commemorate her fifteenth wedding anniversary. *Bata* is a term of endearment that applies to the over 50s and implies respect, affection, wisdom and honour, a secular version of the *gerontos* afforded by the monks to Abbot Cleopa. On a more serious note, Delia had tracked down Dumitru Cătănescu, an eye-witness to Petru Groza's[111] disgraceful threat to King Michael in 1948: 'either you go or I will kill 1,000 students.' Cătănescu, a member of the Royal Bodyguard, had drawn his pistol and told his sovereign that he had no choice other than to leave.

The ladies took me on a conducted tour of Number Sixty Nine Commune Bata. The mansard could sleep thirty-eight students in the summer in comfort; the attic another ten in discomfort. Here was the new lake complete with fish and Japanese bridges. Here was the barbeque area. Here was the shower area for children in the summer. There was the site for a new village museum. There was the site for an outdoor theatre. There was Ion's site for a menagerie of pheasants and other wildlife. It amazed me what they had achieved in the space of five years.

Delia's husband , Ion, joined the party after his daily drive back from Arad where he is a councillor on the regional assembly. Far from the archetypal Romanian politician, Ion is a man of the land, passionate about the country way of life and, with his wife, equally passionate about its culture and history. Doubling reassuring then to learn that he chaired the committees on culture, health and education and if that wasn't enough, headed the Regional Development Committee for the Department of Arad. For Ion, infrastructure meant

---

[111] Prime Minister of the Soviet puppet government in 1945. Known as The Red Bourgeois, the immensely wealthy Groza created the conditions for a complete take-over by the Communists..

mains water and sewage in the villages rather than a multiplicity of grandiose schemes, such as scarcely used motorways, expensive TGVs and environmentally unfriendly airports; education meant keeping students in school by employing motivational teachers like Teodora; health meant accessibility for all, especially the old and the disadvantaged. Politics aside, Ion's great love was hunting and what better way to start dinner than with Cumberland sausages made out of a wild boar shot by Ion.

I asked him about the trophies on the walls, presumably leftovers from the great pre-War days of the Mocsonyi family.

"Certainly not", he replied. "This *cerb* (red deer) was shot three years ago, that *câprior* (roe deer) last year and that *lopâtar* (fallow deer) six months ago".

"What about this collection of wild boar tusks?"

"Well, you have just eaten the owner of that one."

As head of the local Hunting Association, Ion is charged with maintaining the levels of wild life at an 'optimum': this includes bears, wolves, deer and wild pigs. To discharge this task involves a delicate balance between culling and husbandry. Furthermore the Association faces a particular porcine problem; should the wild pigs, who enjoy a nocturnal forest diet of acorns and given half a chance supplement it with a maize, fruit and newly-cut hay, damage the village crops, then the Association must compensate the farmers with cash payments. The answer to this potentially ruinous threat, was to go and feed the wild pigs in the forests with seasonal delicacies such as maize at this time of year. Of course, this also helps to set up the perfect shot!

As if he had not got enough on his plate, Ion also owned and managed a pig farm with 300 Large Whites.

The Mocsonyis were originally Aromanians: Petru served with Prince Eugene of Savoy at the Battle of Zenta in 1697 and thus started a long and profitable relationship with Vienna which culminated in the ennoblement of Andrei as Baron Mocsonyi of Foen by Joseph II in 1780. The Bulci line for the sake of simplicity starts with Andrei (b.1816), who married Josephina, Countess Sztárag, also Baroness Brudern. That may not seem important but their son, Zeno (b.1842), married Maria, Countess Sztáray, which goes to show how crucial a single consonant can be in Hungarian genealogy. Zeno and Maria had one son, Anton (or Antonio) (b.1882), who became a distinguished diplomat and later a senior courtier with the title Le Grande Veneur. Between them, the Mocsonyi clan owned the castles of Bulci, Birchiş, and Căpâlnaş in the Mureş valley, Foen South-west of Timişoara and Vlaicoveţ in Serbia. They sounded rather gregarious and wild for Delia recounted how they would all assemble on Christmas Eve in the house where I was staying and, after a ribald evening of carols, dressing up and dancing, would set off in their carriages at midnight to join the family matriarch at her castle at Foen on the Serbian border in time for Christmas Day celebrations—that meant a 100-mile night-time drive through forests in the depths of winter!

It may come as a surprise therefore to learn that the Romanians of the Banat hold the Mocsonyi family in the highest esteem. The reasons are two-fold. In 1848, the Year of Revolution, when it looked like the Habsburg Empire was about to unravel, the Romanians of the Banat, like the Transylvania Romanians at Blaj, had gathered in great numbers outside the town of Lugoj to articulate their demands. Without the resources of the Hungarians who had openly rebelled against their Austrian masters, the Banat Romanians had to play their hand with great skill, more so since Vienna was playing them off against the Serbs of the Banat who were equally strident in their claim for self-determination. Prince Alexander Mocsonyi counselled non-violence and moderation, a cautious, long-term strategy that avoided the wrath visited on the rebellious Hungarians by the Emperor's Russian allies. Then after the *Ausgleich*, the Prince was one of the twenty-five Romanian deputies who took their seats in the Parliament in Budapest. On 30 June 1870, he eloquently pleaded in favour of racial equality and compromise, arguing, like Archbishop Şaguna of Transylvania, that the unsatisfactory laws that the newly-empowered Hungarians were busy codifying, once sanctioned, could only be undone by legal means. His plea went unheeded.

It was Victor Styrcea's younger brother, Ionel, who had the good fortune to be adopted as his heir by the great Count Anton Mocsonyi. Patrick Leigh Fermor was staying with Count Jeno Hunyadi not far from here: 'A cousin of the Countess lived at Bulci, a few miles away, and their family's adherence to Rumanian causes in the pre-war Hungarian parliament had stood him in good stead when it was over. With a high-bridged nose and receding chin, fiftyish, cosmopolitan, urbane and clever, he was an excellent shot, and King Carol had appointed him Grand Veneur du Roi, or Master of the Royal Hunt; the position involved game, beaters and shooting rather than horses and hounds.'

Ivor Porter in his book *King Michael of Romania* writes: 'It was during the summer of 1942 that a nucleus of resistance to the Antonescu regime began to form around the King. In March Baron Mocsonyi had recommended his adopted son for employment in the King's household—the highly intelligent, highly strung Baron Ionel Mocsonyi Styrcea became head of Chancery to the Marshal of the Court Solescu, and three months later, when Solescu left, was made acting Marshal.'

In the coup against Marshal Antonescu in August 1944, Ionel detained the Marshal and locked him up in the safe containing the King's stamp collection. The next challenge for Ionel was to prevent a Communist takeover. He 'bought a great quantity of arms' and organised the National Resistance Movement[112]. Not surprisingly, he was arrested and put on trial.

In the second half of 1947, the Romanian Communists unleashed their full fury against the country's other political parties, arresting numerous opposition politicians and driving others into exile. The

---

[112] Between 10,000 and 40,000 people were involved in this movement between 1948 and the early 1960s of whom about 2,000 were killed by the Securitate. Spontaneous rather than premeditated, it was based on the tradition of *haiducs*, small groups of outcasts who had fought the Habsburgs in Transylvania. In the 1950s, a traveller came across a member of the resistance in the Carpathian Mountains who implored him to 'tell everyone that there is still a place in the Kingdom of Romania which has not bowed to Communism. As long as our heads are on our shoulders, this corner of the country will be free. Tell the people not to lose faith, for the day will come when the whole of Romania will be free. Pray God for it, so help us God.'

government dissolved the National Peasant Party and National Liberal Party, and in October prosecutors brought Iuliu Maniu, his deputy, Ion Mihalache, and other political figures to trial for allegedly conspiring to overthrow the government. Maniu and Mihalache received life sentences; in 1956 the government reported that Maniu had died in prison four years earlier.

In a letter to Dennis Deletant, the foremost historian of post-1945 Romania, Ionel lists the details of 'my successive jails during the fifteen years and seventeen days of uninterrupted total "legal" detention':

6 September 1947
Arrested at Castel Bulci

7 September-12 November 1947
Interned at the Ministry of Security

12 November 1947—30 June 1949
Imprisoned in solitary confinement at Craiova's Principal Penitentiary, after being found guilty in the trial of Iuliu Maniu.

July 1949
In-patient of Dr Gerota's former clinic in Bucharest with dangerously 'advanced atrophic cachexia', a condition brought on by enforced malnutrition.

1 August 1949—22 October 1949
Imprisoned in solitary confinement at Craiova's Principal Penitentiary

Mid-November 1949
Summoned to appear before the Timişoara court on charges of wartime profiteering; brought to the court in chains, not allowed counsel (they had all been arrested), acquitted but not released.

23 October 1949—25 September 1950
Interned in political section of Cetatea Timişoarei

25 October 1950—16 May 1951
Interned in the military prison at Casa Verde, six miles from Timişoara.

16 May 1951—18 March 1952
Interrogated at Securitate prison in Timişoara as accessory to the trial for treason of the Minister of Justice, Lucretiu Patrascanu[113].

18 March 1952—6 April 1954
Interrogated in the Ministry of Interior's basement II, known as the 'submarine', an underground complex below the river Dâmboviţa in Bucharest where 'the air was conditioned according to one's "positive answers"'; then at the 'Malmaison' Milice jail on Calea Plevnei.

6 April 1954:
Found guilty by the military tribunal sitting at Cotroceni in Bucharest.

7 April 1954—15 February 1955
Started fifteen years of hard labour at Auid's Zarca prison, Count Mercy[114] d'Argenteau's unicellular castle for close confinement

16 February 1955—3 April 1955
Jilava and 'Malmaison' for further interrogation re SIS[115] and CIA contacts.

4April 1955—13 August 1956
Zarca

September 1956
Two weeks interrogation at 'Malmaison'.

---

[113] Held in custody since 1948, Patrascanu was executed in April 1954. He conducted his own defence with the words: 'I have nothing to say, except [that I] spit on the charges brought against me.'
[114] Military and civil governor of the Banat from 1716-34.
[115] British Secret Intelligence Service.

13 August 1956—20 July 1957
Jilava prison outside Bucharest.

21 July 1957—1 June 1959
Piteşti PP including underground solitary confinement during the summer of 1958.
[Father George Calciu, a fellow inmate, explained in an interview how the Pitesti experiment had four distinct steps. First, a team of guards and experienced prisoners would beat incoming prisoners and kill one or two, whoever appeared to be a leader. Next, they would begin to 'unmask', which meant requiring prisoners, under torture, to verbally renounce everything they believed: 'I lied when I said "I believe in God," I lied when I said "I love my mother and my father."' Thirdly, prisoners were forced to denounce everyone they knew, including family. Because a diabolical element of this plan was to employ fellow prisoners as torturers, the targeted prisoners knew no rest. The abuse never ceased, not even in the cell, and every torture imaginable was employed. Last, in order to show they had truly become 'the communist man', these prisoners were required to join the ranks of torturers and assist in the 're-education' of new prisoners. This last step was the most unbearable. 'It was during this fourth part that the majority of us tried to kill ourselves,' said Fr. George[116].]

2 June 1959—7 October 1961
Incarcerated in Dej prison.

8 October 1961
Transferred by train to Brasov and then by Black Maria to new Malmaison (highly secret unicellular reclusion)

---

[116] Father Calciu remained in prison until 1964, when he was released as a result of a general amnesty. He taught French and New Testament studies at the Theological Seminary in Bucharest until he was abruptly dismissed in 1978 for speaking out in defense of religious freedom and human rights. The next year, he was again arrested by the authorities and sentenced to ten years in prison. His cellmates told him that they had been specially selected to assassinate him but they instead came to place their faith in Christ through him. International pressure resulted in Father Calciu's release in 1984 but he was compelled to leave the country.

4p.m. 28 November 1962
Released. 'With a 2nd Class ticket for Cumpulung-Muscel in my torn London jodhpurs' hind pocket but with no cash left to buy a packet of Pulgar gaspers or an apple to try my third set of dentures on!'

Ionel was brought out of Romania by his wife and lived in Switzerland until his death in 1995. For much of that time he assisted King Michael and strove to restore him as King of a free Romania.

He fails to mention in his letter that all his teeth had been forcibly extracted and his finger and toenails pulled out. Michael recalled how his uncle 'would never sleep in a room with the curtains drawn or windows shut.'

A little expedition consisting of Ion, Delia, Teodora and myself set out to visit the last vestiges of the Mocsonyi family, an era which started when Ioan Mocsonyi married Iuliana Panaiot in 1804 and their nine children all needed housing! Before we left, Delia took me on a whirlwind tour of Bata village and I introduced myself to two very polite primary school classes, three extremely respectful secondary school classes, three bemused schoolteachers, and the Mayor, only missing out on the village priest and policeman. We also looked in on the village museum, an impressive collection of wooden utensils and implements, excellent peasant costumes for both sexes and all sizes, and fascinating documents and photographs, all put together by—no prizes for guessing—Delia.

Bulci lay about half an hour away and we passed through several villages, all sharing similar characteristics of wide green verges planted with fruit trees, open brick rather than plastered houses and barns constructed out of timber with wattle stresses. Currently a TB hospital belonging to Arad Health Authority, Bulci's thirty-six patients were installed in a house by the main gate, leaving the main residence empty. The kitchen wing which doubled up as servant quarters was still functioning and three ladies, all clad in grey felt coats fastened with cord, presented themselves to us as guides. Baron Mocsonyi had remodelled the house in 1904 as a comfortable mansion to entertain his guests from Bucharest and Budapest; today, it is on its last legs. Ceilings are collapsing, the external plasterwork bitten off by the unrelenting weather has exposed underlying brickwork, the parquet floors are contracting and splitting and the garden and arboretum abandoned to capricious nature. I have however seen houses in a far worse condition in Transylvania and there is a slim chance that the house could be saved if funds were quickly forthcoming. Positioned on the banks of the River Mureş, Bulci witnessed the XIII Roman Legion pitch its camp here and many hundreds of years later, the execution of thirteen Hungarian generals after the collapse of the 1848 Revolution. It deserves to survive.

Unfortunately, Alexandru Mocsonyi's house at Birchiş did not survive; it was burnt down in 1918, most likely arson, and only the planted parkland of great oaks remains. However, in the next door village of Căpâlnaş, the Mocsonyi house modelled on *une petite Trianon* and built in 1860, continues in use as a hospital for the mentally-ill. The story of its present ownership is intriguing. A former cook of the castle was in possession of a document stating that her son was the illegitimate child of Count Jenö Teleki, the husband of Ecaterina Mocsonyi, the Castle's last chatelaine. When the Communists evicted the family from the castle in 1948, the legitimate heir, Count Bubi Teleki, fell on hard times, became a beggar and ignominiously died in Zam Hospital in 1989. Come 1990, the cook's son produced the letter and is now the owner of Căpâlnaş Hospital which has three more years of its contract left to run.

We wandered round the grounds, yet again the arboretum had become a jungle, in search of the administrator. In front of the main entrance with its fluted Corinthian columns was a life size stone statue of a red deer stag with a strange horizontal cut around its middle. The explanation for this was that before their arrest by the Communists, the family members were rumoured to have hidden their jewellery and money inside the stag. So seriously was this story taken that party officials ordered for the statue to be cut into two. Of course, they found nothing. The administrator finally found us rather than we finding him which would have been difficult for me since he was small, round and dressed in a track suit and trainers with a woolly hat covering most of his head; that part of his face left uncovered was home to a luxuriant moustache. In every respect, he was identical to those Baile Herculane football coaches.

The presence of Ion was a godsend to the administrator since he was able to table a list of all the defects of the property and bend the good councillor's ear about a host of other pressing problems. Delia and I wandered around the corridors and rooms, exchanging greetings with the patients when they passed by; most were elderly and looked sad, timid and distrait. Contrary to many accounts of life inside these institutions in Romania, there was no evidence here of negligent nursing; the impression was one of exemplary care by a dedicated team of doctors, nurses and cleaners. In the centre of the castle, there was what the Romanians describe as a *'luminator'*, a large rectangular glass roof that was replicated by a similar glass awning on the first floor, both of which allowed light to illuminate the corridors and recesses which led off the quadrangular design. It was horrible to learn that Count Teleki's young daughter, Mandy, had fallen over the banisters when running down a corridor and died after falling into the well through the glass window.

It was to Căpâlnaş that the young Patrick Leigh Fermor made his way in 1934 as he 'loped exhausted through the long shadows' on his epic walk to Istanbul. He remembers[117] his host as 'a tall, spreading, easy-going, middle-aged man, with gold-rimmed spectacles and a remarkably intelligent, slightly ugly and very amusing face' and his hostess as 'tall, dark-haired, fine-looking, very kind and very intelligent'. Life at the house revolved around the library from where Count Jenö masterminded his world-class collection of moths, a hobby very much in the traditions of this great Transylvanian family of polymaths, bibliophiles, explorers and politicians.

The last house on our list, but this time with only a tentative Mocsonyi connection, was the castle at Săvâşin lying on the North

[117] Leigh Fermor: *Between the Woods and the Water.*

bank of the Mureş and the property of former King Michael of Romania. Normally it was a simple drive, crossing an iron bridge and then straight into the town of Săvâşin. However the bridge was now a skeleton of creaking girders under repair and to avoid a twenty mile detour, Ion had made a cunning plan. We parked up on the South bank, walked like death-defying trapeze artists along rickety planks fifty foot above the river, clambered down muddy ladders onto the far bank where we were met by a friend of his—the Finance Director of Săvâşin Town Council—and driven to the gates of the castle.

On the site of a seventeenth century hunting lodge later given to the Counts Forray by Joseph II (and later burnt down in the 1784 and 1848 revolutions) Săvâşin is a pretty yellow ochre Maria Theresa-style neo-classical manor house set in a twenty hectare park above the River Mureş. Bought by King Michael from Count Hunyadi in 1942, he appointed Ionel Styrcea its administrator in February 1943 and by Christmas that year the house was ready for occupation. Out of earshot from Bucharest, it soon became the focal point of the young King's plan to remove Marshal Antonescu from power and to take Romania out of the war. In January 1948, after the King had been coerced into abdicating by the Soviet Union's Romanian puppets, Groza and Gheoghiu-Dej, the Royal train left Bucharest and passed through Săvâşin on its way to Lausanne. It stopped and Bibi Popescu, the then administrator of the estate, got off with Azo, the King's Alsatian. It remained as government property after 1948—the Ceausescus stayed here once—until 2001 when it was returned to its rightful owners, the Romanian royal family.

On our way back to Bata, Ion offloaded Delia, Teodora and me into a Dacia pick-up truck driven by Dan, the son of the Mayor of Bata, so that we could visit a hunting lodge at the end of five miles of rough forest tracks. Ion's old Mercedes was not up to it and anyway he had far more important matters to attend to—he had to feed the wild boar. Young Dan nervously set off down the logging track, worried that he would get stuck in a rut miles from the main road with the Departmental Councillor's wife, the village English teacher and a foreigner of unknown temper. His fears were groundless as he skilfully negotiated seemingly impassable potholes and soon we reached the little lodge built on the site of a former castle. Sited just off a ridge, on one side the lodge confronted dense ranks of oaks and on the other, enjoyed magnificent views over a panorama of distant forests. How cosy it was inside with a kitchen, dining room with vast tiled stove and in the loft, accessed by a trap door, beds for seven. With its own well and generator, this was the ultimate get-away-from-it-all hideout except for the multiple tracks of wild pigs, which suggested that they thought of it as home as well.

Ion and Delia gave me a lift to Arad; they were heading to Nadlac for the Hunters' Ball. What fun it sounded! Ion was permanently on his mobile organizing the big shoot at Bata the day after the ball, often juggling three concurrent callers on the line. Fortunately, the car seemed to know its own way to Arad. The occasion would see the election of The Most Patient Wife of a Hunter and the promotion of the keenest hunters to Chevalier de Chasse. Singing and dancing would go on long into the night. What better place to end my journey than this town where I had picked up the first thread of the Ratius of Nadlac. But it was not to be since I had to return to Timişoara the following day. Instead, I had a chance to explore Arad, where previously I had driven through at 2 a.m. one rainy morning on my way back to England and my only memories were a blur of elegant nineteenth century buildings eerily lit by dirty street lamps.

Arad straddles the River Mureş, the great glittering thread of Transylvanian commerce and trade for two thousand years. It was down this river that salt was exported to the rest of Europe, raising in modern terms millions of pounds for the Hungarian and then Habsburg treasuries. Originally mined on the surface by the Romans — salina is pure Latin — the industry developed into massive subterranean mines, the largest at Turda and Praid, others at Vizakna, Kolozs, Desakna and Maros Ujvar. This great river joined the Tisa sixty miles to the West of me at Szeged, from where they both flow into the Danube at Slankamen. The names of rivers reveal their antiquity—Mureş, Maros in Hungarian, Μαριξ in Greek, probably originated as a Thracian word for 'swampy' or 'boggy'.

The problem for a tourist in Arad is that there is nothing particularly distinguished about it. The fort is of a late eighteenth century design by Harsch in the manner of Vauban and annoyingly still occupied by the army. The old town square, Avram Iancu, although modernized in the nineteenth century, manages to retain its colourful eighteenth century charm save for an enormous 1960 Soviet-style war memorial—in fact, the three figures clutching Tommy guns all look like Russian soldiers, which presumably they are since the Hungarians and Romanians were both on the other side. The grandiose theatre is of a standard Viennese 1874 neo-classical design as is the Palace of Administration (1876). The Aurel Vlaicu University building (1894) with a dash of Rococo, the National Bank building (1906), the Cultural Palace (1913) with its mish-mash of different styles and the Church of St Anton of Padua (1904) complete the Imperial architectural identity parade. Even the Orthodox Cathedral was built in the Baroque style in 1865. I should mention that there is a gigantic new multi-domed Orthodox Cathedral nearing completion.

For Hungarians, Arad has great historical importance for it was here in 1848 that General Josef Bem marshalled his revolutionary forces to regain the liberty that had evaded the Hungarians since the fall of Buda in the sixteenth century. By the summer of 1849, the fortress, which had stoically held out for the Habsburg cause, surrendered but it was a pyrrhic victory for the rebels. Forty-six days later it was recaptured by the Emperor's Russian allies and overnight became a prison for 500 rebel officers. The Austrian General von Haynau, a sixty-four-year-old veteran of the Napoleonic Wars known for his uncompromising views about the sanctity of the Empire, ordered the execution of thirteen Hungarian generals in the castle precincts, an action that heaped opprobrium on him and ignominy on the Emperor. Legend had it that during the executions, Austrian soldiers were clinking their beer glasses to celebrate victory over the Hungarians. Since that time, Hungarians will not tap glasses when drinking beer. Haynau retired in 1850 to enjoy a life of travel. However his reputation preceded him and in London he was attacked and beaten up by draymen when visiting the Anchor brewery and was later saved from a mob in Brussels with some difficulty. When Garibaldi visited England in 1864, he insisted on visiting the brewery to thank the men who had attacked the general for Haynau was notoriously remembered in Italy as the Hyena of Brescia.

In case I was missing something, I walked to the Palace of Culture, found a side door marked *Museu* and entered. A lady appeared from behind a curtain and stared at me.

"I would like to visit the museum."

Silence. She beckoned me behind the curtain.

"Two lei."

Tickets were handed over and I looked at her imploringly for further instructions. She made a sign with an upward motion of her head.

"Upstairs? Thank you."

The mime complete, I headed up the stairs and found another lady to whom I proudly showed my tickets. She took no interest and with a sideways nod of her head in the style of her colleague downstairs, indicated that I was clear to go round.

There was, not surprisingly, a strong Romanian nationalistic flavour to the exhibition. George Doya, the barbecued peasant leader, had a stand for his merry band of cut-throats who had burnt Arad to the ground in 1514 (the city was Hungarian at the time). But wait a minute—surely George was really a Székelys captain by the name of György Dózca, who had first appeared in the Ox-roast revolt in 1506, when the Székelys protested agiant this traditional tax on the birth of a male heir to the King? Horea, Closca and Crisan also had a stand to commemorate their 1784 uprising against their hated Austrian and Hungarian landlords in Transylvania, when a frenzied mob of peasants had gone on a killing spree up and down the Mureş valley. The lawyer Iancu Avram featured for his 'heroic' role in the

Revolution of 1848 when he sided with the Habsburgs in the belief that they would recognise Romanian nationality[118], only to find himself completely marginalized by Vienna a year later and ended up a drunken vagabond. And of course there was plenty about the triumph of Trianon. No mention of Prince Ferenc Rákóczi II's *kuruc* attack on Habsburg-held Arad during the valiant Hungarian uprising of 1704-12, when this extraordinary gifted man had raised an 80,000-strong army with international political support to take on the colonial rule of Vienna.

Why is it that Romanian Museums still have this tendency to put a spin on their history and view their evolution as a nation through rose-tinted glasses? I suspect it is more through the perpetuation of past bad practice than today's deliberate design for there is no point in inducting future generations with a distorted and foolish version of the past.

Romanian history has been dictated by the position she has occupied on the crossroads of five Empires—Roman, Bulgarian, Ottoman, Austrian and Russian; thus for most of the last two thousand years, she found herself in the wrong place at the wrong time. That was her fate, not her fault. The fact is that through the adroit efforts of her rulers and through the perseverance and resilience of her people, Romania has not only survived but often prospered. And she has had her share of good fortune in that the Austrians drove the Turks out of Transylvania and the Banat in the late seventeenth century; good fortune in that the result of the post-Crimean War map of Europe led to the formation of the United Provinces of Wallachia and Moldavia; and more good fortune in that the outcome of the First World War, despite the humiliating peace treaty signed with Germany in 1918, resulted in Trianon.

When I reached the last room, the door marked 'Exit' would not open, so I trudged back to the entrance to leave the way I had come

---

[118] It could be argued that his distrust of Kossuth and hence refusal to combine forces with the Hungarians led to the failure of the Hungarian rebellion. Whether Avram's band of 20,000 ill-equipped peasants led by untrained officers would have made any difference is a moot point.

in by. This produced consternation with the 'nodding heads' and a third member of the 'Curating Mummers' escorted me all the way back, fiddled with the locks and mysteriously opened the door as if by magic. Not a word was exchanged between us. At the bottom of the stairs, another lady, taller and possibly more important, silently eye-balled me, watching my efforts to find the unsigned exit with disdain.

Maybe foreigners were not meant to visit the Arad History Museum but I can vouch that fresh air rarely smelt so good. However, I was not prepared to give up on Arad and set off on foot the next morning to explore Aradul Nou or New Arad, new in the sense that the Turks established it on the South bank of the Mureş in 1553. Other than a pretty Catholic Church of 1812 and a good Baroque house of about 1800 opposite it, there is little to commend the town. Crossing back, I spotted a throng of people carrying heavy plastic bags, which meant there was a market somewhere close by. I found it in the Piata Catedralei where covered stalls brimmed with mounds of potatoes, mixed bunches of carrots and parsnips, trays of apples of all varieties, boxes of cabbages, strings of onion and garlic, jars of honey, bags of eggs, all vended by cheery yokels whose ruddy faces contrasted to the pall of their city-dwelling customers. Inside the covered hall, bins of bread the shape and size of footballs were doing a brisk trade; the cheese sellers with glistening white mounds of sheep cheese to offload had to wait to confirm their sales until the housewives had completed their finger-tip tasting.

Between the market and the old town square was the Bohus Palace, a secessionist building built in 1912 by Baron Lazlo Bohus but now sadly in a terrible state of repair, a bit like the historical display in the Museum. But I was not disheartened because Josif Matula, the current President of Arad Council, is on record as saying "if we were to advocate for Arad County, we would concentrate on the past, its present but mostly on its future...the spirit of the city was shaped by its inhabitants: Romanians, Hungarians, Germans, Serbs, Jews."

Add to that, Point 4 of the Declaration of Timişoara in 1990:

'Side by side with the Romanians, there were Hungarians, Germans, Serbians, members of other ethnic groups who sacrificed their lives for the cause of the Revolution. They have all been co-inhabiting our city in peace and goodwill for centuries. Timişoara is a European city where all the nationalities have rejected and reject nationalism. All the chauvinists of the country, no matter whether they are Romanians, Hungarians or Germans, are invited to come to Timişoara to a re-education course in the spirit of tolerance and mutual respect, the sole principles reigning in the future European House.'

Romania has finally come of age in Arad.

CHATER EIGHT

TREKKING WITH THÖKÖLY

Driving North from Bucharest on a late May evening in pouring rain through a deepening gloom occasionally illuminated by vicious shards of lightning accompanied by thunderous barrages—what the American James Noyce, travelling in Romania in the 1800s, described as "the revolving squadrons of heaven's artillery whose reverberations (become) more terrific every moment"—the prospect of walking across the Carpathians began to pall. Like all worthy ideas, it had started innocently enough when I had met up with a group of Romanian eco-tourism operators in London a few months before. Over dinner at Richard and Bronwyn Clutterbuck's, I had found myself sitting next to Dan Marin, a font of extraordinary knowledge about bears and wolves and all matters wildlife—and, most importantly, a shared passion for the obscure but dramatic Battle of Zărneşti in 1690. Dan had convinced me that unless I actually walked the route taken by the opposing armies, I would never understand the real story and so it was at his house next to the Hungarian Catholic Church in the town of Zărneşti that I finally arrived, soaking wet after changing a tyre that had mysteriously shredded itself on the road to Predeal and in desperate need of a ţuica.

Zărneşti lies just to the North of Bran, a village best known for Queen Marie's castle, now cynically marketed as Dracula's. The town itself is deceptively Saxon for the houses all conform to that style of architecture, L-shaped edifices set laterally to the road with gardens and orchards spilling out behind them; in truth it is Romanian and the inhabitants wisely employed expert Saxon builders to construct their homes, particularly after unification with Romania in 1920. The town centre has two typical nineteenth century Austro-Hungarian style buildings, one, a former hotel, is painted yellow ochre with its pediments picked out in white, the other, now the town court, dark purple-pink; opposite them stands the sixteenth century Orthodox church of St.Nicholas, encircled by a floral frieze of livid orange lilies and rampant pink roses. In 1782 the interior walls were painted in the traditional iconographic style with flat-faced impassive Saints lining the walls of the pointed-vault knave, their long fingers guiding the worshipper towards the ornate eighteenth century iconostasis, a curious mix of gold and lavender painted lime wood indented with rows of glass-covered icons, masked by the mirrored reflection of the passing sun. The little enclosed porch is charmingly decorated with peacocks, dog roses, cornflowers and succulent bunches of grapes hanging off a straggly vine, which all combine to offset the stern and unforgiving figures of St Peter and St Paul flanking the entrance.

Although by the end of the nineteenth century Zărneşti was a prosperous forest-products town with its own mill exporting paper as far a field as Vienna, in 1938 life for its inhabitants dramatically changed when a government ammunition factory was erected outside the town. From being an innocuous timber and farming town, it now assumed the importance of a strategic asset and this sobriquet continued through to 1989. During Communist rule, over 15,000 people were employed at the Tohan[119] 'Bicycle' plant, making everything from pistol bullets to rockets and, yes, bicycles but for appearances sake only[120]. Today, only 700 employees remain though the business has

---

[119] Turkish for falcon.
[120] There is a record of an export order for 100,000 to USA: they were all found to be defective.

managed to survive the tortuous transition to the market economy by concentrating on high value export products, namely 82mm and 120mm rockets proudly exhibited at Expomil in 2005. In 1983, an explosion ripped through the factory, killing 56 people and injuring many more. Eight days after this disastrous event, the government blandly announced "Two killed in accident at bicycle factory."

Dan's mother was born in Zărneşti but, when she married, moved to Dobârlau, a village to the East of Prejmer just beyond Brasov. Left a widow with three young children, she struggled to make ends meet; finding himself the male head of the household aged just eight, Dan worked in the potato fields during the long summers determined to play his part as a provider. Finally despairing of life by a creek which regularly flooded twice a year, the family moved back to Zărneşti. Not surprisingly Dan went to work in the ammunition factory when he left school and it was there that he met his wife Luminiţa. It was a restrictive existence; conversations about work were forbidden and there was a heavy military and Securitate presence to enforce this rule. Despite this security, Dan remembers a large sign at the entrance of the works stating "No foreigners allowed in"! He recalls a further absurdity in 1985 when the Romanian government embarked on a peace campaign with the declared aim of reducing arms production by 5%. A huge poster was erected outside the main gate, urging the workers "Let's fight together (with our Communist brethren) against the arms race." Meanwhile, inside the factory, production targets were increased. Such hypocrisy was not lost on the average worker.

With little future at the ammunition plant, in 2000 Dan replied to an advertisement looking for people to join the Carpathian Large Carnivore Project (1993-2003), a programme funded by the World Wildlife Fund and private donors.

"I was already having to moonlight in the forest as Luminiţa and I were bringing up three children." Dan explained. "I used to walk up through the gorges with a stack of young trees on my back, up onto the high pastures and then plant them—mind you, the soil was mainly rock and it took an age to bed one in! When I got home after the walk back, I was so tired that I couldn't hold anything in my hands. There were moments when Luminiţa had to spoon feed me".

The aim of the Project was to study the relationship between man and wild life, especially bears and wolves, in the Carpathian Mountains and to see how they interacted and thus co-existed[121]. Before long, Dan applied to go on a wildlife guiding course organised by the Project and today runs a successful eco-tourism company based on the *Piatra Craiului* (King's Rock) National Park and the Fagaras Mountains, a vast tract of wilderness where human settlements are so scarce that one can walk 60 kilometres without encountering a house or village.

Although my interest in the Battle of Zărneşti revolves around the central character of the mercurial Imre Thököly, its political background spans nearly two centuries. In 1525, the young Hungarian King, Louis, was killed fighting the Ottomans at the Battle of Mohacs. The crown passed to his brother-in-law, the Habsburg Emperor. The Transylvanians, who up until then had been ruled by Hungary, had their own candidate in John Zápolyai and after a bitter struggle, the two parties agreed that the Habsburgs could keep the hereditary title of King of Hungary if the Transylvanians had the right to elect their own Prince. Meanwhile Budapest had fallen to the Ottomans in 1556, so all that remained of 'Royal Hungary' was the Northern hills (now Slovakia), the land West of Budapest and the South (now Croatia and Slovenia). A military frontier was soon established and for the next hundred years little changed save the Transylvanians became more independent and created a prosperous semi-autonomous Principality.

In 1664, the Habsburg Emperor, Leopold 1, won an unexpected victory over the Turks at Szint Gotthard, a crossing on the River Raab

---

[121] Although the Romanian Carpathians cover less than 1.5% of the European surface West of Russia, they are home to almost one third of all European large carnivores: it is estimated that the number of bears is over 5,000, that there are about 3,000 wolves, and some 2,000 lynx. This is the highest concentration of large carnivores anywhere in Europe.

to the South-east of Graz. However, with France pressing on his western territories and little money left in his exchequer, the Emperor signed a peace treaty with the Ottomans at Vasvár for a term of twenty five years. This truce infuriated his Hungarian subjects who had seen the first opportunity in over a hundred years to drive the Turks out of their country vanish before their eyes. Leopold was clearly acting against the interests of Hungary. He should be deselected as King and a new candidate elected by the Estates, one who would pledge to free the country from Ottoman rule. Before this could happen, a strong and efficient Hungarian national army had to be created. There was only one candidate suitable for the job of raising and leading it—Nikolai Zrinyi, the Ban of Croatia, a charismatic blend of soldier, poet and politician.

A week before he was due to meet with the Emperor in Vienna, on 18 November 1664, aged 44, Zrinyi was killed on his estate at Cakovec by a wild boar. The family motto, *Sors bona, nihil aliud*[122] on this occasion let him down. To this day, the Hungarians revere Zrinyi as "a warrior poet":

> '*As long as time endures, my name shall sound*
> *in distant Scythia, whence the Magyars came,*
> *in all lands where their exploits still resound,*
> *to men who know their honour and their fame.*
>
> *I have earned fame not only with my song*
> *But also with this warrior's sword men dread –*
> *I battled with the Turk my whole life long,*
> *And joyed to strew my homeland with their dead.*[123]'

Petar Zrinyi inherited the title of Ban on the death of his brother. Together with his bother-in-law, Fran Krsto ("F.K") Frangepan[124], Ferenc Nádasdy III, the Lord Chief Justice of Hungary, Count Erasmus von Tattenbach of Graz, the Palatine Ferenc Wesselényi and Cardinal

---

[122] Good fortune; nothing else.
[123] From Zrinyi's The Epilogue.
[124] A poet and the translator of Molière's *Georges Dandin* into Croatian.

György Lippay, Primate of Hungary and Archbishop of Esztergom, he formed a cabal to oppose Leopold. The bucolic Count István Thököly quickly pledged his name to the conspiracy. The Thökölys lived in the remote castle of Arva, high up in the foothills of the Tatra Mountains. Having made his fortune out of dealing in wine and cattle, Count István was depressed by the financial ramifications of the Treaty of Vasvár, which threatened to destroy his lucrative trade in driving Hungarian cattle up the Danube through Vienna to Germany. When Miklós Bethlen went to stay at Thököly's castle at Kežmarok in 1666, he found:

> "dreadful entertainment, drinking, dancing, music, hunting and other pastimes, filled more than a week, because István Thököly outstripped all the lords in Hungary, and the other Estates too, indeed, in that wickedness...the master of the house and the other guests around us were drunk every wretched day, and quite often twice in a day."

Wesselényi was now anxious to include the wealthy and influential Rákóczi family in his inner circle. Prince György Rákóczi II had been killed fighting the Ottomans at Oradea in 1660, leaving a 16-year-old son, Ferenc Rákóczi I, as his heir. With their stronghold at Mukachevo and estates at Sárospatak and Tokay, the family had become—along with the Eszterházys—the richest and most exalted in Hungary; they could travel a hundred miles without leaving their lands. Wesselényi came up with a proposition. He suggested marriage between Petar Zrinyi's beautiful, well-educated and high-spirited daughter, Helena, and Ferenc I. Rákóczi's mother, Zsófia, concurred for Helena "had beauty, a penetrating wit and a way to insinuating, that it was capable of gaining the most rebellious of hearts". After their wedding at the Castle of Zborov (today in North-east Slovakia), in 1666 the young couple moved to Sárospatak, one of Rákóczi's many stately homes.

So here were the highest nobles in Royal Hungary, Croatia and Styria—Zrinyis, Frangepáns, Wesselényis, Lippays, Thökölys, Rákoczis, Nádasdys and von Tattenbachs—lined up against their Emperor, more in anger than ambition, frustrated by Habsburg callousness and despairing of Leopold's despotism. But it was no use conspiring among themselves. Real help in finance and arms lay abroad and so the question in 1665, as they gathered at the remote Wesselényi castle of Muráň high up in the Nízke Tatry hills, was: To whom to turn for help?

There were several options. Poland's geographical proximity to the North of Royal Hungary made it the ideal ally. However, Michael Wisniowiecki, elected as King by the Polish Diet in June 1669, married Leopold I's sister Eleanora Maria the following year and thus the door firmly closed on Poland. Their next ploy was to try to put together an anti-Habsburg alliance with Venice and France. The Venetians were not interested since they were over-extended in the Mediterranean. However, France, an ally of the Ottomans since the days of Francis I, was a different story: Louis XIV saw an excellent opportunity to cause trouble for the Holy Roman Emperor without having too much involvement. His envoy in Vienna, Comte Grémonville, met with Nádasdy and Zrinyi in a village inn outside the city walls, all heavily disguised. Letters were set to Versailles and Constantinople, and envoys despatched to Edirne and Warsaw.

Soon the Magnates' Conspiracy, as it was later called, became the worst kept secret in Europe, a daily topic of conversation in the courts of Venice, Vienna, Warsaw and Constantinople. In 1668, a whispering campaign started against Nádasdy in Vienna. Among the more preposterous accusations circulated by the Emperor's agents were that he had set fire to the Emperor's apartment in Vienna, had offered the Emperor a toxic pastry and had poisoned the Emperor's water supply by dropping a dead dog into it.

Rumours about the conspiracy continued to circulate. Take the case of this account of Leopold's illness in April 1670:

"Indescribably gloomy was the chamber of the royal patient: the candles looked as if they burned in a tomb; the atmosphere was mephitic; the king's face wore the ghastliness of the grave; his sallow skin and sunken cheeks, with the thirst which nothing could assuage, gave indubitable signs that some unknown poison was at work upon him. The celebrated Milanese alchemist, the Chevalier Francis Barri, paused and looked round the room. "You are breathing a poisoned air," he said to the king. The patient's apartment was changed, other candles were brought, and from that hour the king began to recover. Within a month, Leopold was cured."

When the candles were analyzed it was found that the unused tapers contained over two and a half pounds of arsenic. A dog, which was given a piece of the wick to eat in its food, died within three hours. It is hard to imagine what motive the Jesuits, who were in charge of Leopold's quarters, could have had for his murder, and there is no evidence that this botched assassination attempt was the work of the Hungarians. The finger might point at Louis XIV, since Leopold had no heir at the time to inherit the possessions of the Spanish Habsburgs. The affair remains a mystery.

After five years of such rumours, Leopold was finally forced to act to forestall an imminent insurrection. When they heard that Protestant preachers in Upper Hungary were giving thanks to God for the Turkish victory over the Venetians in Crete and calling on the Porte to "rescue Hungary from oppression and Papist slavery" and that Ferenc Rákóczi I had summoned the leaders of the Protestant counties to Košice, the Emperor and his advisers reacted quickly and troops were ordered to quash the insurrection. Within weeks, all the ringleaders had been arrested.

In April 1671, Zrinyi, Nádasdy and Frangepán were found guilty of "an innumerable company of crimes and wickednesses" and sentenced to death. Petar Zrinyi's final letter to his wife, Anna Katarina, suggests a man who was never cut out to be a rebel leader:

"My dear Soul! I most humbly beg of you, that you would not grieve your self to excess, at the sight of this letter. Tomorrow, Ah madam, I must tell it you, Alas! Tomorrow about ten of the clock in the morning, we must lose our heads, I, and your brother. To day we have taken our last farewell each of other; and now I come also to take leave of you, my Dear Soul, for ever; entreating you that you will please to pardon me all things, whereby in all my life time, I have ever offended you. God be thanked, I am very well prepared for death, and fear nothing; having a sure hope that God who hath created me, will have pity on me, whom I shall also beseech, for I hope I shall tomorrow be in his presence, that we may see each other in eternal glory before his throne.... God preserve and bless you' and my daughter Aurora Veronica, Amen".

F.K. was distraught; he begged for a stay of execution, protesting he was too young to die and furthermore he was the last of his line. He wrote a last minute appeal to Leopold:

"Dread Sovereign, I am scarcely able to hold my pen for the great consternation wherewith I am seized by reason of the cruel and unexpected sentence which against me miserable wretch hath been pronounced this afternoon: my strength and courage fail me, O Emperor Most Gracious! To write to you, as my necessity requires, so as to excite in your Imperial Breast one small spark of mercy for the saving my life...Neustadt, 28 April about 11 o'clock at night."

The spark of mercy never materialised for Leopold could not have overruled his Privy Council. As they separated, ready for the scaffold, F.K. turned to Zrinyi and said: "I hope that tomorrow we shall embrace and kiss each other with greater joy and contentment than we have now done here below." It was the last time they were to see each other.

F.K. perhaps would prefer to be judged as a poet rather than a politician:

"*Right now come together to the glorious flag.*
Dispel from your heart all vapours of fury;
Put before you the shield of courage;
Dearer to you will be glory, fame and honour
Than one instant, one moment of living in shame:
He who dies honourably lives forever".

This last line served to inspire Hungarian patriots for centuries to come.

On 30 April 1671, Nádasdy was executed in the market square in the centre of Vienna. Hagi Ibrahim, the Turkish Chiaus, together with members of the nobility had been summoned to watch. After the event, they were forced to inspect the body. One witness wrote: "They saw the prince laid in a coffin, dressed in Hungarian attire, with his head on his chest, almost floating in the blood that half-filled the bier." The next morning, Zrinyi and Frangepán were executed in the square at Wiener Neustadt. It was a clumsy performance by the executioner: two blows of the axe fell before Zrinyi was cleanly decapitated. As for poor F.K., the first blow struck his right shoulder, and as he tried to raise himself from the ground, the second severed his head. On 1 December 1671, Count von Tattenbach was executed at Graz; three blows of the axe were needed to remove his head.

Vienna now pursued the Zrinyi family. Petar's son, Ivan Antun, was imprisoned in the mountain fortress of Kufstein, where he was held without trial for the next 30 years. His mother, Ana Katarina, banished to a Dominican convent in Graz, lost her mind and died in 1673. Her two daughters, Judita Petronela and Aurora Veronika, were both confined to convents in Zagreb and Klagenfurt respectively, where they died aged 47 and 75. The Zrinyi estates at Cakovec were confiscated.

The families of the other conspirators fared little better. All Wesselényi's property was confiscated, his widow imprisoned and the Emperor's captain destroyed the family's fortress at Strečno. In 1670, Count István Thököly was besieged at his castle at Likava and killed by Imperial troops, his body left to rot in the cellars for nine months. His son and heir, the 13-year-old Imre, was smuggled out of the castle dressed as a poor villager and then, disguised as a young Polish girl, was spirited through the Austrian lines to safety in Transylvania. His three daughters were sent to Vienna, where they were coerced into converting to Catholicism. Nádasdy's children, stripped of the right to use the family name, were compelled to call themselves Von Kreutz and the males made to wear red silk cords around their necks, imitating the mark made by the Imperial axe on their father.

One conspirator, Ferenc Rákóczi I, conspicuously avoided the executioner's axe. Following the intervention of his mother Countess Zsófia and her Jesuit contacts, Ferenc escaped with his life by paying

Căpâlnaş: post-operative stag

ROYAL TREASURE HUNT

Sărăşin: the Royal lodge

Arad

Joe Boyle

IN MEMORIAM

David Russell

Timişoara plague victims

a massive fine of 400,000 thalers, reduced from an initial demand for two million thalers. Despite his enormous wealth, Rákóczi had to borrow 100,000 from his mother, 20,000 from the Primate and 47,000 from the Jesuits. Forced to leave his castle at Sárospatak, he died at the family's manor house at Borša on 8 July 1676 leaving his glamorous and feisty widow, Helena Zrinyi, daughter Juliana, and three-month-old son Ferenc II.

For the Hungarians, the Magnates' Conspiracy had begun and ended in a shambles. It had never been conceived as a premeditated war of independence, for its origins lay in frustration and anger over the sudden Habsburg capitulation to the Ottomans at the Treaty of Vasvár. Hamstrung by lack of leadership after the untimely death of Nikolai Zrinyi, the conspirators stumbled along the road to perdition, their security compromised by indiscretion and their planning non-existent.

The military occupation now underway in Royal Hungary merely served to inflame Hungarian nationalism. Imperial troops pillaged, raped and committed acts of sacrilege against Catholic and Protestant churches alike. The soldiers, infrequently paid, made up for their lost wages by looting towns and villages. Furthermore, Leopold issued a decree that made every county responsible for the upkeep of each soldier on its territory. By June, after widespread protests, the amount had been halved but the levy still rankled.

A campaign in 1672 to close down the Protestant schools triggered riots in the towns of Upper Hungary. That summer Leopold decreed that all Protestant preachers should leave. Joined by the equally fervent Catholic Bishop Kollonics, Archbishop Szelepcsényi assembled a special court at Bratislava in January 1674. The results were quick and spectacular: 26 Protestant ministers were marched off to the galleys of Naples, 733 Protestant intellectuals exiled or imprisoned and under the personal direction of Kollonics, around 800 Lutheran churches were 'recovered' by the Catholics. Hamel

Bruynincx, the Dutch ambassador to Vienna, circulated an account of these events, causing profound unease throughout Protestant Europe. The response to this heavy-handed Habsburg strategy was predictable and dangerous: from August 1672 the *bujdosok* (from *bujdoso* meaning 'hiding'), small groups of political refugees and displaced persons, went underground or crossed into Transylvania and started a guerrilla war against the Imperial army. Prince Apafi of Transylvania acted as their patron and his right hand man, Count Mihály Teleki, became their de facto commander. International support from France followed, for the very existence of the *bujdosok* gave the lie to Leopold's claim that he had pacified Hungary.

Early encounters between the French-led *bujdosok* and the Imperial troops unleashed a savagery that was to characterise the war. In 1675, Imperial troops captured a French officer, the Comte de Dampierre. He refused to talk under interrogation and when left unguarded in his cell, he bit through his veins and bled to death. The following year, the Comte de Boham confronted General Kopp outside Košice. Kopp's Hungarian soldiers promptly deserted him, leaving him no option but to retreat behind the city walls. Enraged, he proceeded to execute six members of the Hungarian nobility who were his prisoners: two were roasted alive and the others impaled. From then on, woe betide any Imperial soldier captured by the *bujdosok*.

With no sign of immediate results, Mihály Apafi, the canny Prince of Transylvania, began to distance himself from the *bujdosok* insurrection and in 1678 his military sidekick, Mihály Teleki, relinquished command of the rebel forces to the dashing young Imre Thököly (who happened to be engaged to his beautiful widowed daughter). During the dramatic siege of the castle of Likava in 1670, Imre had been smuggled out by two noblemen and given refuge with the Teleki family. Dispossessed by Vienna of his family's estates, incensed by the aggressive activities of the Jesuits and deeply patriotic, the young Thököly was the perfect choice to lead the rebellion.

His tactics were 'hit and run', emerging out of the morning mist and disappearing into the evening gloom. He favoured open country where his horsemen excelled; he avoided fortified towns since he lacked siege engineers and logistical support. In October 1678, Thököly attacked the open town of Kremnica and other mining towns in Upper Hungary and made off with an enormous booty of coin and unminted silver, estimated at 180,000 ducats. His lieutenant, Colonel Joshua, a former monk who had forsaken his robes and turned Protestant, entered Austria with troops gathered from impoverished Hungarian families but contented himself with pillaging rather than a purposeful military campaign.

Leopold tentatively opened negotiations with Thököly at Sopron that winter. After listening to his demands, the Archbishop of Grán suggested that Thököly lay down his arms as a precondition of any talks. Thököly refused. Early in 1678, Thököly had met Helena Zrinyi, the beautiful widow of Ferenc Rákóczi I; by the following year, they were passionately and publicly in love. For Helena, it was a chance to get even with the Habsburgs who had beheaded her father, imprisoned her brother without trial, banished her two sisters to convent life and presided over the death of her grief-stricken mother. Her property on both sides of her family had been confiscated and given to the Imperial Chancellery. Even as Rákóczi's widow, save for her household expenses, all the revenues from his great estates went to Leopold since young Ferenc was his ward. So in 1680, another truce was arranged by Vienna with Thököly, who promptly asked the Emperor for permission to marry Helena. If his request was granted, he offered to convert to Catholicism and support the Emperor, providing his estates were returned. His request was refused.

Now the *bujdosok* became *kurucs* or rebels (from the Turkish word *kurudsch* for rebel); Thököly recaptured his estates at Lipto and Arva, and then took the key town of Košice. Helena was overjoyed:

"If Fortune has lately crowned you, it is love must settle your throne. You have subjects, but you have not any towns where you can keep your court. You may come to Mukachevo when you will, and settle there the seat of your empire. You shall reign, wherever I am

Sovereign. For you have been so long the Master of my Heart, it is but just you should be so of my Dominions."

In February 1681, Leopold, still in a conciliatory mood, summoned a Diet at Sopron. Thököly refused to attend; instead he sent three envoys to demand that Protestants should have rights to worship freely and to own property. Convinced that another war with France was imminent, Leopold afforded religious freedoms in Hungarian towns but ducked the property issue and the confiscated Protestant estates remained in Imperial and Catholic hands.

Sensing that Leopold was now vulnerable on both flanks, Thököly renewed his demands, including pardon for himself and his followers, religious freedom throughout Hungary and, finally, the hand of Helena. Aware that Thököly now had some 25,000 men under arms operating with impunity out of Transylvania, and given that the Turks had made peace with the Russians in February 1681, Leopold consented to Thököly's marriage to Helena. In return Thököly agreed to an armistice. And what a wedding it was. By the end the guests had consumed ten bulls, 36 lambs, 20 pigs, 80 sheep, 800 lbs of fish, two tons of honey; as well as 130 barrels of red wine and 150 of white, 40 barrels of beer and 25 of best Polish vodka. Nine days later, Thököly broke the armistice and seized three important towns in Upper Hungary.

That summer, the Imperial Ambassador to the Porte, Count Caprara, reported to Vienna that the Sultan was obstructing the negotiations to renew the Treaty of Vasvár, which was coming to the end of its term. In his opinion, it was clear that the Porte had another agenda. Thököly, having concluded a treaty with Paşa Ibrahim, was now officially recognised as an Ottoman vassal, Kara Mustafa granted him royal status and in August sent a crown in the name of the Sultan, although even Thököly had the sense to refuse the inflammatory title of King of Hungary. He settled for Prince of Central Hungary.

Leaving her children behind, Helena followed her new husband on campaign. When she had to remain at home, she wrote letters of great passion:

"May God spare me from the fate of living even in the safest of castles without my most beloved husband. I do not want it; it is for me a question of life and death. No misery can make me falter in my attachment to you. Would that you could stand fast by me! I am ready to go to you, even by foot, wherever you may happen to be. What a great thing true love has been, so my sweetest darling, we should rejoice together when fate smiles on us; and should misfortune becloud our sky, we should find consolation in sharing it with each other. Then we shall carry our cross together...."

Still Leopold sought conciliation and extended the truce, leaving Thököly unmolested. Finally in December, the true position of the Porte and Thököly was revealed to Leopold. There was to be no renewal of Vasvár unless the Imperial fort at Leopoldov was raised to the ground, a number of towns near Nové Zámky surrendered and Thököly recognised as King of Upper Hungary, which was to be under Turkish suzerainty. The note conveying this to Vienna read:

"We declare to you that the Count Thököly and some Hungarian Lords, forced by the bad treatment you have a long time shown them, violating the Rights and Privileges of the Kingdom, have rendered themselves our Tributaries and annexed their country to our Empire. Therefore we request you after notice given that they are under our Protection, to restore them their Estates, if you would not break the Truce and draw on you the Punishment your rashness shall deserve."

This was nothing less than a declaration of war. While Austria digested this unwelcome news and sent a reply that Ottoman law did not authorize the 'Protection of Rebels', the Sultan and his Sadrazam set off from Edirne on 30 March 1683 at the head of the imperial Ottoman army. Despite atrocious weather, they arrived at Belgrade in the first week of May, where after agreeing that the first objective was the capture of Györ, the Sultan handed over command to Kara Mustafa. Joined by the Crimean Khan and Thököly en route, the Sadrazam encamped at Györ where he decided it was too well defended. Instead, he gave orders for the army to advance to Vienna.

Suddenly Western Europe found itself once more threatened by a major Ottoman invasion. France, England, the Netherlands, Brandenburg and Spain sat on the sidelines for reasons of self-interest, but Pope Innocent XI managed to rally his German flock, with the German Diet voting money and Bavaria, Saxony and Brunswick-Luneburg sending men to fight. More importantly, Jan Sobiewski of Poland pledged a force of 40,000 men.

As the Turks massed for their attack on Vienna, prayers were offered to Allah: "Blow us with thy mighty Breath like Swarms of Flies into their Quarters, and the Eyes of the Infidels be Dazl'd with the Lustre of our Moon. Consume them with thy fiery Darts, and Blind them with the Dust which they themselves have raised." The bombardment of Vienna started on 14 July and, having installed "his fifteen hundred concubines guarded by seven hundred black eunuchs, amid gushing fountains, baths, luxurious quarters set up in haste but with opulence", Kara Mustafa told the Sultan that soon "all Christians would obey the Ottomans".

On 12 September under the overall command of Sobiewski, the relief of the city began. A contemporary report reads: "After a Siege of Sixty days, accompanied with a Thousand Difficulties, Sicknesses, Want of Provisions, and great Effusion of Blood, after a Million of Cannon and Musquet Shot, Bombs, Grenadoes, and all sorts of Fire Works, which has changed the Face of the fairest and most flourishing City in the world, disfigured and ruined most part of the best Palaces. In the Night the Christians made themselves Masters of all the Turks Camp." It had taken just eight hours.

The morning after the battle revealed bizarre sights. Sobiewski wrote to his wife: "The Rarities which were found in the Prime Vizor's Tent, were no less Numerous than Strange and Surprising, as very curious Parrots, and some Birds of Paradise, with all his Banios, and Fountains, and some Ostriches, which he Chose rather to Kill, than let 'em fall Alive into our Hands; Nay his Dispair and Jealousy transported him so far, as to Destroy his very Women for the same Reason."

After their catastrophic defeat at Vienna, certain quarters of the Porte tried to blame Thököly. After all, his performance had been lacklustre; on reaching Bratislava, he had quickly retreated when confronted by the regular troops of Charles of Lorraine, and had then refused to redeploy to Vienna when ordered by the Sadrazam. Then, conspicuous by his absence from the Ottoman order of battle at the disastrous defeat at Párkány on 9 October, which led to the loss of the key Danubian fortress of Esztergom, he hastened to Edirne to defend himself before the Sultan. His erstwhile friend and commander, Kara Mustapha, was executed in Belgrade on Christmas Day, strangled with a silk scarf and then decapitated. Heads rolled when defeat was visited on the Ottomans.

With the Turkish cause lost, Thököly offered new terms to Leopold. He would desist from rebellion if, first, the Emperor confirmed the rights of Protestants in Hungary and, second, he was granted the North-eastern provinces of Royal Hungary with the title of Prince. The answer from Leopold was an emphatic 'No' and sensing he now had the upper hand, he used this opportunity to try and win over the remaining rebels. He offered free pardon and security of the estates of Thököly's former followers who presented themselves before the end of February to swear allegiance. Thököly's career as a rebel leader appeared to be at an end.

Leopold now decided that despite continuing French hostility— Louis XIV had attacked Luxembourg at the very time Vienna faced the Ottoman siege—the moment had come to concentrate his forces in the East. Consequently he signed the Holy League with Poland and Venice to prosecute the war against the Porte in which no one power would sign a separate peace. It was to be a turning point in European affairs. A series of almost unbroken victories began with the successful siege of Nové Zámky and the investment of Buda.

The Turks, perhaps under the impression that Thököly could be traded with Vienna in exchange for favourable peace terms, decided to sacrifice their former ally. Paşa Ibrahim issued a warrant for his arrest and instructed the Paşa of Oradea to invite him to dinner on 15 October 1685. Thököly accepted. Seized, then bound and chained, he was delivered on a peasant's cart to Belgrade. Without soldiers, captains, territory or funds, Thököly lost all his military and political influence. His captivity immediately drove the remainder of the *kurucs* into the Habsburg camp. Seventeen thousand *kurucs* gave their allegiance to Leopold who accepted their 'repentance' in good faith; under Habsburg control, they now formed the basis of a regular standing army which could be deployed against the Porte.

The Sultan, realising that Ibrahim had scored an own goal, ordered him strangled and had Thököly rehabilitated. In January 1686 he despatched him to Transylvania with a small army. A glimmer of hope remained for the *kuruckirály*.

But it was too late: all but one of the key fortresses had fallen to the Imperial troops. Only the Rákóczi's Zamkova castle at Mukachevo still held out, with 4,000 of Thököly's *kurucs*, together with his family and diplomatic corps, who had sought refuge there the previous year. In November 1685, Vienna ordered General Caprara to capture this last remaining *kuruc* stronghold. Described as 'unenterprising, avaricious, envious and cruel, careless of the comforts of his soldiers, and never possessing their confidence', Caprara sent a letter to Helena, instructing her to surrender the castle, reassuring her that, if she broke with Thököly, he would spare her and her children. She quickly seized the propaganda initiative and replied that while she was not afraid of weapons, she hoped that the Emperor would not wage war on a woman who was protecting her children: setting the king's soldiers on widows and orphans was surely not a recognised custom of war.

During this exchange of letters, Helena and her castle captain, Sándor Gáspár, prepared to defend the castle to the last man. In military terms, her assets amounted to 4,000 troops and a formidable fortification, defended by three curtains of high walls and a wide moat. Her liabilities were a shortage of ammunition and supplies, limited funds and a mélange of refugees encamped within the castle precincts. Proceeded by a week of intense bombardment directed by the feared Italian mercenary General Caraffa, the siege of Mukachevo began in February 1686. Infamous for his statement, "If I believed I had in my whole body a single drop of blood favourable to the Hungarians, I would have my veins opened," Caraffa made a ruthless adversary. However, the attack did not go well: rainy weather, coupled with a shortage of ammunition, severely hampered the effectiveness of his artillery. On 9 March, Caprara sent Helena another letter, ordering her to surrender. She again refused, telling him she found it unbelievable that he was waging war against a mother and her two children. This was not the act of a glorious emperor or of his army's commander.

The Imperial army restarted their bombardment in earnest. This provoked Helena to order red flags flown from every turret as a sign of defiance. Her coolness under fire became legendary. On one occasion, a cannonball landed beside her and Ferenc as they walked along the battlements, killing a young maid who was following a few feet behind them. Helena continued her patrol in full view of the enemy. In late March, the Imperial forces directed their fire at Helena's personal living quarters, causing extensive damage to the buildings and killing her horse in the process. A 200-pound unexploded mortar bomb lodged itself in her bedroom.

By mid-April Vienna, alarmed by escalating costs and a rising tide of negative publicity, was exasperated by Caprara's failure to take the castle and ordered the siege commander, Caraffa, to rejoin the main army. A small contingent of cavalry remained behind to observe activities in the castle. Meanwhile, Helena had become the toast of Europe: Louis XIV pronounced her the reincarnation of Joan of Arc and sent her presents of jewellery; the Polish royal family wept tears of pride for her and in London, she was the Whig heroine of the day. Helena wisely used the respite to bring money and supplies from Poland and, on the diplomatic front, she sent envoys to Vienna and Paris to elicit continuing support.

However, the position of Mukachevo became increasingly isolated when, on 26 October 1686, Christian flags were raised over the ruined towers of Buda Castle by Charles of Lorraine's soldiers, signifying the end of 150 years of Ottoman rule in Hungary. News of this reached Mukachevo in a letter from Thököly. On 4 November, Helena sent an envoy to Sobiewski in Warsaw, requesting his help to ensure Hungarian interests were protected during this period of upheaval. But that autumn Imperial troops were once more redeployed to Transylvania and before long, Mukachevo was again blockaded.

The military picture was bleak. Although she had managed to re-supply and re-equip her forces, Helena knew that the continued long-term defence of the castle was impossible. The surrounding villages had either been ravaged by Imperial mercenaries or milked dry by their new German owners. Furthermore, Vienna now resorted to black propaganda and accused Helena of cutting off the hands of prisoners of war.

Events began to overtake her. On 12 August 1687, at the second battle of Mohács, the Turks were soundly beaten by Charles of Lorraine and lost 30,000 men, leaving the way open for the Habsburg armies to invade all of Transylvania. Two months later on 27 October, as news of a widespread mutiny in the Ottoman army reached Cluj, the Prince and the Diet capitulated to Austrian demands, handing over twelve major forts and making a cash payment of 700,000 forints to the Imperial army. In the meantime, Thököly had been released from Turkish captivity and had made his way to Wallachia where he fought a series of minor skirmishes against troops from the Holy League.

The situation at Mukachevo was now desperate. No one had been able to leave the castle since the previous November and food and ammunition stocks were running dangerously low. Yet to prematurely relinquish it to the Imperial forces would remove Helena's only card - her international reputation as a latter day Joan of Arc. She wrote to Thököly and Sobiewski for help but none was forthcoming. At the end of 1687, she wrote to the French ambassador in Warsaw telling him that if she did not receive military assistance, she would have no choice but to enter into negotiations with the Imperial forces.

Realizing that the rebellion was nearly over, Thököly now proposed to the Pope that if his Holiness obtained advantageous terms for him from the Emperor, not only would he become a Catholic but also contribute to the persecution of the Lutherans. According to one contemporary source, he sent his letter in code to Helena for her comments; somehow she allowed it to fall into the hands of her chancellor, Dániel Absolon, a stalwart Protestant and former secretary to Prince Apafi. Appalled at Thököly's treachery, Absolon and the fortress commander, András Radics, deliberately squandered two months worth of supplies in a single week.

Thus on 17 January 1688, Helena had no choice other than to capitulate. The terms were not harsh: all the defenders were pardoned, she was allowed to keep her estates and those belonging to her Rákóczi offspring, but she had to take up residence in Vienna where the Emperor became the guardian of her children. Six days later, the valiant Hungarian garrison left Mukachevo, after a siege that had lasted for 813 days. Helena arrived in Vienna on 27 March, on the twelfth birthday of her son Ferenc II. Three days later he was taken from her and sent to Bohemia to be educated as a Catholic. He was never to see his mother again. Accompanied by her daughter, Helena was retired to an Ursuline convent, where they both remained for the next three years.

The irrepressible Thököly obstinately refused to give up. Nailed to every village tree, his Declaration of March 1688 read:

"Ye People of Hungary, it is long ago since your Enemies and mine have published my Death, and nevertheless I am alive still, God be Thanked, to defend your oppressed liberty. How long will ye bear, ye brave Hungarians, their Triumph over your Innocence? If you had been designed to perish, is it not better to do it having your Arms in your hands, than to be put to death by an infamous hang-man? Make sane endeavours to get out of the shameful slavery wherein you are, seeing you want nothing else but the will to do it: the Power of your Enemies is not as great as you think."

Within months, on 8 September, Belgrade fell to the Habsburg armies after a desultory defence. The Elector of Bavaria easily overcame Thököly's covering force outside the city. The only light on the horizon for Thököly was Louis XIV's invasion of the Palatine, which once more meant that Leopold had to fight on two faraway fronts.

The peace initiative, started by William of Orange in 1688, whereby the Dutch offered to mediate between the Ottomans and the

Emperor, had been making slow but sure progress. When the Anglo-Dutch Austrian alliance was signed in May 1689, the Sultan was on the point of accepting the Habsburg conditions for peace. Then Paris proposed a French-Ottoman alliance. Encouraged by the prospect of Imperial troop diversions to the western front, the Porte saw a chance to launch a major counter-offensive and make good some of their losses.

The long-serving Prince of Transylvania, Mihály Apafi, died on 15 April 1690. Thököly was immediately named Prince by Süleyman II. The Habsburgs, who supported the Transylvanian Estates' nomination of Apafi's son, Mihály II, reacted by sending an army under the command of Generals Heissler and Mihály Teleki to remove Thököly.

It was therefore hardly surprising that as the Habsburg armies marched East, the interests of the Wallachians (who as vassals of the Porte had to trim their sails to the prevailing Ottoman winds) and Hungarian *kurucs* coalesced with the Ottomans and an army assembled at the Prince of Wallachia's estate at Potlogi, a few miles West of Bucharest. News of this quickly reached the Habsburgs and General Heissler deployed his troops around Bran Castle, knowing that this was the only entrance into Transylvania that the Ottomans could force. As the Ottoman army left Rucăr, their scouts appeared outside Bran and the first shots were fired. Everything appeared to be going to plan for the Habsburg army.

It is now that Dan and I enter the story and like Doctor Who, arrived in our time machine at Podul Dâmbovitei, a small village on the main road to Bran, in time to join the Ottomans on 19 August 1690. To the North lies the impassable, jagged limestone mountain range of *Piatra Craiului*; to the East the toll road to Bran and beyond that the key garrison town of Brasov. But were these mountains really impassable? Brâncoveanu and Thököly had daringly decided that they could in fact be crossed and if their gamble worked, the Imperial army would be taken by surprise.

As we headed North out of the village, we soon found ourselves driving through a narrow defile with cliffs reaching up into the sky on either side; at one point the track cannot have been more that 40 foot across and it almost seemed possible to reach out of the car window and pick the wild blue *Clematis Alpina* and tufts of alpine forget-me-not or *King of the Alps*. Then, as if a gate had opened, we found ourselves in a lush valley following the course of the Raul Dambovitei. After about twenty kilometres, the valley closes in again and, leaving our car, we walked along the banks of the river through hornbeam, alder and sycamore thickets which teemed with grey wagtails, avoiding the yellow-bellied toads who sprang fearlessly into our path until we reached the foot of a steep hill. Dan, who had been chatting about the woodpeckers and owls who inhabit these woodlands, suddenly stopped and pointed at a sign.

"You see that sign? It says: No entrance except for forestry vehicles." He became agitated and irascibly animated. "You should know what happened to me. Really. I walk up that track with some hikers and a truck driver yells at me to clear off. He says from the cab of his ten-ton truck that we are disturbing the wildlife!"

"Ridiculous," I said, stating the obvious.

"You would think so but next day I get letter informing me that I have broken law and must pay large fine."

"You're joking?"

"No, not joking. Anyway, I don't pay fine and go to court. Judge rules not guilty."

I was relieved at this happy ending since I had been about to ask him how long he went to prison for.

The absurdity of this story is best illustrated by the 2006 wildlife census of the *Piatra Craiului*. According to Dan, on his patch there were four wolf packs, varying between two and seven, ninety chamois, fifty bears, fifteen lynx, up to two hundred wild boar and an indeterminate amount of red, roe and fallow deer. For the shepherds who spend months up in the high pastures of these mountains, the wolf and bear represent the greatest threats to their livelihood and not just physical. Dan explained that in addition to the practical defences like large dogs and kraals of thorn trees, the shepherds and their villages employed spiritual defences as well. Based on *The Master of Wolves* legend, on 16 January no less a personage than St Peter himself comes to meet with the wolves and with a large book in his hand in which are written the names of all those who have given themselves over to the devil, he tells them whose livestock they are to eat that year[125]. And on 30 November, St Andrew supervises a second promulgation of the list.

The story of the Lame Wolf is more sinister, for due to his impediment, he arrives last at the meeting with St Peter after all the food has been distributed. All is not lost for there is a villager up a nearby tree who has been spying on the Saintly confabulation and the wolf is given permission to eat the intruder. Vasko Popa, the Serbian-Romanian poet, used this story[126] as a symbol of the twentieth century:

The lame wolf walks the world
One paw treads the sky
The others pace the earth
He walks backwards
Erasing each pawprint before him
He walks half-blind
With terrible bloodshot eyes
Full of dead stars and living parasites
He walks with a millstone
Forced round his neck
An old tin can
Tied to his tail
He walks without resting
Out of one circle of dog-heads
Into another
He walks with the twelve-faced sun
On a tongue which lolls to the ground

---

[125] Many legends also tell of the Master of Wolves distributing food to the wolves on a given saint's name day.

[125] Translated by Anthony Weir

"By the way," continued Dan, "do you know why the wagtail wags her tail?"

"No idea. Enlighten me."

"Well, it's quite simple really. To start with the wagtail had no tail. Then one day she was invited to the wedding of the lark and feeling embarrassed asked the wren whether she could borrow her tail. The wren agreed but after the wedding the wagtail refused to give it back which explains two things. Why the wren hardly has a tail and why the wagtail keeps moving hers! In Romania, we like to know the reason for these things—in fact, we like to know the reason for everything."

While we had been chatting, Dan had been scrutinising the hill above us and having identified the way, scampered up the bank with me in tow. As we clambered up a slippery 45 degree slope, the *Plaiul Turcilor* or Turk's Trail was marked every now and then by ancient beech trees, whose twisted trunks and lanky branches indicate long-gone open spaces. Usually two foot wide and nevermore than five, this was the secret track that Prince Brâncoveanu's Wallachian scouts had chosen for the army, so that it could bypass the Imperial forces at Bran and take them by surprise from behind. The maps today still show this trail passing *Piscul Turcilor* (The Turks' Peak) and then descending through *Valea Turcilor* (The Turks' Valley) to *Lunca Turcilor* (The Turks' Meadow). I found it hard to believe that along this treacherous route no less than two infantry and six cavalry regiments had travelled undetected, without stopping for over sixteen hours. The descent had been so perilous that a Turkish chronicler recounts how they had had to tie trees to the tails of the horses to prevent them sliding to their death.

Retracing our steps back to the car, we then drove in a long loop back through Bran to Zărneşti to the place where the Ottomans had descended and pitched their camp, where the *Bôrsa Tâmas* and *Bôrsa Groşet*[127] meet. On our way we passed a horse and cart hurtling towards us with no one on board. I had seen such sights before but always the driver was slumped in the bottom of the wagon fast asleep and usually inebriated. About a mile on, a farmer came running towards us.

---

[127] An old word for sheep's milk.

"Have you seen my horse and cart? She was scared by a bear at the river and took off like a thunderbolt!"

"A bear?" I looked at Dan. He shrugged.

"These things happen a lot round here."

I told the frantic farmer to jump in and we turned round in pursuit of the driverless cart. We found it more or less where we had first past it, quietly standing in the shade of the new National Park Information office.

"What's she called? I asked.

"Nellie". Poor Nellie, what a dreadful shock she must have had.

The ground by the Information Office is called *La Morminte* — The Graveyard — and is where they buried the dead after the battle. I thought of those macabre stories told by visitors to Waterloo shortly after the battle of how the ground had a spring in it. By now it was getting late and Dan realised that we had yet to see the battlefield itself. Coincidentally it lies next to the ammunition factory, a large field of rich grassland sprinkled with red poppies. Here, on 22 August 1690, the two armies met; the Ottomans order of battle included Brâncoveanu, Thököly, Cerkiz Ahmed, Kuciuk Gazi Ghirai, Sitahdari and two infantry regiments. The Austrian line-up featured Count Teleki, once the mentor and protector of Thököly, and Generals Castelli, Nordkermer and Magni. Their commander, General Heissler, was still en route from Bran in haste.

The battle itself was one-sided. With most of their troops deployed around Bran, the Austrians were off-balance, outnumbered and disorganised. In the face of a confident cavalry attack, they broke ranks and fled, leaving their generals either dead or taken prisoner. Thököly was elated by the capture of Heissler. His immediate response was to arrange a trade: Heissler for his beloved Helena. But circumstances, as ever, changed and the Sultan decided to keep the captives as insurance.

Cheese making

The Cheese House

Shepherd's hut

Despite this famous victory, there was no respite for Thököly: a month later he was forced to move on by the ubiquitous and omnipotent Prince Louis of Baden. Once he had crossed over the Bodza Pass with the remnants of his army on 25 October, he was destined never to return to Transylvania. He again offered terms to Leopold – he would side with the Holy League if Vienna recognised him as Prince of Transylvania and honoured him with the title of a duke. Any agreement needed to be guaranteed by Venice and Poland. Nothing was heard from Vienna.

In February 1691, Helena, frustrated by her detention in Vienna, wrote to Thököly:

"God bless your Lordship. I am able to write to your Lordship because General Heister Ephebus has come to me and asked me whether or not I would be willing to write to your Lordship. I was surprised that your Lordship had not written to me nor sent any news through the said Ephebus; but he excused your Lordship because no-one knew where they could get hold of you.

Therefore I write to your Lordship that I am in good health, and I desire to know what my position is. Does my Lordship wish to abandon me or to recognise me as his wife? And to arrange my return to him through an exchange of hostages? For it will not be able to happen otherwise. May he be merciful, I ask, towards the prisoners, for I fear that something similar my happen with me. In one word, I have committed myself to Almighty God and to your Lordship's love for me. A great thing between those who are married is true love and duty, in which I remain your Lordship's acknowledged spouse."

The long years of separation were beginning to take their toll.
During that summer, Mustafa Köprülü continued to lead his army westwards from Belgrade to Peterwardein, where he was intercepted by Prince Louis at the battle of Novi Slankamen on 19 August. The Turks were defeated and Köprülü killed. This massive but costly victory by Prince Eugene made the Ottomans' formal proclamation of Thököly as Prince of Transylvania on 22 September an empty gesture.

Although Thököly had led the cavalry at Slankamen, his Turkish allies knew they had lost Hungary and Transylvania forever. It had been a disastrous year.

On Christmas Day 1693 a deal was finally signed in Vienna, whereby Thököly could exchange General Heissler for Helena. The following spring, at Bačka Palanka on the lower Danube, his battle flags flying in the strong breeze, Thököly waited in high expectation, his men camped in the flowering meadows along the banks of the river. Escorted by a troop of Imperial cavalry, Helena dismounted from her carriage and embraced her husband for the first time in eleven years. Here they lived in some style, bankrolled by the French King, but the years of war and deprivation had taken their toll on Thököly. Wracked by gout, grey-haired and stooped, he looked to Helena for support and strength.

The Turks were unsympathetic to their former proxy and Defterdar Ali, the Grand Treasurer, summoned Thököly to Belgrade to warn him that only strong men were required to serve the new Sultan, Mustafa II. In 1695, under pressure from Vienna which still maintained an 8,000 strong army of occupation in Transylvania, the Sultan ordered Thököly and Helena to Constantinople, where they settled in Galata on a meagre allowance. So dire were their financial circumstances that they sold Helena's jewels and then bought an inn where the legates of the Transylvanian Princes had once lived. The news of Thököly as an innkeeper raised wry smiles in Vienna.

At the Peace of Karlowitz (Sremski Karlovci in today's Serbia) on 26 January 1699 the Turks and Austrians signed a treaty which began the process of disengagement after over 150 years of conflict. With the exception of the Turks retaining the Banat of Temesvar (Timişoara), the whole of Hungary reverted to Vienna; Podolia and Kameniec were restored to Poland and the Venetian conquests in Dalmatia and the Morea confirmed. Russia retained Azov for the duration of two years. Specifically excluded by name from the Treaties, on 24 September 1701 Thököly was sent to Gemlik, a village to the South of Istanbul. At least the cost of living was cheaper there and Thököly's health improved; his gout was cured, he went hunting and in 1702 he bought a summer house two hours from the village.

Surrounded by her garden of roses, pomegranates and lavender, Helena died at Gemlik aged 59 on 18 February 1703, close to her beloved husband but five hundred miles from her son, Ferenc. She never knew of his renewal of the rebellion against the Habsburgs. "If she had known it," wrote Thököly to his stepson, "in her happiness, she would have been born again." Her tombstone read: "Here rests the pride and glory of her sex and her country after a life of heroic suffering".

After yet again flirting with conversion to Catholicism as a way to facilitate his passage home, Thököly reaffirmed his Protestant faith in September 1705. Shortly after, aged 48, he died. His secretary, Komáromy, arranged for him to be buried under a tree in the Armenian cemetery, since the Sultan had refused the repatriation of his body. On the simple gravestone, under the Thököly crest, his epitaph read: *"Bene sperando et male habendo transit vita"*—"Our life passes, hoping for good but experiencing evil."

Thököly's remains were repatriated to Hungary in 1906. After a state funeral at the Lutheran Church in Deak Square in Budapest, he was finally laid to rest at the family seat in Kežmarok. The speech at the interment service ended: "Leave now, wanderer, remember the deceased, and ponder that the heavens may be conquered only with such weapons."

Born into the crucible of dissent, Thököly was a worthy standard-bearer of Hungarian nationhood. If his political judgment was poor and his motives occasionally questionable, his courage and resilience in the face of extraordinary odds was unsurpassable. His military achievements may not have been spectacular but they turned the idea of rebellion, as espoused by Nikolai Zrinyi and the Magnates' Conspiracy, into a reality. This was the challenging legacy he left to the next generations of Hungarian patriots.

Thököly's erstwhile ally, Prince Brâncoveanu of Wallachia, betrayed to the Turks by his courtiers, was arrested on Good Friday 1714 and charged with treason:

"seeing that Preda Brancovano has had a secret understanding with Austria, Russia, Poland and Venice; that he has accepted from the Emperor the title of Prince of the Holy Empire, and from the Czar the Grand Cross of St.Andrew; seeing that he has forwarded his treasures to Vienna, and has only rebuilt the palace at Tirgovist that he might the more easily be able to flee; seeing that he possesses property and castles in Ardialia[128], and that he has agents in Vienna and Venice; seeing that the desertion of Thomas Cantacuzene is only the fruit of his counsels; seeing that he has made cymbals of silver and has struck coinage bearing his effigy, the Sultan Achmet condemns him and all his family to be beheaded[129]."

Brancoveanu was philosophical about this turn of events. 'Such will always be the fate of those who serve tyrants' were his final words. Archimandrite Bartholomew describes Constantine's last day:

'On that terrible 15th August 1714, Constantin Brancoveanu turned sixty in the prison of Istanbul, while Princess Marica, in prison as well, remembered it was her name day. That was the day chosen by the Sultan for beheading Brancoveanu and his four sons after having them devilishly tortured for four months, day after day, sometimes under the unfortunate Princess's eyes of a wife and mother. Barefoot and dressed only in shirts, the convicts were taken to the scaffold in Ialikiosk market and aligned, like cattle to be slaughtered, before the whole of Europe, whose ambassadors had been invited to the bloody performance. In keeping with the Sultan's order, the first to fall was the head of the eldest son, Constantin. Stefan was beheaded next. Then the axe cut off Radu's head. Deeply shaken, the youngest son, Matei, aged barely eleven, threw himself at the Sultan's feet promising he would become a Muslim if his life was spared. His request was

---

[128] Transylvania
[129] Ottoman archives

neither accidental, nor hopeless. Already while they were tortured the mufti had promised their pardon provided they agreed to turn Muslim—an offer rejected by the prisoners. Matei was begging for it now, in front of the block splashed with his brothers' blood, under the executioner's arm awaiting the Sultan's decisions. After having learnt of his request through an interpreter, the Sultan asked Brancoveanu if he agreed. The son's life was now in the father's hands. It would have meant the certitude that Brancoveanu's descent continued. How harrowing must have been that moment's split in the old man's soul! If he had given Matei his life, as the latter wished, this would have shattered the perfection of the work of 'an old boyar and Christian prince', tragically rounded off by fate. Perfection cannot be conceived other than round. The unfortunate father did not have time to voice his thoughts. He motioned to his son: redeem your soul, not your life! Matei put his head on the block and the axe fell like lightning! Some people think that Brancoveanu's beautiful head (he went next) remained attached to his body by a strip of flesh. I, however, see it tumbling to the ground and stopping near Matei's, cheek to cheek, in godlike tenderness."

After the execution, the victims heads were displayed on the walls of the Seraglio[130] and their bodies thrown in to the streets below to be eaten by dogs. However, fearing a revolt by the city's Christians, the Sultan's servants recovered the corpses and dumped them in the Bosphorus where they were fished out by the Patriarch's men and buried on Halki island off Constantinople. Princess Marica finally managed to arrange for her husband's remains to be secretly brought to Bucharest in 1720, where they remained undiscovered in the Church of St George until early this century. The tomb Constantine had prepared for himself at Hurezu Monastery remains empty to this day.

---

[130] In London, traitor's heads were usually exhibited on a bridge or gate of the City; in Constantinople, 'senior' heads were on white marble pillars in the First Courtyard of the palace, 'lesser' heads in niches on either side of the Imperial gate. Only 'senior' heads were stuffed with straw.

Dan had had enough of military history by now and had switched to one of his favourite subjects, folklore.

"Did you know that only very recently in a village in Oltenia they asked a child jump over grave on a horse and when the horse refused, they disinterred the body and cut its heart out, which they then burnt, ground the ashes and put in a drink which all present had to have a swig."

"Why?"

"Well, this is about *strigoi* and *moroi*."

These are not words to be taken lightly since they are at the heart of the Romanian vampire[131] myth. Both *strigoi* and *moroi* are the evil souls of the living (*vii*) or the dead rising from the tombs (*morți*) that transform into animal or phantomatic apparitions during the night to haunt the countryside, troubling whoever they encounter, the difference being that the *moroi* are subject to the *strigoi*. They are close relatives of the werewolves known as *pricolici* or *vârcolaci*, the last meaning goblin at times.

The name *strigoi* is derived from *strigă*, meaning witch or barn owl, similar to the Italian *strega* for witch and descended from the Latin word *strix*, for a shrieking vampiric bird. The origins of the term *moroi* are less clear, but it is thought to have possibly originated from the Old Slavonic word for nightmare, *mora* .

In her 1926 study of *The Vampire in Roumania*, Agnes Murgoci collected numerous accounts, some of which tally with Dan's.

> Some twenty or thirty years ago (from 1914) in the commune Afumati in Dolj, a certain peasant, Mărin Mirea Ociocioc, died. It was noticed that his relations also died, one after the other. A certain Badea Vrajitor (Badea the wizard) dug him up. Badea himself, going later into the forest up to the frontier on a cold wintry night, was eaten by wolves. The bones of Mărin were sprinkled with wine, a church service read over them, and replaced in the grave. From that time there were no more deaths in the family.

---

[131] *A Transylvanian term is șișcoi.*

Some fifteen years ago, in Amărăşti in the North of Dolj, an old woman, the mother of the peasant Dinu Gheorghiţa, died. After some months the children of her eldest son began to die, one after the other, and, after that, the children of her youngest son. The sons became anxious, dug her up one night, cut her in two, and buried her again. Still the deaths did not cease. They dug her up a second time, and what did they see? The body was whole without a wound. It was a great marvel. They took her and carried her into the forest, and put her under a great tree in a remote part of the forest. There they disembowelled her, took out her heart, from which blood was flowing, cut it in four, put it on hot cinders, and burnt it. They took the ashes and gave them to children to drink with water. They threw the body on the fire, burnt it, and buried the ashes of the body. Then the deaths ceased.

Some twenty or thirty years ago, a cripple, an unmarried man, of Cuşmir, in the South of Mehedinp, died. A little time after, his relations began to die, or to fall ill. They complained that a leg was drying up. This happened in several places. What could it be? "Perhaps it is the cripple; let us dig him up." They dug him up on Saturday night, and found him as red as red, and all drawn up into a corner of the grave. They cut him open, and took the customary measures. They took out the heart and liver, burnt them on red-hot cinders, and gave the ashes to his sister and other relations, who were ill. They drank them with water, and regained their health.

In the Cuşmir, another family began to show very frequent deaths, and suspicion fell on a certain old man, dead long ago. When they dug him up, they found him sitting up like a Turk, and as red as red, just like fire; for had he not eaten up nearly the whole of a family of strong, young men. When they tried to get him out he resisted, unclean and horrible. They gave him some blows with an axe, they got him out, but they could not cut him with a knife. They took a scythe and an axe, cut out his heart and liver, burnt them, and gave them to the sick folk to drink. They drank, and regained their health. The old man was reburied, and the deaths ceased.

In Văguileşti, in Mehedinţi, there was a peasant Dimitriu Vaideanu, of Transilvanian origin, who had married a wife in Văguileşti and settled there. His children died one after the other; seven died within a few months of birth, and some bigger children had died as well. People began to wonder what the cause of all this could be. They took council together, and resolved to take a white horse to the cemetery one night, and see if it would pass over the graves of the wife's relations. This they did, and the horse jumped over all the graves, until it came to the grave of the mother-in-law, Joana Marta, who had been a witch, renowned far and wide. Then the horse stood still, beating the earth with its feet, neighing, and snorting, unable to step over the grave. Probably there was something unholy there. At night Dimitriu and his son took candles and went to dig up the grave. They were seized with horror at what they saw. There she was, sitting like a Turk, with long hair falling over her face, with all her skin red, and with finger nails frightfully long. They got together brushwood, shavings, and bits of old crosses, they poured wine on her, they put in straw, and set fire to the whole. Then they shovelled the earth back and went home.

Closer to home, Agnes informs us that in Zărneşti, when a female vampire is dug up, iron forks are put into her heart, eyes, and breast, and she is reburied with her face downwards!

Well into his stride, Dan then told me the tragic story of Irina Cornici, a nun at the remote Holy Trinity monastery in Tanacu in Moldavia. Brought up in an orphanage, 23-year-old Irina suffered from schizophrenia and joined the monastery as a novice in 2005. After three months, the principal monk and four nuns diagnosed that she was possessed by evil spirits, so tying her to a makeshift cross, they prayed for three days and nights for the devils to leave her. Deprived of food and water, by the time they cut her down, Irina was dead. In February 2007, the monk was sentenced to 14 years in prison for murder and the nuns received terms of between 5 and 8 years each.

"You know you can register your business as a witch in Romania. One only has to read the adverts in the newspaper and they are full of offers by fancifully named ladies, Deadly Nightshade or Mrs *Atropa Bella Donna*, to work miracles. Technically they are called healers but believe me, when there is a full moon, the black cockerel needs to make himself scarce."

The finale to this liturgy of superstition involved young unmarried girls in the Maramures. "On New Year's Eve, they go into the shed where the family pig is kept—the one that was not slaughtered on 21 December—and hitting it with their bottom, ask 'On pig, what year will I be married?'. The number of grunts from the pig indicates the number of years the maiden will have to wait."

Emily Gerard, the author of The Land beyond the forest, identified five strange people to watch out for when walking in the forests of Transylvania. First, she warns us of the *damieni micuit*, or the small men, grey-bearded dwarfs who, attired like miners with axe and lantern, haunted the gold and silver mines. Three knocks on the door of a miner's house was their warning to the wife that her husband had perished. Although in principle well disposed towards human beings, they were very quarrelsome among themselves and were often to be heard hitting each other with their sharp axes or blowing their horns as signals of battle. Next comes the *Om ren* or wild man of winter, the terror of all hunters and shepherds. He is followed by the Mountain Monk, a malevolent spirit, who specialises in breaking tools. Then there is *panusch* who lies in wait for helpless maidens in forest glades; this is, of course, the pagan Pan who has been up to his philandering tricks for thousands of years. And, lastly, *gana*, a beautiful but malicious witch, out to 'doom' any man weak willed enough to succumb to her charms.

The following day, Dan had a group of visitors from the US Embassy in Bucharest to look after, so I headed for the nearby Peasant Fortress at Râşnov. The Mongol invasion of 1241 had devastated this part of Transylvania and the Hungarian King wisely lifted his former limitation of building non-royal castles only in wood. The good burghers of Râşnov took advantage of this and on the limestone outcrop behind the town, Die Rosenauer Burg, started to construct a robust stone fortress. It may well be the case that the Teutonic Knights had already started one before they were evicted in 1215 but we do know that when the next Tartar invasion swept through in 1335, it encountered stiff resistance at Râşnov. Over the next centuries, the citadel provided refuge to the townsfolk on many occasions and finally fell into disuse[132] in 1848. It had been captured only once when

---

[132] It is now a tourist attraction under Italian management.

in 1602 Báthory's army besieged it after the inhabitants had thrown their lot in with Moses Székelys's revolt. After he had interdicted their water supply, the defenders capitulated from thirst and although they made two attempts to retake the fortress later that year, they ended up having to buy it back from Báthory for 3,000 florins. Two Turkish prisoners were co-opted to dig a well in exchange for their freedom: seventeen years later, they walked out as freemen having dug down for over 146 meters.

There is no account of what happened to the inhabitants of Zărneşti during the Mongol invasions; most likely, they were slaughtered like their neighbours. However, there are records of the villagers taking refuge in a cave during the Ottoman invasion of 1421 and that afternoon I set off to find it. A small cart track on the Eastern outskirt of the town marks the start of the path to *Colţul Chililor*. It gradually ascends through the hay meadows, at this time of year a riot of wild flowers—including Globeflower *transsylvanicus*, electric-blue alpine gentians, butterfly orchids and pale pink fragrant orchids, fingerleaved and heartsease violets, Austrian Viper's-grass, Vipers Bugloss, Kidney-vetch, plantains, Dyer's Greenweed, Solitary Harebells, Ajuga and Masterworts— until it reaches the bottom of the massive limestone cliffs which reach up to over 6,000 feet and culminate in the *Crucea di Carpati*. Meandering through fir woods, the plaintive mewing of buzzards and throaty bark of ravens overhead, it ends at a tiny monastery where there is a minute wooden church and across a small clearing, living quarters for three monks by an *isvor* or spring. A more peaceful and remote place is hard to imagine.

The walk had taken me an hour and a half, so it was with a sense of astonishment and admiration that I imagined the Zarnestians, a child clutched under both arms, fleeing for their lives from the advancing horde and reaching the cave in time to live another day. I took a different route back, following a stream up the *Valea Ursilor* (Valley of the Wolves) to the *Padina Popii* (The Priest's gully) through woods of beech and pine trees that soared up like medieval perpendicular columns to join together in a latticed canopy, a loosely ordered web of foliate tracery ribbed with stiffening branches. Then, as I turned to descend, a flock of sheep and goats suddenly appeared and blocked my path, urged on by a shepherd, a small boy and four large dogs. I had passed them at their camp earlier on and now they were making their way up to the high pastures for the night.

Shepherds own these mountains; even the highest *Varf* or peak at 7,640 feet, although officially called *La Om*, "The Man", is unofficially known as the shepherd's peak. To learn more, I set off the next day with Dan's son, Bogdan, to walk to the high pastures where the shepherds had set up their summer camps. Like his father, Bogdan had reached the profession of mountain guide through a rather circuitous route though more compressed. At fourteen, he had enrolled at a military academy determined to be a fighter pilot in the Romanian Air Force. A slight defect in his left eye cast a shadow, albeit a small one, over his long-term future at the controls of a Mig-21, so he opted to read political science at Bucharest University. Whilst politics can be a well paid profession over the long term, in the short term it was a recipe for poverty, so Bogdan switched to reading civil engineering and having duly graduated, found himself engaged in the burgeoning family guiding business.

We headed off down the gorge towards Magura village and then pressed on to the *Falizu Arcadei*, the Arcade of Cliffs, where Bogdan stopped to show me 'the spiders' cave'.

"You know American film company come here to make Dracula-style movie and they wanted cave." It struck me as a relatively normal request by a location manager under pressure.

"Problem," continued Bogdan, "is there is indigenous spider living in cave. So when they ask permission of National Park, answer was No. So they went to Mayor of Zărneşti who can also give permission and explained problem."

"Mayor said: look if problem is only that there are spiders in cave, I sent the town hall cleaning ladies with brushes, they tidy cave and then no problem!"

Fortunately for the spiders, the Mayor was overruled by the National park.

The walk through the gorge was every bit as dramatic as the previous expedition on Thököly's trail; on either side sheer limestone cliffs born down on us, shutting out the heavens which were the aerial preserve of crag martins and alpine swifts. After half and hour, we left this penumbral trail and climbed up into the woods, a natural arboretum of pine (and its small relation the dwarf pine), larch, spruce, fir, rowan, beech and sycamore. And like the Teddy Bear's Picnic, "If you go down to the woods today, you're due for a big surprise", the first sign we saw of bears was a large scratch mark about six foot up a tree.

"This is made by females", Bogdan said in a reassuring voice. "Originally people though it was males marking their territory but research has showed that it is females telling males to buzz off."

I pondered on this anomaly of nature. Why?

"Females spend two years rearing their cubs, so they don't want sex. Male bear different. He has been known to kill cubs to persuade female she needs to reproduce again."

"What do you do, Bogdan, when you meet a bear?"

"Look, for last half hour, bear knows you and me in woods. Number one. Then, if we meet bear, bear probably run away. Best thing to do is walk slowly backwards, like diplomat avoiding war."

"And if bear comes towards us?"

Bogdan paused.

"If bear still come towards you, you go towards bear."

"Is that what the book says? When I was a keen climber in the French Alps, the book said if one of you fell off a razorback ridge, the other had to throw himself over the other side as a counterweight. I never tried it."

"I understand. This has not happened to me yet but concern is not ordinary bear but seriously bad tempered old male. They do not conform."

As the conversation continued, we passed a second bear sign, a rotten pine which had been given the full claw treatment in the search for large black ants.

"Bears have poor digestion, so they look for big black ants with plenty formic acid. This stimulates the enzymes in their stomachs and hence aids the ingestion process." Thinking that he had lost me with science, Bogdan added, "They're not stupid."

Bear talk abruptly stopped when we found the path blocked by a deadfall. This was no ordinary deadfall caused by wind or old age for the stump and the base of the deadfall, riddled with holes of varying size, looked like the army had been using them for target practice. This was the handiwork of woodpeckers; Great Blacks were responsible for the largest holes, then White Backed for the medium-sized and lastly *Alpinus* Three-Toed for the small. It was a magnificent team effort.

By now, we had emerged from the woods into the alpine meadows and before long heard the tinkling bells of grazing cattle and goats, which meant we were nearing a shepherd's camp. The etiquette on approaching these remote communities of men and beasts is dictated by the shepherd dogs. Trained to see off wolves and bears, they have scant regard for strangers and rarely hesitate before attacking them. So the drill is to pick up a large stick, walk very slowly towards the camp and look for the shepherd/cowman/ goatherd with a view to him calling off his fervent canine defenders. Those that have not followed this etiquette have to put it politely retired hurt, often in the backside.

The centrepiece of the camp was a large log cabin, which turned out to be a cheese factory. In the first room, Bogdan introduced me to the head shepherd who was sitting on his own, stitching a piece of pine bark into a tubular container for cheese, very traditional apart from the heavy duty plastic thread. This was solitary work that required concentration, so after inspecting the cheese maturation room, we departed to the Şea or saddle which straddled the ridge. Another one of Noyce's thunderstorms erupted and, sodden and bedraggled within minutes, we set off down the mountain, discussing music to keep our spirits up in the hammering incessant rain. I suddenly remembered that I had not collected any stories in Zărneşti about the moon or aurochs and appealed to Bogdan for help.

"Well, we do have a story about the moon in these parts which of course involves a shepherd. Long ago the moon was a brilliant white, pristine you know, and much closer to the earth. This infuriated a crotchety shepherd who could never get to sleep at night because the moon was too bright. So one day he picked up a handful of dung and threw it at the moon, telling her to go away. And that is why you can still see the blotches of dung on her face and why she is now so far away."

As Dan said, there is an explanation for everything in Romania.

EPILOGUE

The Romanians' love of the moon is reflected in their contemporary poetry, which is full of enchanting and enthralling lunar imagery. Some phrases that come to mind are 'the moon's rays tapping on my window', 'the moon took its carriage of milk for a walk', 'the bones of the moon...', 'the moon has circuses', 'he who....wants to swallow the moon.' The genesis of that imagery can be found in much earlier traditions, many espoused by the Roma. George Borrow, during his travels round Spain in the nineteenth century, came across this gypsy couplet:

> '*At midnight, when the moon began*
> *To show her silver flame,*'

Luminița Mihai Cioabă is an extraordinary bilingual poetess and dramatist, writing in Romanes as well as Romanian, who is internationally recognised as a cultural icon of the Roma people. The Sibiu-based Cioabă family has been at the head of the Roma for several generations. It was the late Ion Cioabă who, after striving to integrate the Roma into society on a national and international level in the 1960s, became the King of the Roma in the 1990s to represent them in their fight for human rights.

Described by the Romanian poet Mircea Dinescu as having 'slipped out from the native linen tent into the insecure paper tent, governed by doubt and wakefulness', Luminița arranges the simple elements of existence—air, wind, fire, stone, flowers, moon, sun, water, sky, night—into a deeply religious verse-form, on the one hand dark and mysterious, on the other clear and translucent.

What better way is there is finish my journey than to rejoice in the magic words of Luminița?

My Eyes on the Sky

by Luminiţa Mihai Cioabă

One night or one day
I'll no longer be here
To breathe earth's air
My eyes on the sky.

No longer blow
Like poppies brushed
By a breath of wind
My heart
Will cease beating.

I'll arrive
On the other side
Beyond
The many skies
One day or one night.

In the death-swaddling
Darkness
I know
I'll have to cross water
But
I'll always remain
Bright light
Because the word I've written
Will glow there for you.

Translated by Adam J. Sorkin and Cristina Cîrstea

'*old....*': Queen Marie's photograph album (Kent State University); '*new....*': ac; '*from the trap....*': ac; '*to the pot*': ac; '*river traffic*': ac; '*mile 23*': ac; '*Mazepa on way*': ac (from Horace Vernet); '*Mazepa arriving*': ac (from Horace Vernet); '*to become hetman*': National Museum of Art, Stockholm, Sweden; '*Zăbala*': ac; '*Turia*': ac; '*Mikes*': ac; '*Csoma*': ac (from Csoma Museum); '*Mihail today*': ac; '*....yesterday*': Michael Styrcea; '*Csoma memorial*': ac (detail from picture in Count István Széchenyi Museum, Hungary); '*buffalo boss*': ac; '*bonny ploughmen*': ac; '*Sachsiz*': ac; '*Sighisoara*': ac; '*sinners*': ac; '*river of fire*': ac; '*Jesse's tree*': ac; '*Akathistos*': ac; '*saints etc*': ac; '*father Cleopa*': unattributed; '*moldavian hermit*': ac; '*painful death*': ac; '*stylite*': ac; '*Enescu*': ac; '*Grigorescu*': ac (from self-portrait); '*Cantemir*': ac; '*Valeni*': ac; '*houtsoul verger*': ac; '*last judgment*': ac; '*Râşca*': ac; '*Simona*': ac; '*Râşca panel*': ac; '*Peles*': ac; '*theatre company*': unattributed; '*Queen Marie*'(top L): Queen Marie's photograph album (Kent State University); '*Queen Marie*'(top R): ac (Postcard); '*Queen Marie*'(bottom L): ac (Postcard); '*Queen Marie*'(bottom R): ac (Postcard); '*Cotroceni*': My Dream Houses 1935; '*Pelisor*': My Dream Houses 1935; '*Copaceni*': My Dream Houses 1935; '*serbian*': ac; '*orthodox*': ac; '*RC*': ac; '*Baile Herculane*': ac; '*Russell*': ac; '*Delia, Ion*': ac; '*Bulci*': ac; '*Câlpănas*': ac; '*stag*': ac; '*royal lodge*': ac; '*Arad*': ac; '*Joe Boyle*': Len Taylor Estate; '*Russell*': ac; '*Timişoara*': ac; '*cheese making*': ac; '*cheese house*': ac; '*shepherd's hut*': ac

Written and Photographed by Alan Ogden
ISBN 988-97764-1-3

"Winds of Sorrow" is an eclectic collection of essays compiled by the author during his travels to Transylvania in northern Romania between 1998 and 2004. What was at first a mere inkling of a name on a map in a faraway Ruritanian land unfolds into an exotic medley of fascinating people and picturesque places. The complex truths behind the convoluted history of Transylvania are revealed as the reader journeys to the medieval towns and villages of this former Principality, once famous throughout the courts of Europe. These are journeys not to be missed!

"In this meticulously researched account, Alan Ogden swiftly drives a stake through the heart of the vampire myth....Ogden is an energetic – and eccentric guide- scampering around churches in search of crumbling frescoes..."
The Guardian, 4 December 2004

"Ogden demonstrates with tremendous enthusiasm that, far from being an irrelevant backwater, Transylvania is crucial to a true understanding of Europe.... Winds of Sorrow adds significantly to a body of work that amounts to a valuable contribution to European culture, testifying to the tenacity of its virtues as well as to its horrors."
The Spectator, 20 November 2004

"The rural areas, a microcosm of mediaeval life, are filled with proud and generous inhabitants. Images of smoke, darkness and inclement weather contrast with gorgeous vistas, the luminosity of church art and the beauty of an unsullied countryside."
Geographical magazine, January 2005

THE DISCONTENTED:
Betrayal, Love and War in Habsburg Hungary

Written by Alan Ogden
ISBN 988-97764-3-X

"The Discontented" tells the heroic story of the Hungarian rebellions against the Habsburgs in 17th and 18th centuries. Led by the charismatic trio of Imre Thokoly, Helena Zrinyi and Ferenc Rakoczi II, there were moments when the rebels nearly succeeded in securing the independence of Hungary from the Habsburg Emperors.

Against a background of international intrigue and superpower politics, the valiant actions of the kurucs were ultimately doomed and their leaders forced into exile in Turkey.

Here is a tale of hubris, betrayal, love and reckless courage that remains inspirational centuries later.